Islam at War

ISLAM AT WAR

A History

George F. Nafziger
and Mark W. Walton

PRAEGER

Westport, Connecticut
London

Library of Congress Cataloging-in-Publication Data

Nafziger, George F.
   Islam at war : a history / George F. Nafziger and Mark W. Walton.
      p. cm.
   Includes bibliographical references and index.
   ISBN 0–275–98101–0 (alk. paper)
     1. Islam—History.   I. Walton, Mark W., 1949–   II. Title.
   BP50.N335   2003
   297′.09—dc21   2002044957

British Library Cataloguing in Publication Data is available.

Library of Congress Catalog Card Number: 2002044957
ISBN: 0–275–98101–0

First published in 2003

Praeger Publishers, 88 Post Road West, Westport, CT 06881
An imprint of Greenwood Publishing Group, Inc.
www.praeger.com

Printed in the United States of America

The paper used in this book complies with the
Permanent Paper Standard issued by the National
Information Standards Organization (Z39.48–1984).

10 9 8 7 6 5 4 3 2 1

CONTENTS

CONTENTS

INTRODUCTION

On September 11, 2001, America suddenly discovered the Islamic world. The word *jihad* became commonplace in the spoken American lexicon. An unknown people with unusual customs and even more unusual ideas struck at the American heartland and secured our undivided attention. Yet, despite the thousands of words spoken by the media since September 11 the history of the Islamic world has barely been exposed to our view. And we are even less aware of what has motivated this attack on our peace and tranquility.

Many in the Islamic world see the events of September 11 as a military operation. Surely Osama bin Laden did. Many will be surprised to discover that this is not the first blow struck by the Islamic world against the Christian world or the West, nor the worst blow. It is merely the latest. Indeed, a large part of the Islamic world's history revolves around armed conflict, much of it with the Christian and Western worlds. War has been part of the Islamic world since the Archangel Gabriel first spoke to Muhammad, and it is the principal process by which Islam spread throughout the world.

It is the intent of this work to explore that ancient and rich military history. It begins with Muhammad, the first Muslim warlord, and follows the first world superpower, the Ottoman Empire, as it rose from the obscurity of the central Asian steppes and vanished at the stroke of a pen in 1918. It explores the history of suicidal religious zealots that fought the crusaders in 1100 and their modern counterparts driving airplanes into buildings filled with innocent civilians.

It was not the intention of this work to provide a detailed, scholarly examination of the military history of the Islamic world. Such a work would be far too massive to be anything other than the work of a lifetime. Instead, this survey touches on the high points of Islam's military history. It also seeks to set straight the record on the military nature of Islam, which has been broadly represented as being a peaceful religion. It certainly has a peaceful side to it, but its military history is so rich and so long that any attempt to suggest that it doesn't exist is a disservice to the truth.

Chapter 1

BIRTH OF ISLAM: ISLAMIC EXPANSION AND MUHAMMAD AS BATTLEFIELD COMMANDER

> Warfare is ordained for you, though it is hateful unto you; but it may happen that ye hate a thing which is good for you, and it may happen that ye love a thing which is bad for you. Allah knoweth, ye know not.
>
> Koran, Surah II, 216

Muhammad was born, it is thought, in the year A.D. 571, at Mecca. The name given him by his mother is lost to history, but not the name given him by his peers—Muhammad. His father, Abdullah, died before his birth, and his mother, Aminah, a member of the Yathrib tribe of Medina, lived only until he was six. The honor of raising Muhammad fell to his grandfather, Abd-al-Muttalib, and when he died it fell to his uncle, abu-Talib.

Legend relates that at the age of twelve Muhammad accompanied his uncle on a caravan journey to Syria and that during the course of this trip Muhammad met a Christian monk that legend identifies as Bahira. From this encounter he may have learned some of the tenets of the Christian faith. Little else is known about Muhammad's youth except that some years after the trip he went into the service of a wealthy Meccan widow named Kadijah. So faithfully did the young man transact her business, and so excellent was his demeanor, that she married her young agent. The marriage proved a happy one, even though she was fifteen years older than he. Throughout the twenty-six years of their life together, he remained devoted to her. Even after her death, when he had taken many wives, he continued to speak of her with the greatest love and reverence.

This marriage, however, was pivotal in Muhammad's rise to power. It gave him wealth, position, and status within the ranks of notables of Mecca. These men gave him the title Al-Amin, the "trustworthy" a tribute to his honesty and ability.

Having gained a position of wealth, Muhammad had leisure, and in that leisure time he pursued his own inclinations. He took to secluding himself and meditating in a small cave on the hill outside of Mecca called "Hira." While meditating in this cave Muhammad heard a voice commanding, "Read!" He responded, "I cannot read." Again the voice commanded him to read and he responded he could not. A third time, and more terribly, the voice commanded, "Read!" Muhammad said, "What can I read?" The voice responded, "Read thou in the name of thy Lord, who created man from a clot and it is thy Lord the Most Bountiful who teacheth by the pen, teacheth man that which he knew not."[1] When his trance broke, Muhammad stepped out of the cave and heard a voice say, "Oh Muhammad! Thou art Allah's messenger, and I am Gabriel." Before him stood, in likeness of a man, an angel. This was the first of many revelations; Muhammad had received the call of Allah. Highly distressed and filled with emotion, he rushed home in alarm. Kadijah convinced him that Allah would not send a harmful spirit to him.

Inspired, Muhammad became as prophetic as any of the Hebrew notables of the Old Testament, preaching initially only to his family and closest circle. At first his message was God is one. He is all-powerful. He is the creator of the universe. There will be a day of judgment. Splendid rewards await in paradise those who follow God's commandments. Those who do not, face terrible punishment in hell.

As his convictions grew stronger, Muhammad went out among his fellow Meccans with his revelation, initially to be met with derision and scorn. His message changed to one of dire warnings, and he became a prophet of doom, alternating between stories of the pleasures of paradise and the torments of hell. Muhammad's wife and her cousin Waraqh ibn-Nawfl were among the first of his followers. However, the aristocratic and influential Ymayyad branch of Quraysh[2] stood against him. They believed his heresy would damage their commercial interests because it attacked the pantheon of deities that stood at the center of the pan-Arabian pilgrimage upon which their commerce rested. This was the Ka'bah, the holy place to which all Arabia made pilgrimages, and Mecca was the node of this sacred place.

Despite this resistance, over a period of about four years Muhammad slowly gathered recruits from the slave and lower classes drawn to the promise of relief from their earthly sufferings. Alarmed, the Meccan authorities began to actively persecute Muhammad's followers and forced the migration of eleven families to Abyssinia. In 615, a further eighty-three families followed. They found sanctuary in the domain of the Christian Negus, who refused to deliver them into the hands of their oppressors.

Muhammad did not flee to Abyssinia, but remained shut up in his family's stronghold. At first, the defenders of the status quo tried to bring Muhammad to a compromise in his preaching against polytheism. They offered him a throne as king if he would give up his preaching. When negotiations failed to work, they turned to ostracizing him. His entire clan was shunned by the powers of Mecca.

Undaunted by the persecution of his fellows, Muhammad continued to preach and convert. He continued to have revelations. The people of Mecca, tiring of the ban against the new prophet's clan, brought out the documents prepared to establish the ban against communication with Muhammad, only to discover that white ants had destroyed all of the writing, except the words "In thy name, Oh Allah." When the elders saw this "marvel" they had the ban removed and Muhammad was again free to go about Mecca.

Despite his restored freedom, resistance to Muhammad's preaching had become hardened. He turned his attention to the city of Taif, where he failed utterly. Undiscouraged by this setback, he continued to preach—and soon found a receptive and useful audience.

In A.D. 620, as the pilgrimage season arrived, he encountered a small group of men from Yathrib, a city more than 200 miles from Mecca, who heard him gladly. These men had heard Jewish rabbis speak of a prophet who would arise among the pagan Arabs, and with whose leadership the Jews would destroy the pagans. The men of Yathrib—or Medina as it is now universally known—took Muhammad for this man, and on their return home they related what they had seen and heard. During this meeting the Yathribs swore allegiance to him in the pact of Al-ʿAqabah. The oath they swore to Muhammad is the same oath that was later extracted from female converts, with no mention of fighting as existed in the original. This would become important later—and it would change for the men of Yathrib. When they returned to their homes, they took one of Muhammad's converts with them. This teacher spread the word in Yathrib and soon every house in the city knew of Muhammad.

Two years later, during pilgrimage season, a deputation of seventy-five men was sent from Yathrib with the purpose of meeting Muhammad. They invited Muhammad to return with them and make Yathrib (al-Madinah or Medina) his home in the hopes that he might reconcile the hostile Aws and Khazraj tribes.

Seeing the value of this idea, he authorized 200 of his followers to slip quietly to Yathrib and then followed them, arriving on September 24, 622. This was the famous "hegira" *(Hijrah)*. Some question if this was truly a "flight" or a scheme of migration that he had carefully considered for about two years. His followers had quietly sold their property and then quickly disappeared into the desert. Some say that the Meccans realized what was happening and planned Muhammad's murder, fearing what might happen if he were to establish himself in rival Medina.

It is possible that Muhammad had a timely revelation that warned him of the plot. He was ordered to make war upon his persecutors "until persecution is no more and religion is for Allah only.[3] But he would flee, realizing that the time was not right. Muhammad and two faithful followers, Ali and Abu Bakr, remained in Mecca until Muhammad received God's command to flee. God's command came the night ordained for his murder. When the would-be assassins were before his house, Muhammad gave Ali his cloak and bade him lie down so that it would be thought that Muhammad lay there. He was sure that when they saw it was Ali, they would not harm him. A "blindness" fell upon the assassins as Muhammad slipped out of the house, and he joined Abu Bakr. Together they slipped into the desert and hid in a cave until it was safe to travel to his new haven. Because of the significance of Muhammad's move to Yathrib, Caliph Umar,[4] decreed that the lunar year, beginning on July 16, become the official starting point of the Muslim era.

The move to Yathrib, or Medina, proved a turning point in Muhammad's life. He was despised in his birthplace of Mecca, but well received in the home of his mother. Thirteen years of humiliation, persecution, and unfulfilled prophecy had ended. For Muhammad the change was even greater, as he now rose from the role of scorned prophet to ruler of a state, albeit a small one. And yet, from this tiny state in ten short years would grow the Arabian Empire.

In the first year of his reign in Medina, Muhammad made a solemn treaty with the Hebrew tribes. This treaty secured for them equal rights of citizenship and religious liberty in return for their support of his hold on power. The Hebrew idea of a prophet was more of one that would lead them to power and dominion rather than one who made them the equals of another non-Hebrew tribe. It is apparent to western readers that these were not the first Hebrews to have trouble with a prophet! It is believed that they attempted to manipulate him to their ends, and this struggle appears in the Medina surahs in the frequent negative references to the Hebrews and hypocrites. Prior to this time, the Qilbah, or place toward which the Muslims faced when in prayer, was Jerusalem. The Hebrews had interpreted this as an indication of leaning toward Judaism and that Muhammad required their instruction in religious matters. However, probably because of the looming conflict, Muhammad received a new commandment from God to change the Qilbah from Jerusalem to the Ka'bah at Mecca.

As ruler of a state, Muhammad immediately turned his attention to establishing the proper method of public worship and laid down the foundation of the state. He did not, however, forget his enemies in Mecca nor that he had been commanded by God to fight against them until they abandoned their persecution of Islam. To this end he began making military preparations. The Meccan followers of Muhammad had been, for thirteen years, pacifists, and it is clear that many of them had a strong hatred for warfare, even if fighting in self-defense. If Muhammad was to overcome his enemies in Mecca he must also overcome this strain of pacifism. Surah II was revealed to him at this time, and the notable passage II, 216 (see the top of the first page of this chapter) is the most relevant passage in this surah to what was about to come. Some cynics believe that Muhammad had a convenient revelation to suit his purposes, while true-believing Muslims consider it divine revelation.

The commandment to warfare having been received, Muhammad began a process of training his new army. Small expeditions led by him or by other, closely trusted fugitives from Mecca went out. These armed bands, however, consisted solely of Meccans and no Medina men. These reconnaissance missions served both to explore the region and to meet and persuade surrounding tribes not to side with the Meccans. Though military operations, these excursions do not appear to have resulted in any major battles, though in one instance blood was shed and booty taken. This was apparently against Muhammad's orders; these were intended more as training exercises designed to build up the morale and inject some fighting spirit into Muhammad's followers. Still, the call to loot would be a powerful and natural inclination to the soldiers of the day. In later years as Muslim armies occupied the rich Persian and Byzantine holdings to the north, loot and fervor would be powerful twin pillars of Muslim success.

In the second year of the Hijrah, now that his hold on power was firm and his army exercised, Muhammad sought to take advantage of the periods of "holy truce" which served pilgrims to the Ka'bah. He used this truce as a screen to attack a wealthy summer caravan as it returned from Syria to Mecca. This was not just a looting foray, but a strike at the vital commercial interests of the Meccans.

The caravan leader had learned that the attack was coming and sent to Mecca for reinforcements. It is debatable if the caravan could have been saved or if the relief force sent from Mecca—more than 1,000 men,—was actually a defensive measure, or a punitive expedition designed to punish Muhammad. In either event, it was a disaster.

Muhammad had apparently deliberately let word escape of his intention to attack the caravan in order to draw out the Meccan army, his real target. Commanded by God to attack his persecutors, he had carefully lured the Meccan army out where he could engage it. The engagement occurred at Badr, eighty-five miles southwest of Medina, during Ramadan, A.D. 624. Before the fight occurred, Muhammad gave the Ansar (supporters), as the natives of Medina were called, leave to return to their homes, as their oath did not include the requirement to fight in the field. Unwilling to abandon their ruler, they refused to leave and went into battle. With these brave men and his original band of Meccan followers, the Prophet's forces were unstoppable. Muhammad's inspirational leadership brought his 300 men victory over a force of more than 1,000 Meccans. During the engagement the Meccan chief, Abu Jahl, one of Muhammad's greatest enemies, was killed. This engagement is also described as the first jihad, or holy war, because it was an aggression by infidels who were intent on the destruction of Islam and the Muslims.

The battle was hugely significant to the establishment of Muhammad's temporal power. The victory was interpreted as divine sanction of the new faith that he was spreading. Accordingly, we must examine this in terms of what had been revealed to Muhammad in the surah, prior to this engagement. There are two relevant passages:

> Surah IV, 74. Let those fight in the way of Allah who sell the life of this world for the other. Whoso fighteth in the way of Allah, be he slain or be he victorious, on him We shall bestow a vast reward.

> Surah IV, 104. Relent not in pursuit of the enemy. If ye are suffering lo! They suffer even as ye suffer and ye hope from Allah that for which they cannot hope. Allah is ever Knower, Wise.

Surah IV, 74, is a passage that we will frequently discuss. It promises paradise to those who die fighting for Allah. Imagine if you will the influence this would have on a man who believed it to be the revealed word of God, spoken to him by God's own prophet. Surah IV, 104, is far more practical. It rightly points out to those who might be fainthearted that their enemies are suffering as much they are, and if it is bad for them, it is equally bad for the enemy. In fact, militarily speaking, an army's position is always far worse when pursued than when pursuing. In fact this surah foreshadows the famous pursuits of Napoleon, and even the blitzkriegs of World War II. It is difficult to say if the Prophet perceived this specifically, but his words certainly provoked his men to push harder. If they were pursuing a broken enemy, the necessity to pursue that enemy and complete his destruction was critical if Muhammad was to break their power.

The victory at Badr manifested the Muslim's spirit of discipline and contempt for death. These two factors would become the hallmark of Muslim warfare for the next 1,500 years. It is interesting that Muhammad at first refused the service of his Medina Ansar. This may be an indication that he had formulated the requirement that none might fight as his allies unless they were Muslims. This idea would be important in the years following, as many tribes flocked to his banner. It was very much the tradition of that country—and many more since—that people followed a winner and deserted a loser. The Prophet's idea may have been to use this as one more tool to persuade conversion.

This idea is supported by Surah IV, 89.

> They that long that ye should disbelieve even as they disbelieve, that ye may be upon a level (with them). So choose not friends from them until they forsake their homes in the way of Allah; if they turn back (to enmity) [abandon Islam] then take them and kill them wherever ye find them, and choose no friend nor helper from among them.

This is a clear indication that the decision to join Islam was irrevocable. Defection would not be tolerated by the armies of Muhammad.

The Battle of Badr also seems to have been followed quickly by the revelation of Surah VIII. Militarily, this surah is extremely interesting. Within it are the following passages:

12. When my Lord inspired the Angels, (saying) I am with you. So make those who believe stand firm. I will throw fear into the hearts of those who disbelieve. Then smite the necks and smite of them each finger.

13. That is because they opposed Allah and his messenger. Whoso opposeth Allah and His messenger, (for him) lo! Allah is severe in punishment,

14. That (is the award), so taste it, and (know) that for disbelievers it is the torment of Fire.

15. O ye who believe! When ye meet those who disbelieve in battle, turn not your backs on them.

16. Whoso on that day turneth his back on them, unless maneuvering for battle or intent to join a company, he truly hath incurred wrath from Allah, and his habitation will be hell, a hapless journey's end.

Surah VIII, 12–14, implies that Allah will smite nonbelievers through his soldiers. This is the carrot to the faithful. Surah VIII, 15–16, is the stick. The Koran clearly says that running away from the enemy will condemn the Muslim warrior to hell. It is fascinating to see that the phrasing of these passages does allow for soldiers to maneuver at appropriate times. This was completely within the tradition of the hit-and-run style of warfare practiced by the nomadic desert tribesmen. One can consider these passages in the context of Muhammad's next battle, Mt. Uhud.

Unfortunately for Muhammad, his victory at Badr was not decisive. The very next year the Meccans, under Abu Sufyan, would avenge their defeat at the Battle of Mt. Uhud in A.D. 625. Muhammad was heavily outnumbered, but, nevertheless, came near victory. The Muslim army numbered about 700 men, and the Meccan forces, under Abu Sufyan, were around four times their strength. However, Muhammad, victorious in the initial engagement, was betrayed by a force of fifty archers that had been ordered to block a pass and prevent the Meccan cavalry from passing through. While Muhammad's men looted and pillaged the spoils of their victory, these fifty archers abandoned their post to join the pillage. As fate would have it, the Meccan cavalry arrived and moved through the now unguarded pass to strike the disorganized Muslims in the midst of plundering. Muhammad was wounded and initially thought slain. His uncle, Hazrat Hamza, was killed. When Muhammad was found only wounded, his band circled around him and fought their way clear of the field, escaping into the desert. The Meccan victory at Uhud was short-lived, though, and the initiative returned to Muhammad.

The following day, Muhammad again went out with his army to show himself and to deter the possibility of a Meccan attack on Medina. He encountered and conversed with a friendly Bedawi tribesman. This Bedawi then met the Meccan forces, where he was questioned by abu-Sufyan, the enemy leader. On hearing that Muhammad was alive, in the field, and thirsting for revenge, abu-Sufyan decided to withdraw and returned to Mecca.

This drawn battle was not positive in its immediate effect. As some will always wish to support the winning side, many Arab tribes and the Hebrews, who had a treaty with Muhammad, saw the defeat at Uhud as meaning that the Muslims were losing. They shifted their allegiance toward Mecca. Perceiving the Muslims as weakened, these groups attacked and murdered them when they could be found in small parties. One of Muhammad's close followers, Khubeyb, was captured and sold to the Meccans, who publicly tortured him to death in Mecca. The Hebrews became openly hostile and frankly stated that the pagan religion of the Meccans was superior to Islam. Again, this was not the first time that Hebrews underestimated a prophet.

In A.D. 627 a force known as the "Confederates" *(al-ahzab)* that consisted of Meccans with Bedouin and Abyssinian mercenaries had begun to take military action against Medina. In a gathering to discuss strategy, a Persian follower of Muhammad, named Hazrat Salaman Farsi, suggested to Muhammad that he dig a trench around Medina. This was done by 3,000 Muslims, apparently in a day. When the confederates arrived before Medina the moat defense prevented them from attacking, so they camped and contented themselves for several days with showering arrows on the city.

As the Muslims waited for the assault, word came that the Banu-Qurayzah tribe of Hebrews had abandoned their loyalty to Muhammad and had gone over to the Confederates, combining their fighting men. It is possible to say that this news signified the absolute nadir of Muslim fortunes in all of what had passed, and all that was to come. In 1,500 years of Muslim history, at no point does the entire fate of the Prophet's people rest on a small, dispirited, besieged garrison such as that at Medina in 627.

But Muhammad was neither discouraged nor helpless. Matters would quickly change.

These combined enemy forces sat before Medina and contemplated their next action. While they discussed their options, agents from Medina spread dissent between the Confederates and their new Hebrew allies. As distrust brewed, a storm came in from the sea so strong that the besiegers' tents blew over and no fires could be lit either to cook or keep warm. The leader of the Confederates, having had enough, quietly slipped away in the night. His mercenaries and adventurers followed. When the Banu-Qurayzah awoke in the morning, they found they'd been abandoned and also quickly decamped. The Battle of the Ditches, or Battle of Ahzab, as the blockade of Medina was called, ended with both sides losing about twenty men.

Muhammad felt obliged to take action. The Bani Nadir Hebrew tribe of Medina had actually been expelled a full year before the Confederates attacked Medina. But now the Banu-Qurayzah tribe was singled out for destruction. Muhammad caught the Banu-Qurayzah in their stronghold and began a month-long siege. When it ended, they surrendered unconditionally, except that they begged judgment by a member of the Arab tribe to which they were adherents. This was granted them, but the judgment rendered was brutal. The 600 able-bodied men were condemned to death and slaughtered. Their women and children were sold into slavery. The slaughter of the men and the enslavement of women and children of a defeated tribe or city would become a common practice as the Islamic Empire expanded.

Muhammad now distributed the spoils, such as the Banu-Qurayzah tribe's ownerless date groves, to his followers. The process of expelling Hebrew tribes continued, and in A.D. 629 the Hebrews of Khaybar were expelled from their oasis north of Medina. Thus the religious purification of the pilgrimage sites began.

In A.D. 628 Muhammad had a vision[5] of himself entering the holy place in Mecca determined to attempt the pilgrimage. His recent victories had encouraged those tribes whose loyalties belonged to the strongest to swing to his support again. He called upon them to support him, and many came, but not all. He drew together a band of 1,400 men and dressed them as pilgrims to the Ka'bah. Again, word of Muhammad's advance leaked into Mecca and Meccans prepared for war.

Muhammad heard of their preparations and stopped his advance, choosing to send a messenger ahead to request that he be admitted as a pilgrim. The messenger was abused and returned without delivering the message. Further messengers were sent and finally the Meccans sent out proper envoys. The Truce of Al-Hudeybiyah was signed, agreeing to no hostilities between the two parties for ten years. Muhammad was not permitted to visit the Ka'bah, but after a year of no hostilities, he and his comrades were to be allowed to do so. Meccan deserters were to be returned, but deserters from the Muslims were not. The truce was opened to any of the other Arab tribes that might wish to sign it, as allies of Mecca.

It might appear as if Muhammad had received the poor end of the bargain, but in fact, he gained the ability to openly penetrate into Mecca and spread his message and his religion. He co-opted the city from within using a fifth column of propagandists that undermined the religious power base of the pagans.

That same year, the Meccans violated the Truce of Al-Hudeybiyah and slaughtered a tribe allied with Muhammad. Fearful of the consequences of their act, they sent emissaries to Muhammad asking for a renewal of the truce, hoping they would arrive before Muhammad learned of the massacre. They did not.

Muhammad summoned all the Muslims capable of bearing arms and amassed a force of 10,000 fighting men. This, coupled with spreading internal dissent, was too much. The Meccans were overawed by the Muslim numbers and fled the field without shedding any blood. Muhammad proclaimed a general amnesty, but held the enemy leaders accountable. The relief and surprise caused the city to swear allegiance to Muhammad.

Having unrestricted access to Mecca, Muhammad entered the sacred temples of the idolaters and smashed the idols, said to have numbered 360. He proceeded to declare the area around the Ka'bah as sacred to Islam and issued Surah IX, 28, which forbade non-Muslims from approaching it. This was probably intended to break the back of the polytheists and their annual pilgrimage to the Ka'bah and may not have been intended to be a permanent exclusion, but it has become one, and to this day no non-Muslim is permitted there. Apparently, however, in at least fifteen recorded instances Christians penetrated the two Holy Cities and escaped alive. The first was Ludovico di Varthema of Bologna in 1503.

Angry at the destruction of their idols, the remaining pagan tribes sought to regain control of the Ka'bah. They gathered 12,000 troops and at Huneyn in a deep ravine ambushed Muhammad and his bodyguard. The fight was horrible. Although outnumbered and in a tactically awkward spot, the Muslims were victorious. The booty was tremendous, as many of these nomadic tribesmen had brought all their wealth with them. Having crushed his enemies, Muhammad sent out emissaries to continue the destruction of pagan idols. Only the Taif appear to have made any considerable effort to resist Muhammad, so he laid siege to their city. This appears to be Muhammad's first use of siege artillery, and its first use by any Arabs.

Muhammad had become the major power in the region and could now increase his power without engaging in battle. In 632 he stationed a garrison in Tabuk and signed peace treaties with the Christian chief of Aylah and the Hebrew tribes in the oases of Maqna, Adhruh, and al-Jarba to the south. These non-Muslims taken under the protection of the Muslims were obliged to pay a tribute or tax known as the *jizyah*. This tax would be imposed, as the empire grew, on all non-Muslims who became part of the empire. It was the penalty for not converting and would become a lever for subtly forcing conversion.

That same year Muhammad heard that the Byzantine emperor was gathering a force in Syria with the goal of destroying him. The Byzantine force is reported to have 100,000 men. Though such figures are notoriously unreliable, it is probable that the force gathering was considerably larger than what the Muslims would deploy against it. Sources agree Muhammad sent 3,000 men into Syria under the command of Zeyd (or Zaid). Some claim that this campaign was unsuccessful, but the reckless valor of the Muslims so impressed the Byzantines that they decided to leave this hornet's nest alone. The most reasonable source claims that the shattered remnant of Muhammad's force retreated to Medina after losing three commanders.

When sources conflict on such issues we must attempt to evaluate the possible motives that might result in such divergent opinions. The great problem is that ancient history is not the complete record that we would like. Journalism did not exist, official records were either not kept or did not survive, and what has come down to us must be examined for self-serving intent. Simply put, we can conjecture, but not know.

Bearing all of this in mind, Muhammad would likely have known of the power of the Byzantines. A force of 3,000 men might have made a useful raiding party, but would have been too few for a major attack. The Byzantines had a high military reputation, and such a small force would have been too weak to seriously hinder a full-bore Byzantine effort. It might reasonably be considered a suicide mission. On the other hand, at the time the Byzantines almost certainly had their hands full with their long-time Persian opponents, and the proposed imperial threat was just a sideshow. In this case, 3,000 men might have been enough. It is certainly not reasonable to think that 3,000 Muslims prevailed against 100,000 Byzantines.

We do know that Muhammad's total armed force was certainly larger than 3,000 men, so it could not have been a serious effort to attack and defeat an enemy. This would violate the first and most obvious rule of war—concentration of force and effort. Muhammad's many engagements clearly indicate that he understood this principle. If one looks at it callously, the sacrifice of 3,000 men who were expected to fight with fanatic ferocity might well encourage an enemy to think twice about the damage possible from engaging the entire force of such an enemy. Whatever the result of this abortive Syrian adventure, Muhammad did not suffer from it, nor did his rule.

In A.D. 630 once again rumors arrived in Arabia that the Byzantines planned an invasion of Arabia. The Muslims mobilized to face the rumored invasion and preparations for a jihad were made. A force, reputed to be 30,000 strong, was organized and dispatched north to Tabuk, where the Byzantines were rumored to be massing. When they arrived, the Muslims found no Byzantines. After waiting a few days, they returned to Arabia.

After the Banu-Qurayzah were slaughtered, particularly between 630 and 631, there came what was known as the "year of delegations" *(sanat al-wufud)*. Delegations from the various tribes of Arabia flocked to him to offer their allegiance to Muhammad, if not out of conviction, then out of convenience. Muhammad accepted them, exacting a verbal profession of faith and the payment of the *zakah* (poor tax). Tribes that had, heretofore, bowed to no one, bowed to the will of Muhammad—the Tayyi, the Hamdan, and the Kindah.

In the tenth year of the Hijrah, Muhammad entered Mecca triumphantly at the head of his annual pilgrimage. This would be his last pilgrimage, as three months later, back in Medina, he took unexpectedly ill and died complaining of a severe headache on June 8, 632.

Looking at Muhammad's military operations, it is clear that he understood how to motivate men. He offered them great rewards in either victory or defeat with Surah IV, 74. He showed that he understood that the enemy's situation is as hard as that of his own army and by revelation in Surah IV, 104, made it a matter of religious dogma. How could a tired, hungry, and cold soldier not believe that his enemy was suffering when God had said it was so?

A fair amount can be deduced about his tactical capabilities. As an inspirational leader, his first battle at Badr in 624 shows him the equal of any of the great soldiers in history. At the battle at Uhud we find that Muhammad understood the value of terrain and how by holding appropriate positions a small force should be able to stop a larger force. Unfortunately, at Mt. Uhud, the band of fifty archers failed to hold their key position. It would be interesting to discover what punishment Muhammad meted out to those greedy men who so nearly caused his death.

Muhammad also showed both a willingness to listen to subordinates, as when he adopted Salaman Farsi's suggestion to dig a moat around Medina in A.D. 627. He was also willing to accept new ideas. His use of the moat and his use of siege artillery at the reduction of Taif were both major innovations in the traditional form of Arab warfare.

If more evidence is needed of the Prophet's military skill, one can only point out that he had a well developed sense of the military ideal—maintaining the objective. He was willing to accept the unfavorable terms of the Truce of Al-Hudeybiyah to achieve his long-term goal. He traded a paper victory to the Meccans in return for the time and ability to spread his message to the Meccan population as well as unfettered access to the other surrounding Arab tribes. He'd seen the success of his proselytizing and knew that he could gain strength faster than the Meccans. Quite possibly he understood the arrogance and ignorance of the Meccans toward what he was doing and played to their weakness.

If one looks at his first battle, the attack on the caravan at Badr, one also finds that Muhammad had realized that conquest lies not in simple booty-gathering raids, but in the destruction of the enemy's forces. At Badr, Muhammad targeted not the rich caravan but the Meccan army. This concept of destruction of the enemy's army as the key to victory would repeat itself throughout the expansion of Islam. The Romans had practiced wars of annihilation, but this process disappeared in the Western European military tradition, not to reappear until Napoleon Bonaparte's 1796 campaign where he set about the destruction of the enemy armies, knowing that to be the quickest and surest path to victory.

For a man whose first experience of combat appears to have occurred when he was fifty-three years old, Muhammad proved a remarkably capable leader, tactician, and strategist. Where he would have gone had he not died in A.D. 632 we of course will never know, but it is unlikely that his successors deviated far from his chosen path.

CHRONOLOGY

571	Muhammad is born in Mecca.
615–22	Muhammad preaches.
622	Hijrah to Medina.
623	Muhammad has authority in Medina, war with Mecca.
630	Occupation of Mecca
630–32	Muhammad consolidates control of Arabian Peninsula.
632	Muhammad dies, June 8.

NOTES

1. Koran: Surah XCVI, 1–5.

2. For the sake of those not comfortable with Arabic names, the Quraysh will, henceforth, be referred to as the "Meccans," since they lived in Mecca.

3. Koran: Surah VIII, 39.

4. Hazrat 'Umar Ibin-Al-Khattab, the second caliph, who ruled from A.D. 634 to 645.

5. Koran: Surah XLVIII, 27.

Chapter 2

THE GREAT CONQUESTS

In 622, at about the time that Muhammad was beginning to construct his power base at Medina, the two great powers of the Mediterranean world were in the final phases of a great war. This war, fought between the ancient Persian Empire and the organized power of the Byzantine Empire, had six more years to run. The two huge warring empires forgot about the seemingly ephemeral events in the Arabian Peninsula. Neither of them could have foreseen the mistake in this.

Of the two, the Persians had been familiar to the western powers since the days of Xerxes and the Greek city-states in the fourth century B.C. The great empire, now ruled by the Sassanid dynasty, had its power base in what is now Iran and Iraq, but it stretched as far as India, and traded beyond. The English-speaking world knows little of the Persian Empire, but it was probably the mightiest imperial construct of all time. Made rich by its position astride Oriental trade routes, and strong by the number and valor of its warriors, the fire-worshipping Zoroastrian Persians were both vigorous and competent. They had been troubled by Greeks, and then by Alexander, and even by the Romans, but at the end of the day the Persian Empire stood as it had always—the greatest power in the Middle East. Or so it was in 622.

The Byzantine, or Eastern Roman Empire, had grown up around the city of Constantinople in the fourth century A.D. Although this Eastern Empire considered itself Roman in all except geography, it had been sufficiently distant and powerful to survive the destruction of the old Western

Empire centered in Rome itself. As with the Persians, the English-speaking world has generally paid little attention to the Byzantines. These Eastern Romans had inherited the intellectual, organizational, and military skills of the old Western Empire and had systematically improved upon them. By the seventh century, the Byzantine Empire controlled most of the Mediterranean seacoast. Her navy ruled the Middle Sea in the same way that her army generally dominated Greece, Northern Africa, Turkey, Syria, Italy, and even Spain. The Byzantines were thus not only the heirs of the most successful of the old western powers, but they also produced the first modern sea-based empire in western history. By the second quarter of the seventh century, Byzantine skills had been honed to their highest degree, and nothing could stand against Byzantium—or so it seemed.

When Muhammad died in June 632, the new Islamic state was thrown into confusion and uncertainty. Like so many warlords before and since, Muhammad had failed to provide for a succession. Indeed, no one knew if there was to be a succession, or even a continuing government. With the Prophet's death, many of the nomadic tribes surrounding Mecca and Medina fell away—they refused to pay their taxes and renounced their allegiance to the faith. This became known as "The Apostasy." Had it been allowed to persist, it would probably have meant the end of Islam and certainly would have prevented the great Muslim Empire that soon would come into existence.

At the very hour of Muhammad's death, Abu Bekr was appointed—virtually by acclaim—to lead the new Arab state. A deeply devout and well-respected man, Abu Bekr combined piety, humility, honesty and solid common sense. After the death of the Prophet, he was almost certainly the only man who could sustain the core religious and political foundations of the Islamic state. His reputation was such that he had no rivals—he was acceptable to both Meccan and Medinan followers.

Abu Bekr held together the core of Islam, centered in Mecca, as the nomadic tribes that had earlier offered allegiance to Muhammad, fell away. In July 632 within days of his accession to authority, the new caliph, as he was now called, sent a raiding force under Usama, the son of the Prophet's adopted son, north to raid the Byzantine frontier. This force took many of the fighting men away from the seat of power, but left enough to mount a sharp retaliation against tribes that attempted to stray, or refuse to pay their taxes.

When the raiding party returned from the Byzantine frontier, Abu Bekr deployed the returning warriors to stamp out any hint of apostasy or rebellion. The new commander of this force was Khalid ibn al Waleed. Khalid soon proved himself one of the great natural military leaders in all of human history. He would be instrumental in two of the world's most decisive campaigns. Even more remarkably, these campaigns were conducted almost simultaneously against two stronger powers.

Khalid marched south and east with perhaps 4,000 warriors and at the Battle of Buzakha defeated the combined tribes of rebels and apostates. This was in the fall of 632, and when coupled with the later Battle of Aqraba, marked the end of serious opposition to the Caliph Abu Bekr. A good story about one of the chiefs of the apostates—Tulaiha—illustrates the ready humor of the nomadic Arabs of the day. Tulaiha had claimed prophetic inspiration and revelation such that he would rival and replace Muhammad. At the Battle of Buzakha his forces were scattered, and later Tulaiha repented, became faithful and went on pilgrimage to Mecca. When chided for his murder of the faithful Muslim Ukkasha during his revolt, he is reported to have said, "Why, was it not better that by my hand Ukkasha should ascend into heaven, rather than that I should by his descend into hellfire?" And, when asked what had become of his prophetic gift, the old rebel answered, "It was but a puff or two, as if with a bellows." Humor of this sort shows the rough but hardy character of the desert warrior. It would not have been out of place coming from a Viking at the opposite extreme of the Eurasian continent. Just as the seafaring raiders would batter the centers of European power, so would the desert raiders crash into the great Middle Eastern nations.

As Khalid subdued the rebelling tribes and brought the entire Arabian Peninsula under control, the caliph in Mecca recalled most of his fighting men to reinforce the Syrian expedition against the Byzantines. The redoubtable warrior, with probably fewer than 1,000 men, pushed on to the northeast toward modern-day Iraq, arriving in the lands of the Beni Bekr tribe in early spring of 633. This tribe of Arabic nomads had not professed Islam during Muhammad's life, and Khalid had no particular argument with them. He was, in fact, well greeted by Muthanna ibn Haritha, a subclan chief. Muthanna and most of his tribesmen were willing to become Muslims and allies, because this would give them weight to raid into Persian territory. This union was the beginning of the destruction of the fabled Persian Empire at the hands of an insignificant band of nomads.

The Sassanid Persian Empire had been established 400 years earlier in A.D. 226, and by the seventh century had very much recovered the grandeur of the fabled Achaemenid Empire that had so troubled Greece in the classic era. In the early years of the seventh century King Chosroes II fought a generation-long war with the Byzantines. This epic war came to an end in February 628 when Byzantine Emperor Heraclius decisively defeated the main Persian host at Nineveh. Chosroes was assassinated by his son, Siros. Siros made peace with Byzantium and then proceeded to butcher every conceivable family rival. This practice of destroying rival siblings would become a regular event during any dynastic change in later Islamic kingdoms.

Siros's treachery was not rewarded by any success, for he too fell to an assassin after an eight-month reign, and the realm fell to pieces. The proud empire fell into such total chaos that the term "civil war" is hardly appropriate. Anarchy is much closer to the truth. Finally, in 632, a king was found—Yezdegird, a young and inexperienced lad with some royal blood, but nothing like the experience that would have been required to lead the ruined Empire back onto its feet.

Had the Byzantine war not ruined Persia, it would have had little difficulty with the Muslims. At its prime, the Persian army was a formidable array. The fine Persian cavalry—famous since Alexander's day—was the cream of the army. It included not only heavily armored lancers, similar to later Western knights, but also hordes of lightly armed horse-archers, including Hun and other steppe tribes as allies. The infantry was not as well thought of, being mostly peasant levies rudely equipped with bows or spears. However, when accompanied by Indian elephants, they were a terrifying opponent to any foe. Under normal circumstances it is unlikely that the Muslims would have had the strength even to confront the main Persian armies, but the Sassanian strength had been terribly reduced by the long war with the Byzantines.

The Persians had created a chain of buffer states to guard their frontier from the nomadic tribes living in the desert between Iraq and the Arabian Peninsula. Of these, the chief were the Beni Bekr, whom Khalid encountered in March of 633. The Beni Bekr had been paid by the Persians to police their frontier with the wilder tribes to the west, but the financial drain of the wars had shrunk the subsidy. The result was that Khalid found a willing ally who was not only familiar with the frontier's geography and his enemy's forces, but also his weaknesses.

Reinforced by his new allies, Khalid moved quickly, and in March 633 he defeated a small Persian force at Kadhima, south of the Euphrates, close to the Persian Gulf. He then moved through the fringes of the desert to capture the port city of Ubulla, which surrendered on terms. Crossing the river, the Arabs found themselves in the rich farmland of the Tigris-Euphrates basin, which must have seemed a land of plenty to the nomadic desert warriors. The force actually operated east of the river briefly, but Khalid, a clever strategist, preferred to keep the desert at his back, not the river.

In fact, all of Khalid's campaigns show that he truly understood the concept of "desert power." Simply put, his men could move into the drier lands, and his heavier Persian opponents could not. This meant that he could offer battle or refuse just as he chose. If threatened, his men could withdraw into the desert where they could not be pursued.

This tactic was certainly obvious to the great warrior. First, his men were accustomed to the harsh conditions of the desert, and the Persians were not. Second, the Persian horses would require a great deal of water daily, and that was not to be found in the sandy wastes. Third, the Arabs quite naturally employed their camels as mobile supply columns, rather like convoys of trucks in modern warfare. "Ships of the desert" is an appropriate phrase.

In late April or early May of 633 the Persians gathered another force to oppose the raiding Muslims. This probably included a core of Persian soldiers, but also included a contingent of Arab tribesmen, freshly bribed by the imperial government. Khalid, hearing of this force, withdrew west of the Euphrates and gave battle at Ullais. This famous Battle of the Blood River was apparently a hard fight. The battle name reflects the fact that Khalid slaughtered all of the enemy prisoners that came under his hand. Massacres like this were not unheard of in that time, but neither were they the norm. It is likely that the Muslim leader used the slaughter to send a clear message to the other tribesmen of the area. This would be a particularly useful message—the Arab desert tribes were the only ones who could possibly interfere with the "desert power" strategy that the veteran warrior was employing. Thus, Khalid both defeated a threat to his rear and made a recurrence less likely.

With the victory at Ullais, and with some reinforcements from the Beni Temeem, the Muslims moved north, again on the west bank of the Euphrates. They soon confronted and besieged the fortified city of Hira in May or early June 633.

Hira represented a unique problem to the Arabs, and a common one to the besieged. As brave as they might be, the lightly equipped desert raiders would certainly lack the equipment and skills of siege warfare. Defended walls would present an insurmountable obstacle against which the raiders could only blockade and harry the surrounding country. This sort of work, although rewarding, was slow, and brought the attackers to a standstill. If they remained in place long enough, it was always possible that a fresh enemy force could arrive from across the Euphrates. It should be noted that Hira was by far the largest and most formidable city that the Arabs had yet encountered.

For the residents of Hira, though, the situation was also difficult. Although the townspeople could defend their walls, they could not cope with the Muslims in open battle—and so they could not protect the surrounding farms and villages. These farms were the food supply for the city, and if they stayed in enemy hands, the city would starve or be forced to capitulate. The best solution, of course, would be relief by a mobile Persian army. The disarray of the Persian government made that unlikely.

With both sides well aware of their own weaknesses, a compromise was in order. Hira surrendered to the point that tribute was collected and a tax set to be paid. But the city fathers were unwilling to convert to Islam. They were Christians, and that faith they kept.

Khalid's skill as a general becomes apparent when one examines his actions at the Battle of the River of Blood, and the Siege of Hira. He could be murderous, and he could be generous. Neither or both could be said to be his character. Ultimately, the desert warrior had the flexibility of mind to adapt the course that would best further his goal. Modern military theorists consider this the "maintenance of the objective." The uneducated desert warrior had an inherent understanding of strategic concepts.

In September Khalid's force moved a few miles north and captured the walled city of Anrab by the novel expedient of filling its moat with the bodies of its weakest camels. In December 633 the Arab army moved back into the desert to deal with yet another threat to their desert lines of communication mounted by Arab tribes more northern than those crushed at the Battle of the Blood River. These tribes were either unaware of the Blood River battle or unimpressed by it. With the aid of a small Persian garrison they threatened to cut Khalid's line of retreat, and he turned back to the west to deal with them at Ain el Tamr.

The Arab general was generous in most dealings with the Persian cities that he occupied, but he was ruthless with the nomads who opposed him. After this victory, all of the losers were slaughtered and their families were sold into slavery. In this instance, it served Khalid's needs to secure his line of retreat, and he annihilated anyone who threatened it.

This was the Khalid's last victory over the Persians. His original instructions from Caliph Abu Bekr had been to eliminate opposition in the Arabian Peninsula. He had exceeded that authority by his attacks on the Persian Empire. While he had been attacking one giant in the east, the caliph's main interest lay to the north and the invasion of Byzantine Syria. In December 633 Khalid was recalled to assist the Muslim main effort, where his military genius would shine yet again.

The new commander of the Arab forces opposing Persia, was Muthanna, a tribal sheik of the Beni Bekr, from central Arabia. It is probably fair to say that Muthanna was a less capable leader than Khalid, but he was nonetheless a resolute man and one of considerable personal valor. Refitting his reduced force from Hira and Anrab, he moved to the ruins of ancient Babylon on the banks of the Euphrates, and awaited the Persian response.

This came in the spring of 634 when the new boy-king, Yezdegird, brought up such troops as he could, and attempted to drive the raiders away. His forces included an elephant, which must have seemed strange indeed to the Arabs. One also assumes that the Persians had a significant numerical superiority over the invaders, for Khalid had gone off with his chosen troops and Babylon was nearly in the heart of the Persian Empire.

In the event, the Persians advanced with their ferocious elephant and caused some dismay among the Arabs, but Muthanna himself ran forward and killed the huge beast. Perhaps as a Beni Bekr tribesman Muthanna would have had some familiarity with the Persians and may even have seen elephants. However it was that he dispatched the beast, its death heartened the Arabs, who pushed the enemy back and held the field.

Now victorious, Muthanna must yet have known that his isolated force could not long resist the enemy in their own heartland. After the battle at Babylon, he rode to Medina to see the Caliph Abu Bekr and beg for reinforcements. He arrived in late July and met the caliph. Old and frail, Abu Bekr died in August 634, to be succeeded by Umar ibn al Khattab. The new caliph recognized the value of Muthanna's requests and called up additional levies for the Iraqi front.

There is an interesting anecdote from this visit. As recruits came forward, the old friends and companions of the Prophet were notably absent. Umar was asked who would command the new force, and the names of several of these companions were brought forward. But the new caliph would have none of it, and he said that the man who had first volunteered should lead. In this manner the obscure Abu Ubaid ibn Masud found himself a leader of men—in fact he was to lead the whole army on the Persian front, with Muthanna as his subordinate. It was a casual process by any standards!

With reinforcements being gathered, the two commanders returned to the front, and none too soon. The King of Kings, as the Persians called their monarchs, had appointed a wise old general named Rustem to command his armies. Rustem had been harrying the much-reduced Arab force with mobile columns while a large army gathered under command of a general named Bahman. As the fresh Arab warriors arrived, the two armies consolidated and prepared to fight.

Before they could join in battle though, the obstacle of the Euphrates must be overcome. In ancient days great rivers were impassable military obstacles, at least if defended. If too deep to ford and too wide to allow archers to support a bridge or boat crossing, they simply could not be crossed. Of course if both armies wanted to fight, then an accommodation could be made by the simple method of inviting the enemy to cross.

Thus, in the fall of 634, General Bahman invited Abu Ubaid to decide who should cross the river. Although his veteran leaders—Muthanna among them—suggested that the Arabs keep the friendly desert to their rear, and not the dangerous river, the brave Abu Ubaid retorted, "What? Shall we fear death more than they?" And so battle was joined, the Persians happily conceding passage across the river on a bridge.

The fight took place south of Babylon and east of the Euphrates. The Persians probably outnumbered the Muslims, who may have had 10,000 men. Additionally the Persian host had its usual contingent of elephants and was fighting on ground of its own choosing. The nomads came on with their usual courage, but the new levies from Arabia were fearful of the elephants, and the lines began to waver. At this, Abu Ubaid ran forward to slay one of the beasts personally. Probably he intended to emulate the great Muthanna, who had also slain one of the monsters. However, the Arab general was misinformed that the trunk was an elephant's vulnerable point, and so slashed at it with his sword. Sadly, the elephant's reaction was predictable and, far from following in Muthanna's footsteps, Abu Ubaid fell into the elephant's. With the death of their leader, the Arab forces fled back to the bridge in panic. The rout was bad enough—about 6,000 were lost—but it would have been worse had a rear guard not held the bridge for a time.

This battle, probably occurring in October of 634 became known as the Battle of the Bridge. Muthanna resumed command and led the remnants of the army back into the desert fringe, where they were safe from the enemy. It would be a year before sufficient reinforcements arrived for the Arabs to renew their offensive, meanwhile the desert terrain protected them from attack by the King of Kings.

The battle that Muthanna fought at Buwaib in November 635, was his last and greatest victory. In this fight the Arabs had the desert at their back and the Persians had the Euphrates behind them. When the Persians gave way, Muthanna rushed forward to the bridge—the same one across which his own army had fled—and held it against the fleeing enemy. Few Persians escaped. This was the battle that Muthanna wanted, and Abu Ubaid had denied. Shortly after the Battle of Buwaib, Muthanna died, perhaps of old wounds.

It would be autumn of 636 before the new Arab leader appeared on the Persian front. He was Saad ibn abi Waqqas. He was a thick-set and fierce veteran, said to have been the first to draw blood in the behalf of Islam. He may, in fact, have been a part of the first raid on the Meccan caravan in 624. If Saad was a fierce nomadic warrior, he was also an experienced fighting man. He possibly fought on the Syrian front against the sophisticated Byzantines, and this service may have impelled him to actually train and organize the Arab armies. What had been a simple cloud of nomadic warriors with no organization above the clan or household, now became a real army. It was divided into divisions to serve as advance and rear guards, main body, and flankers. Each division was further divided into smaller units. Thus he created a fighting machine much more responsive to its commander's will. Of course, little had been wrong with the earlier force—the comfort for fighting men to serve with their kinsmen around them allowed a kind of cohesiveness that civilized armies do not always enjoy.

In the late winter of 636, Saad moved his army forward from his desert marshalling areas. Although the Persians had lost the last battle, they were still strong enough to deny the line of the Euphrates, so the Arabs had accomplished nothing of import until Saad had completed his training and brought his army up to a strength of perhaps 30,000.

The Persians had also been active. King Yezdegird had consolidated his power, somewhat, and General Rustem had gathered a strong army. It was the view of the general that his nation could not be defeated while his army was intact, and that his army could not be defeated while the river was to its front. Since the Arabs occupied only a tiny sliver of the great Persian Empire, there was no point in offering battle. Perhaps time or dissension would wear down the Muslim enthusiasm. He was perfectly correct in his strategy. Sadly, the Great King wanted the destruction of the Arab army to be the showcase of his new reign. He ordered Rustem to cross the Euphrates and attack.

The Arab force was drawn up in battle array near Qadasiya with the desert at their back. The Persians advanced in their usual style, preceded by a numerous force of elephants. Saad himself watched the battle from a rooftop in the village. Possibly he was acting as a modern general would, although his troops would not have appreciated this style of command. Possibly he was ill. In any event, the battle was a heavy one, and although the Muslims suffered deep losses on the first day, they did succeed in driving off the great beasts that so troubled them. On the second day the Arabs were reinforced by a strong contingent from Syria. These men, who had been victorious against the great Byzantine army, now lunged straight against the Persian force. Fighting continued into the night. On the third day, the elephants were put back into the fight, but their magic was gone, and Saad ordered the brave chief Qaqaa to deal with them. This he did by dismounting his men and attacking the beast's eyes with long spears.

Again, after the sun set, fighting continued into the dark. This time it was probably a planned attack. The nomads, who loved to compare themselves to wolves, liked to raid at night, and now their individual skill would be more of an asset against the serried ranks of the more formally trained Persian soldiers.

On the fourth day, with both armies nearing exhaustion, a sandstorm blew out of the southwest, and the Persians, with wind and sand in their eyes, broke. Rustem was killed and the King of Kings' army was irretrievably shattered.

This Battle of Qadasiya, fought in spring of 637, sounded the death knell of the old Persian Empire. Only ten years earlier their armies had occupied Syria and Egypt and had been battering at the gates of Byzantium. Despite additional tokens of resistance, after Qadasiya the empire fell to pieces. The Arab forces were slowed more by the weight of their loot than by Yezdegird's rear guards.

This victory was astonishing in its own right. A mighty nation had been defeated on its own ground by a motley assortment of tribal nomads. No wonder Muthanna said, "In the days of Ignorance a hundred Persians could defeat a thousand Arabs, but now, God be praised, a hundred Arabs can put to flight a thousand Persians."

Even Western skeptics may wonder about the divine nature of the Islamic conquest, for the campaign against Persia was but one of two fights that the infant religion fought simultaneously. The two enemies of these campaigns, Persia and Byzantium, were the greatest powers in the Middle East, and both were simultaneously smashed by an enemy with neither experience, nor wealth, nor numbers.

The Byzantine Empire draws scant attention in the English-speaking world today. Instead we focus on the Roman Empire, which may have had two or three centuries in the sun, but the Byzantine, or Eastern Roman Empire, lasted for a thousand years. The Byzantines, Greeks, or Romans—they were known as all three—were the heirs to the political, cultural, and military legacy of the whole Mediterranean basin. They were also the keepers of the military might of Christianity. Rome had become Christian officially in the fourth century. By the seventh century, the most powerful bishops were appointed by the Orthodox Church in the east. Thus, the Islamic storm about to break on Byzantine Syria would challenge the empire on every level.

In the first quarter of the seventh century, the empire engaged in a war of twenty-six years with the Sassanid Persians. For much of that time, Persian armies had occupied the vital Byzantine provinces of Egypt, Syria, and Anatolia. Even denied the taxes and revenues of these core areas, the Byzantines still held the great city, kept a mobile field army, and maintained the greatest fleet in the Mediterranean. The Emperor Heraclius, who would face the Muslims in Syria, had employed a wonderfully adept combination of offensive and defensive strategies to battle the Persian hosts. The end of this great war came in 628. Heraclius had moved his army from the Lebanese coast to the eastern extremity of the Black Sea. There, with hired Hunnic mercenaries, he had defeated the Persians in their heartland and dictated peace.

Heraclius and the empire were thus at their height when the Muslims came into the scene. And yet, for all of its power, the Byzantine Empire had serious weaknesses. The lack of imperial authority in the key Syrian, Egyptian, and Anatolian provinces had crippled the bureaucracy. The local residents were beginning to lose their identity as imperial subjects. The army brought in no recruits from these provinces, and so when the Byzantine army did appear, it was as foreign as that of the Arabs. Money was also a problem. War expenses and disruption of the tax base made it difficult to keep the armies and fleets paid. Byzantine armies expected to be paid and paid regularly. They were not like the Arabs that they would soon face.

Finally, a deep schism existed in the Christian world, and the Byzantine throne permitted its bishops to persecute heretics rather than to persuade them. When the Arabs moved against the Empire, generally the Muslims would be seen as liberators and not conquerors because of the religious intolerance within the Byzantine Empire. The sophisticated Byzantines enjoyed no comfort and little support from their religion, while to their enemies, the new faith of Islam gave a coherence and zeal that propelled them and magnified their commitment.

The earliest Muslim attack on Syria was in 629, while Muhammad was still alive. What may have been a mere raid met resistance—probably only local Arab tribes with a small Byzantine column—at the Battle of Mota. In this affair the Muslims were turned back with heavy losses, and Zeid ibn Haritha, the Prophet's son, was slain.

From 629 on, Syria became the main target of Islamic expansion. This may have been because the Arabs were eager to avenge Zeid's death. It may also be that they were familiar with the riches of the province because annual caravans traded with Mecca and Medina. It may have been that they considered the enemy weak, because the Persians had occupied the province for so many years. Whatever the reasons, the Byzantine target was always first in the eyes of the caliphs, and it was always the front to which the recruits clamored to be sent. It will be remembered that Khalid's first attacks on the Persians had been little more than a casual extension of his campaign to reduce the apostasy that followed Muhammad's death. Byzantium was always the main enemy from the day Muhammad had consolidated power in Arabia.

Abu Bekr dispatched the first real invasion in the winter of 633–34. Three columns, led by Amr ibn al Aasi, Yezeed ibn abi Sofian, and Shurahbil ibn Hasana marched north in a three-pronged attack. Shurahbil was to take the coastal plain to the west of the Dead Sea, Yezeed was to move up the east side of the same sea, and Amr was to strike into southern Palestine in the direction of Gaza, from farther east yet.

This opening campaign closely mirrored the Arab attacks against the Persians. They first met and defeated the tribal buffers that the empire had erected, and then moved on cautiously. The raiders kept their backs to the desert when facing heavy opposition. As on the Persian front, they had little difficulty with the local defense forces, and used their mobility to strike when and where they chose. While there was no Euphrates River to hold back the Muslims, the Byzantines did manage to field an army that held off the small raiding armies. This army held the Arabs at bay near Deraa, and although outflanked by Khalid, kept the enemy out of Damascus during the winter and into the spring of 634.

With the Arabs halted in the west, the Byzantines prepared a counter-blow, and a clever one. A large field army was assembled from the garrisons of Syria and Palestine—probably reinforced by troops moved by sea from the central army—and marched down the coastal route. The Byzantine plan was to strike Amr's army before it could be reinforced from the main Muslim force stalled at Deraa. The imperial force could then isolate the main Arab armies from supplies and reinforcements arriving from the south. This plan was much a part of Heraclius's traditional strategy of using defenses to hold an enemy while launching an attack in an unexpected quarter. It might well have worked, but the Emperor was fighting against Khalid, arguably the greatest desert warrior of all time.

While the imperial force, commanded by Theodorus, the Emperor's brother, marched south, Khalid led the main Arab forces south and the east of the Dead Sea. They crossed to the west at the Pass of Moab. In spite of their longer march, the Arabs arrived to bolster Amr's force before the fight took place. This rapid movement was typical of the Muslim armies, and the slow pace of the Byzantines was, and remains, symptomatic of sophisticated military forces. The Byzantine army drawing on the legacy of the old Roman legions, and the experience of fighting mounted warriors in the east, was a formidable foe. The core of the army was heavy cavalry armed with lance and bow. These were supported by various light troops. All were well trained and equipped—at least in theory. Even in literature the Byzantines were strong; since they enjoyed several military manuals that carefully guided every aspect of a campaign and were based on centuries of military experience. All of this reflects the care and attention that the Byzantines lavished on their military. It is not surprising that they did not seriously regard their rude opponents.

Battle was joined at Ajnadain, about twenty-five miles southwest of Jerusalem. It is not well chronicled, but the exploits of one Zarrar ibn al Azwar are wonderful. Possibly they are even true. Other events seem more possible, as they are illustrative of Byzantine and Arab practices.

Both armies were divided into divisions. Left, right, center, and rear guard. This would have been normal for the imperial forces, and innovative for the Arabs. The Byzantines then sent a black-robed monk to offer negotiation with the enemy, but actually to spy. This seems possible, for the Byzantines used trickery and treachery when it suited them. Their surviving military manuals detail some of these tricks. The Muslims responded to the monk by offering conversion or *jizyah,* the payment of a tax, and a token of submission. In keeping with Arab practice, as can be seen in the account of the Battle of Badr in Chapter 1, the fighting may have started with a contest of champions. In this fabled duel, Zarrar slew several Byzantine leaders, including two city governors. This wonderful heroism sadly, is unlikely to have occurred. Imperial leaders were taught to use their armies as weapons and would have considered personal challenges dangerous and backward. Fighting continued through the day with significant losses on both sides.

At the beginning of the second day, the Byzantines may have attempted to reopen negotiations with Khalid, intending to kill him by treachery during the parley. In the event, as the legend goes, Zarrar foiled the plot, and slew the enemy leader. This wonderful tale may be true. The Byzantines considered assassination a useful military tool. If true, this event caused fury in the Arab lines and confusion in the imperial ranks at the same time. The Muslims charged and swept the field.

The Battle of Ajnadain left both sides exhausted with heavy casualties. Not even Khalid could organize a pursuit, and the beaten imperial troops fled north to shelter in the walled cities of the provinces. The Arabs returned to the Deraa front, confident that their rear was secure. They still had their eyes on Damascus. As for the Byzantines, it is likely that the field army's defeat weakened the morale of troops occupying the positions at Deraa. They were easily broken and streamed away toward the great city of Syria in September 634, just a few weeks after Ajnadain. The single important Arab loss was Khalid. The enemy did not hurt the great leader, but the new Caliph Umar demoted the army commander to lead a single division. However Khalid's personal reputation was such that he was able to remain with the army. Abu Ubaida became the commander in chief.

With the enemy in retreat, the Arabs reached out for Damascus, the strategic prize of the whole campaign. However, they were to have the same problems with this fortified city that they had at Hira on the Iraqi front. Damascus held out for six months, a time the Emperor Heraclius put to good use assembling a new army. Had Muslim siege techniques been perfected, they might have taken the city much earlier and might have broken up the emperor's new forces. As it was, Damascus fell in almost comical fashion. Abu Ubaida had carefully and honorably negotiated a surrender with the governor of the city to take place on a certain day in the summer of 635. He did not, however, inform his subordinates, and thus it was that on the very night prior to the surrender, Khalid contrived to mount the wall near the east gate, overcome the guards, and storm into the city with his men. Khalid the great warrior, be it noted, was not much of a soldier. He failed to notify his superior. As dawn broke, Khalid's division was storming into the city at the east gate, while the governor was surrendering to Abu Ubaida at the west. All was made well, but it was a good example of Abu Ubaida's quiet methods and Khalid's warrior skills. They complemented each other nicely.

While the Arab forces, perhaps 20,000 strong, sat in front of Damascus, Emperor Heraclius was forming a new army around Antioch. It was a large one, but not a particularly good one. One large contingent was Armenian, recruited in the heart of the Anatolian province renowned for its good soldiers. But the Armenians insisted upon fighting under their own Prince Gargas in their own formations. This was, perhaps, the fruit of the long Persian occupation and recent imperial defeats. Another contingent was of Christian Arab tribesmen of the northern part of Arabia led by Sheikh Jabala. These might well have found themselves in the Muslim army, for they were the tribe that had formed the traditional buffer between the empire and the Arabs. During the long Persian wars they had not been subsidized by the Byzantines and were thus quite ready to join the Muslims out of pique. However, their leader had been insulted in Medina when he, a desert prince, was treated to a Koranic display of equality with a low-born townsman. As a result, Jabala and his men found themselves once more in the Byzantine camp. The third portion of the new army was of regular regiments drawn from the capital. These were probably few, because much of the central forces had probably been spent at Ajnadain and Damascus. Nevertheless, it was an imposing force, if only in numbers, and it may have been as strong as 60,000 men.

In spring of 636 the imperial army marched south into Syria. Khalid, who was by now the de facto commander of the Arab army, promptly abandoned Damascus, the prize that they had so patiently besieged the previous year. It is not surprising, since his army would be no better at defending a city than they had been at attacking one. Their strength was mobility, and their safety was the desert at their backs. Khalid moved back to something like the old lines near Deraa, taking up position in about April 636.

The imperial army approached its old positions, and—not surprisingly—settled into a defensive posture. The Byzantines had a sophisticated, seemingly modern theory of warfare. The army's goal was to defend Syria, which they could do from the Deraa position. The destruction of the Arab army would have been desirable, but the Byzantines saw no reason to risk a battle if the same outcome—the defense of Syria—could be obtained without hazard. As a result, the armies faced each other for weeks on end, stretching through the summer of 636.

Both armies held strong positions for the same reasons—the eastern flank was covered by the rocky volcanic lava fields of the Jebel Hauran, and the west flank by the deep canyon and shallow water of the Yarmouk River. The course of the river itself ran between the two forces. Thus, both armies may have had relatively secure flanks, and the Muslim forces had the desert to their rear. It is quite likely that the imperial forces may have ditched or otherwise fortified their camps, and possibly portions of the lines.

Much of the detail about the Battle of Yarmouk, as it was styled, is not known for a certainty, but several theories and threads provide possible explanations. Over the course of the summer, additional levies were sent forth by the caliph at Medina, strengthening Khalid's force. It is likely that the Byzantines were weakened by desertion at the same time. If this was so, it may explain why the Byzantines offered battle in August. They were growing weaker and the enemy stronger, so an early battle was more to their advantage. If this was the case, it is likely that the imperial forces attacked, and, once out of their positions, were destroyed by the ferocity and zeal of the Muslim forces.

Another possible explanation is that the Arabs had infiltrated both flanks with small parties to block Byzantine communications to the north. When a great sandstorm blew up from the southern desert—reminiscent of the storm at the Battle of Qadasiya in 637—the Arabs attacked with the wind and sand at their back, more able in these circumstances to fight as individual warriors than their enemies were in their formed ranks. The battle is said to have gone on for six days, which seems a long time for men to fight with muscle-powered weapons. We do know the Muslims were completely victorious, and nothing remained to stop them from snapping up the entirety of the Palestinian and Syrian provinces.

Although Yarmouk is little known today, it is one of the most decisive battles in human history. With this victory, Islam became the dominant religion in all of the modern Middle East. Palestine and Syria became Muslim nations. The road to Egypt was opened, and through Egypt and Syria, Muslim caliphs acquired the naval force to spread the religion and their power throughout the southern Mediterranean basin, all the way to Spain. Had Heraclius's forces prevailed, the modern world could be so changed as to be unrecognizable. The governments and people of Syria, Jordan, Israel, and Egypt would be most unlike what they are today.

The conquests of Syria and Persia completely absorbed the energy of the Caliph Umar's new state for a time. Two astonishing and overlapping campaigns had drained the Arabian Peninsula of manpower. Even after the conquests were well in hand, there were garrisons to be held, field armies to be maintained, and an administration to be built for the new empire. The strategic situation of the caliphs was generally favorable. Persia was no threat, Byzantium was in sharp decline, and no other enemies had appeared. If warriors were in short supply, gold was not. It had become the standard practice of the invading Arab armies to send a tithe of their loot to Medina. The Muslim state was rich. In the seventh century wealth could buy warriors and could pay for the maintenance of those already in service. The conquered peoples were not slow to accept the new religion and the military service that went with it. Leaders too were available, and few states have been as fortunate in the loyalty and skill of their generals as the early Arab Empire. It is interesting that the loyalty and devotion shown by Khalid, the greatest of the Arab generals, was not repaid by the caliph. Like any successful warrior of the time, Khalid had taken his share of the vast loot won by the armies that he commanded. He became immensely wealthy, and although his honor was never in question, he was not a devout man. Caliph Umar, however, required devotion. Two years after Yarmouk, Khalid was dismissed in disgrace and never served again. It is fortunate for the new empire that no great foreign challenges emerged at this time.

The Caliph Umar probably authorized some action against Egypt in 639 when he was visiting Jerusalem. Amr ibn al Aasi was permitted to make an attempt with a smallish army traveling along the Mediterranean coast. The first tentative expedition set out with only 3,500 men, crossing the frontier in late winter 639. This may be looked on as a reconnaissance-in-force rather than a real invasion.

Egypt was the richest of the provinces of the Eastern Roman Empire, just as it had been for the Western Empire. Egypt straddled the rich trade routes to the Indian Ocean, and the incredibly rich alluvial soil of the Nile delta made the land prosperous. For centuries the large Mediterranean cities had counted on the Egyptian corn fleets to feed their populations.

This rich province should have been perfectly invincible against Arab invasion, if only by reason of geography. The coastal road from Palestine was blocked at Pelusium, just to the east of the easternmost arm of the Nile Delta by a major fortress. This strongpoint could be easily resupplied or reinforced by the Byzantine navy. The Nile itself was a major obstacle on a scale that completely dwarfed the Tigris and Euphrates. The great river of Egypt was navigable for hundreds of miles and unbridged. Thus it could be a highway for Byzantine military and naval operations and a barrier to those of the Arabs. A nearly impregnable fortress called, inter-estingly enough, Babylon, held the apex of the channels to the south of the Delta. Finally, Alexandria itself lay at the extreme western end of the Delta and was a strongly fortified coastal city, again easily relieved by the Byzantine fleet. To successfully attack these positions with fewer than 4,000 men was not possible. Had the Arabs attacked this stronghold when the Empire was in order, Egypt could never have been taken. As it hap-pened, Byzantine efforts in Egypt were completely futile, and in some cases actually counterproductive.

When Amr ibn al Aasi's little force arrived at Pelusium in the early months of 640, they were reduced to the slow siege that was the only way that they knew to capture a fortified city. How long the town might have been held is uncertain, but in late January the garrison made a sortie. When the Arabs counterattacked they managed to enter the town before the gates could be barred, and the fortress fell. Even in Arab hands Pelusium re-mained a problem; Amr had too few troops to garrison it, and if he left it open, the Byzantines could easily reoccupy it with an amphibious force and thus threaten his rear. To resolve this problem, the Arabs destroyed the fort and then turned to the southwest to make for the huge fortress of Babylon.

This Babylon—not the one in the Tigris Euphrates area—may have been first named by Persian troops who conquered Egypt in the sixth century B.C. Another story is that the fort was named by Babylonian pris-oners who had been captured by an ancient pharaoh's army. Whatever its origins, the fortress was the most strategic place in Egypt. While Amr's troops sat waiting at Pelusium, Theodore, the governor of the province, had moved troopships down the Nile and completed the garrison. When the Arabs arrived outside the fortress they were in a difficult spot. To cross the Nile they would have to find boats and not only risk attack by the Byzantine ships, but also risk being cut off from reinforcements, or escape if matters turned sour. Laying siege to a city on a great and navigable river was out of the question, and a storming attack would have been impossible against the sixty-foot-high walls of the great citadel. Amr, perhaps judging his opponent correctly, simply marched fifty miles south, forced boats from the local inhabitants, and crossed the river. The Byzantines stood by passively and did not interfere.

Once across the Nile, Amr skirmished and raided up and down the west bank of the River but had too few men to accomplish much more. His problem had already been remedied, for the caliph had sent reinforcements, a body of 12,000 men from Medina to operate under Amr's command. These arrived in June, and again the Byzantines watched both parts of the Arab army, and struck neither, thus giving up an opportunity to defeat an enemy in detail. In July, though, with the Arabs united and on the east bank, Governor Theodore finally brought his army into action.

The Byzantine force of unknown size marched out of Babylon to attack the Arab camp at Heliopolis. Possibly Theodore was desperate, and possibly he thought that the Arabs should be attacked before they became even stronger. Amr, for his part, deployed his main force to block the Byzantine attack but concealed two small flanking parties in front of his main line. When the imperials attacked, these struck in succession, and shattered the Byzantine army. Remarkably, this tactic was well known in Byzantine military manuals. It says something for the growing sophistication of the Muslim armies that they could plan such a clever trap. It also says something about their opponents, who were tricked by one of their own devices!

The Battle of Heliopolis, fought in July 640, was the only major field action in the conquest of Egypt. Babylon was such a strong position that it held out until April of the next year. Even then, the garrison accepted generous terms. The surrender was not a military necessity but a political one, caused in the end by the throne's support in the suppression of the heresies that the Alexandrians so loved. Alexandria itself, the greatest city in the Mediterranean basin, surrendered meekly in September 642. Again, politics, not swords caused the fall of the city.

It would be difficult to overstate the feebleness of the imperial defense of the Empire's richest province. The Byzantines had many problems and dealt well with none of them. Heraclius had died, and his succession was an unhappy affair that left the throne in the hands of weak and temporary rulers. The empire was wracked with religious controversy. The Orthodox Church in Constantinople decreed to be heretical any church that did not completely adopt Orthodox doctrine. Heretics were ruthlessly persecuted. The Muslims, with their mild tax, were generally welcomed as liberators, not conquerors. Worst of all, the Arab attacks came at a time when the empire was deeply in debt and when civil administration in Syria, Iraq, and Egypt had been in Persian hands for ten years. Full bureaucratic control was not yet reestablished.

Thus, Egypt fell almost by default. It became a key part of the growing Muslim Empire in 642, and so has remained a Muslim country for nearly fourteen hundred years.

There was to be a footnote, though.

With Egypt subdued, Amr ibn al Aasi marched west, occupying the coastline as far as Tripoli, with little opposition. Amr was clearly a capable military leader, but like Khalid, he was relieved at the height of his power. As in Khalid's case, Amr was charged with corruption. These groundless charges were believed by the caliph. The conqueror of Egypt might have faded into obscurity, but he did not.

In 645 the new Caliph Othman demanded more taxes from his Egyptian governor. The new governor, who had replaced Amr, went to work, and soon Alexandria was seething with anger. A secret deputation was sent to Constantinople, and in the fall of 645, a Byzantine fleet and army descended on the city and captured it without difficulty. Amr was immediately recalled by Caliph Othman, and he promptly defeated the Byzantine army when it sortied from the city. In the summer of 646 Alexandria was retaken by Amr, who was, as a reward, then dismissed!

With the conquest of Egypt, Syria, and Persia, the new Islamic Empire was firmly established. Persia was the springboard to Afghanistan and northern India, Egypt was the base for the consolidation of North Africa and Spain. The Muslims grew accustomed to their new power bases quickly. As early as 649 an Egyptian fleet with Arab soldiers descended on Cyprus. In 652 another fleet held back a Byzantine attack on Alexandria. Thus the naval resources of Egypt and Syria brought to an end the long era of Roman and Byzantine naval monopoly in the Mediterranean. The wealth of men, money, and equipment that the new empire provided made Muslim armies the material equal of any in the world. They had already demonstrated their moral superiority in convincing terms.

The record of these conquests is simply astonishing. Between 633 and 646, a period of only thirteen years, the Arabs had completely defeated one of the two greatest empires in history, and had eviscerated the power of the second. This amazing feat was accomplished by previously disorganized and unruly tribal nomads who lacked wealth, equipment, and large numbers.

The question is, how did this great feat take place? Certain facts must be considered. Obviously the Persians and Byzantines were exhausted and may not have given much credence to the Islamic threat at first. However, neither great state seemed able to instill much loyalty in its subjects. Great cities and whole provinces meekly accepted the new conquerors. Likewise, neither of the mighty empires could compete with the Arabs on the battlefield. Between them, they lost every serious engagement except the Battle of the Bridge in Iraq in 634. This Arab superiority is even more telling, for Byzantium was led by Heraclius, one of her most notable soldier-emperors. Additionally, Persia and Rome represented the most advanced cultures in the world. Their religion art, literature, and architecture were the products of many proud centuries. With these facts in mind, only one possible explanation remains for the Arab success—and that was the spirit of Islam.

There is no question that Muhammad inspired his early followers with a profound spiritual zeal. That zeal, shared by soldiers and commanders alike, made the Arab armies more than a match for their better equipped and more formally disciplined opponents. It is a military truism that a willing soldier is a good soldier. The generous terms that the invading armies usually offered made their faith accessible to the conquered populations. And if it was a new and upstart faith, its administration by simple and honest men was preferable to the corruption and persecution that were the norm in more civilized empires.

In the end, the Great Arab Conquests were won by the faith of the conquerors, nothing else. The unified Arab Empire built from the conquests would last only a short time. Greed, corruption, inefficiency, and civil war would break the monolithic caliphate irredeemably—but the faith remained. After nearly fourteen centuries Islam has surrendered almost nothing of the great conquest.

CHRONOLOGY

622–28	Final stages of Persian-Byzantine War
622–29	Abu Bekr succeeds Muhammad as the first caliph.
632	Khalid defeats apostates at the Battle of Buzakha.
633	Khalid marches on Persia.

633–34	Three Arab columns march on Syria.
634	Damascus is occupied and lost.
634	Muthanna commands on the Persian front.
635	Abu Bekr dies and is succeeded by Umar.
636	Battle of Buwaib, Muthanna defeats main Persian army.
636	Battle of Yarmouk; Byzantines lose Syria, Palestine, and Lebanon to the Arab armies led by Khalid.
637	Battle of Qadasiya; Saad defeats King Yezdegird and Rustem, the last serious defense of the Persian Empire.
639–42	Conquest of Egypt

Chapter 3

ISLAM AND THE CRUSADES

In A.D. 1071, Alp Arslan led his Seljuq Turks to victory at the Battle of Manzikert in what would one day be called Turkey. The entire Byzantine army was destroyed, and Emperor Romanus was killed on the field. This victory, besides being the beginning of the end for old Byzantium, was also the single most important catalyst in the onset of two centuries of crusading warfare. These crusading wars would be unlike any that had been seen before, and they would have an influence on the Islamic lands of the Middle East that is still curiously evident.

After Manzikert, the Byzantine state compounded its military defeat with an internal struggle for the throne. This struggle for succession was eventually won by Alexius Comnenus, who realized that the imperial losses to the Seljuq Turks could not be repaired by the remnants of the Byzantine army. New forces would have to be found. Alexius chose to appeal to the Roman pope for troops. He couched his appeal in religious terms, pointing out that the new soldiers would be regaining Christian lands that had been lost to the "infidel." He rather assumed that these troops would flock to Constantinople, enlist as mercenaries, and then regain the lost provinces for the Byzantine Empire. The appeal of this to the westerners was that they would be aiding Christianity by regaining lands that had recently been surrendered to Islam but had been Christian for centuries. It was normal for Byzantine armies to be formed with large mercenary contingents, but Alexius's appeal for troops had been couched in religious terms, and he had appealed not to a king, but to a churchman.

When the western troops came to the Eastern Empire, they would come with an idea different from Alexius's. They would come to create conquests in their own name and to acquire land for themselves, not for the old empire. Thus, the crusaders came as a response to Emperor Alexius, but not the one that he wanted.

In the modern mind, the Crusades are poorly and erroneously defined. Virtually everything thought about them is wrong. The Crusades were not a war; they were a series of wars. They were not fought between the "Saracens" and the Franks, they were fought between Turk and Syrian and Egyptian and Byzantine and Mongol and at least three "crusader" kingdoms, most of whom allied with and against each other at various times. The alliances only rarely followed along religious lines. The Crusades were also not national wars in any sense at all. They were medieval wars in which the feudal overlords of cities, castles, or provinces made war against each other with greed as the motivator and loot as the object. The Crusades were not religious wars. Lands were conquered not for Christ or Allah, but for warlords. The followers of a religion were as likely to be killed by their co-religionists as by their infidel opponents.

The first of the Crusades to descend upon the Muslim world was that of Peter the Hermit. Peter was viewed as a deeply religious man and a powerful speaker. He undoubtedly believed himself inspired, and inspiring he was. He gathered and then led a crowd of some 30,000 souls on a larcenous and murderous rampage across France, Germany, Hungary, and into the empire. Alexius was courteous but glad to see the mob depart into Asia, as he had clearly hoped for an army of crusading soldiers, not a swarm of felons.

When Peter's crusade moved south from Constantinople into Anatolia, it entered the lands recently conquered by the Seljuqs. Here the inhabitants were Christians, for the Byzantines had held Anatolia for hundreds of years, and the Seljuqs for less than twenty. The crusaders, who had come to slaughter Muslims, immediately began systematic forays of looting and murder against the local country folk—all of whom were Christians—and set their eyes on the city of Nicaea, only some forty miles from Constantinople. This was the capital of the Seljuq Turk, Kilij Arslan, whose father had conquered the area and broken the Byzantine army.

When the crusaders, or "Franks" as the Turks called them, had foraged all of the available food near their camp, they moved against Nicaea en masse. Kilij Arslan ambushed the poorly equipped and undisciplined mob, and by the end of the day, the crusade was over. Most were captured or killed, but Peter the Hermit would survive to preach in the armies that were following. This battle, fought outside of Nicaea in 1096, was to be the first major engagement in a series of wars that would last for nearly two hundred years. It was also the only victory for Kilij Arslan. His army would be cut to pieces in the next year, as what became known as the First Crusade crossed into Anatolia.

The First Crusade had marched across Europe in the wake of Peter's rabble. This group was much more formidable than the earlier host, for it was mostly composed of Norman knights and men-at-arms. They may have numbered 30,000, and they were led by great warlords who vied with each other in both valor and greed. As these men passed into the empire, Alexius was rapidly disabused of any idea that they had come to help Byzantium in the name of Christianity. They had come to carve out kingdoms, and if they remained in Constantinople, they might well start their carving there. The emperor was as glad to see them go as he had been to hear of their coming.

This host bowled over Kilij Arslan's Turks in 1097. That potentate had been busily making war on a relative—the normal occupation of the Muslim Middle East, when the crusaders arrived. He gathered his army and offered battle at the city of Dorylaeum in June 1097. The Frankish knights marched in separate columns to engage the Turks because their leaders had too much pride in themselves and too little trust in each other to march together. The Seljuqs were engaged frontally, pinned, and then enveloped by two independent columns. The Normans, whose characteristic habit was to throw themselves into headlong charges, actually surrounded the Turkish force. Poor Kilij Arslan was probably the only commander who was ever outmaneuvered by a Norman army.

The Battle of Dorylaeum cleared the path through Anatolia. The Franks had come to conquer the Holy Land, and not the Turkish peninsula, and onward they marched, or at least most of them. Count Bohemund detoured to the east to topple the kingdom of Edessa, betraying its aged and friendly ruler. This became the first crusader kingdom in the east. It would endure from 1098 until 1144.

As the Franks moved south, the Turks and Syrians watched for them and were perhaps somewhat concerned, but made nothing like a concerted effort at mutual defense. Indeed, the caliphs and emirs of Syria were habitually at war with each other. If the Franks posed a threat, each ruler hoped that the foreigners would weaken his hereditary opponents, and thus make his own position stronger.

Antioch, ruled by the Turkish emir Yaghi-Siyan, was the crusaders' target. Yaghi-Siyan was an able commander and Antioch a superbly defensible city. Although he did what he could to hold out, the hapless garrison had to watch as two blundering relief expeditions, one from Damascus, and one from Aleppo, were defeated. After a desperate defense of six months, the city fell to treachery. Bohemund the Norman became the first Count of the city.

The crusaders themselves did not have an easy time of it during the siege. Food supplies were used up and local forage depleted. Knights were forced to eat their horses. Men sickened and died, and some turned to cannibalism. Even with the capture of the city, supplies remained low as the garrison had devoured most of the foodstuffs during the long siege. It was during this period of famine and depression that a famous incident occurred—that of the Holy Lance.

In June 1098, immediately after the fall of Antioch, the Turkish governor of Mosul in Persia arrived with a great army composed of Turks, Persians, Arabs, and Egyptians. The crusaders were badly outnumbered and unable to stand a siege in the unprovisioned city. Fortunately, they were saved by a miracle. One Peter Bartholomew, a priest traveling with the army, claimed that the Holy Lance that had pierced Christ's side was buried under the floor of a chapel. Miraculously, or so it seemed, when the chapel floor was excavated, Peter himself found the holy relic. Thus inspired by the wonderful discovery, the Frankish army marched out of the city and attacked the combined host confronting them. The Muslim army was scattered and the last mobile Muslim force in the Middle East was defeated. Lacking an army to defend it, Jerusalem and nearly the whole of Palestine fell to the invaders.

There is an interesting footnote to the story about the Holy Lance. In the early months of 1099, the crusader army was having difficulties reducing a pair of small fortresses. As spirits sank, Peter Bartholomew continued to have visions and revelations. He was treated with increasing skepticism, as his miraculous insights ceased to bear fruit. He furiously demanded the right to defend the honor of his revelations, and so on Good Friday 1099, a huge bonfire was prepared. To show his divine approval, Peter calmly and deliberately walked into the middle of it, paused, and walked out the far side. This would have been a powerful sign, had he not died almost immediately from the burns that he received. In Peter's defense, he seems to have shown an honest belief in what he was about, and he did provide what was taken for a miracle at the crucial moment. He was by no means the worst of the crusaders.

With the capture of Antioch and the defeat of the great Muslim army, the crusaders were able to set about building their kingdoms. From 1099 until 1144 the feudal lords built their fiefs and castles. Like their Muslim predecessors, they engaged in civil wars with one another and generally squandered the time of peace. The conquest of Middle Eastern states by newcomers was nothing new. The lands where the crusader kingdoms were being built had been captured more than once before and would be—more than once—again. What made the crusaders somewhat different is that for the first time since the Great Arab Conquests, an idealistic element entered the fighting. For the first time the Muslims met a militant religion championed by people with military potential. This was something of a shock, for although religious war was becoming an outmoded idea in most Muslim states, it was still very much understood that jihad was something that Muslims did to their neighbors, not the reverse. The general contempt with which most Christian rulers treated their Muslim subjects and neighbors also would eventually enrage, and help consolidate the neighboring states.

Thus the Christian warlords failed to do more than survive. They offered their Muslim subjects and neighbors little. The European lords persecuted their own subjects and frequently massacred those Muslims that came under their power. At the same time the Christian Europeans represented a tiny portion of the population of the Middle East. The wiser lords, of whom there were few, realized that their fiefs would survive only as they used and accepted the Muslim merchants and farmers that provided the wealth of the land. When waves of additional crusaders arrived from Europe, usually after a Christian disaster of one sort or another in the Middle East, they were welcomed as fighting men—the European knights could be formidable warriors—but not as feudal competitors. Their ardor was squandered in abortive offensives against Egypt in 1149 and 1249 and a successful one against Byzantium in 1204. Worse, the new arrivals were totally ignorant of the Middle East. It was not unusual for them to slaughter the peaceful inhabitants of whatever city they first entered, even if it was already held as a crusader fief.

Islamic resistance to the Frankish newcomers remained unfocused, as the various Arab, Persian, Egyptian, and Turkish nobles squabbled amongst themselves, but slowly a wave of antipathy built up against the newcomers. Eventually men of sufficient stature and vision came to the fore to launch successful counterattacks against the invaders. These leaders, of whom we will examine three, were able to acquire sufficient influence among their rivals to work against the Franks.

The Turkish *atabeg* (Prince Father) Imad al-Din Zangi became ruler of Aleppo and Mosul in 1128 following the murder of his predecessor by the Assassin sect.[1] Zangi was in all respects a remarkable leader. He was a gifted soldier, not unusual for Turkish princes of the day, but also a gifted politician. He kept his troops and their commanders under a severe discipline, and in the field, lived under the same conditions. Zangi led his troops from the front, in the tradition of the Turkish warrior caste. He was among the first Turkish rulers in Syria to attempt real government—his predecessors had been mere warlords who treated their Syrian lands to looting and rapine.

Zangi ruled in the midst of internecine Muslim warfare. His early years saw a series of confusing and vicious struggles as he sought to consolidate power in Syria. He dared not challenge the Christians at this time, but so remarkable was his character, that in 1130, Alix, the daughter of Bohemund II, king of Jerusalem, offered him an alliance against her own father! This he declined, as it would have made an impossible alliance for him, and he had too many concerns in his own lands.

During a Seljuq quarrel for the succession of the throne in 1133, Zangi marched on Baghdad. Ambushed en route, he was assisted by an enemy— a Kurdish officer named Ayyub. In years to come, Zangi would remember this noble gesture and help Ayyub's son to his first position of authority. This man would become the scourge of the crusader kingdoms—Saladin.

In 1135, Zangi was nearly made ruler of Damascus, the principal city of Syria, but intrigues continued to hold him back. In 1137, he marched on Homs in central Syria, intending to take it as a steppingstone to Damascus. Caliph Unar, who ruled the city, craftily called upon the Knights Templar to aid him in his defense and then, as the Christian army approached, offered to assist Zangi in the destruction of the infidels. This Zangi did. In June 1137, the Templar army was trapped in the fortress of Barin by Zangi's forces and forced to surrender. After the battle, however, Unar renounced his allegiance and Zangi besieged Homs, which he could not take because a combined crusader-Byzantine army was besieging his city of Shayzar. Fearing the loss of this vital city, he withdrew his army and broke the siege.

This Byzantine-crusader alliance could have been serious to the Muslim-dominated Middle East. It was, in fact, the only time that the crusaders acted as the pawns of the old empire, and had the Frankish vitality been combined with the empire's organization, the results for Syria could have been fatal. Zangi responded with propaganda to tear the two allies apart—warning the Byzantines of the huge army that he was gathering and warning the Franks of Byzantine designs against their own newly conquered lands. He swept the enemy away, more with guile than arms, but this victory made him the preeminent man of Syria. In May 1138, he was offered a wedding alliance to princess Zumurrud of Damascus and received Homs as her dowry. It was supposed that her son Mahmud would then turn Damascus over to his new father-in-law. However, despite the agreement, Mahmud refused to turn the city over to

Zangi. In July 1139 Mahmud was murdered, but before Zangi could take control of the city, the old Caliph Unar—Zangi's ally and enemy at Homs—seized control and began plotting a new alliance with the crusaders. Thus Zangi was stalled again, more by the clever old Caliph Unar, a master of the political game, than by the crusaders.

Unable to cement his control of Syria, Zangi turned his attention north and in 1144 retook the kingdom of Edessa, the first of the crusader states to be captured and the first to fall. It was also Zangi's last great achievement, for a servant murdered him in 1146. His kingdom fell apart, and his son Nur-al-Din was left with only Aleppo.

Zangi's life was not dedicated to the destruction of the crusaders, but to the acquisition of personal power. At his death, his realms dissolved into the hands of various strongmen, and his son was left with a sliver of his father's power. But Nur-al-Din, a man very different from his father, would decisively change the balance of power in the Middle East. An austere man, more at home in the library than on the battlefield, the new ruler of Aleppo would fight the Franks with his own wisdom, and others' swords.

Nur-al-Din's first act upon reaching the rump of his father's old realm was to march his army to the relief of Edessa. Raymond of Antioch and Joscelin, the ousted king of Edessa, were moving an army to recapture it. Accompanied by emir Shirkuh, a seasoned Kurdish warrior, Nur-al-Din and the Aleppan horsemen arrived in time to put the Christians to flight and save the city. It is worth noting that Shirkuh was of the family of Ayyub who had helped Zangi in 1133, fourteen years earlier. He was Saladin's uncle, and would be his mentor.

But the capture of Edessa had alarmed the Christian west, and in 1147, what became known as the Second Crusade arrived in the Middle East. This was led by two kings—Konrad III of Germany, and Louis VII of France, and brought an impressive number of fighting men to aid the crusaders.

This Second Crusade accomplished little. Instead of recapturing Edessa, the two kings decided to attack their only friend in the area—Damascus! In July 1148, the Christians arrived and were resisted by the wily Unar. Unar's strategy was familiar and effective. He wrote to the neighboring leaders saying that he would turn the city over to the Franks if they did not raise the siege. To the Franks he said that the vast host of the sultan was coming, and that if they did not withdraw, he would turn the city over to the sultan! The Franks dithered for only four days, and then retreated. This was perhaps Unar's finest hour, and nearly his last. He died in the next year, and once again Damascus was a prize for the taking.

Nur-al-Din took the city in April 1154. He struck no blow, but simply presented himself as the champion of the people. His astute politics and virtuous nature accomplished the job. The city was opened to him, and he was made its ruler by acclaim. Finally, more than fifty years after the fall of Jerusalem, Muslim Syria was in the hands of one ruler. Thus, for the first time, a united resistance to the crusaders could be mounted.

But any campaign against the invaders had to be delayed, for in 1156 a great Byzantine army, led by the Emperor Manuel, advanced south from Constantinople. This was the last great Byzantine army, and the last military revival in the empire's thousand-year history. The imperial soldiers recaptured much of Anatolia from the Turks and then turned south into Syria. The emperor's host had come, not to make war with the Muslims, but to retake Antioch. It had always been an imperial city and the crusaders had vowed to return it to the empire if they took it. This vow, of course, meant nothing more to the Franks than any of their other vows, and Manuel meant to have his city back. He took it in the summer of 1156. This was important to Nur-al-Din, for no attacks against the crusaders were possible while the Byzantines were in the field.

In 1163, Egypt fell into a worse disorder than normal even for that debased caliphate. Caliph Shawar, the new ruler, appealed to Nur-al-Din for help. The Damascene ruler sent an army, commanded by Shirkuh and accompanied by the general's young relative Saladin. The principal reason for this expedition was to keep the crusaders out of the Nile caliphate, which would be impossible without better government than the Egyptians had been providing. The Franks also intervened, and in 1164 Shirkuh, who had been successful, was threatened by a large army from Jerusalem. In response to this threat, Nur-al-Din responded brilliantly by threatening the fortress of Harim, near Antioch. In an open battle, he crushed the remaining crusader army in Syria and menaced the heart of the Frankish kingdoms, thus forcing the Christians to withdraw from Egypt. But the strategic fruit of Nur-al-Din's victory was minor, and his general had to withdraw from the south in the face of growing Egyptian hostility. Soon, in fact, the Egyptians under Shawar openly allied with the crusaders against the Syrians.

In March 1167 at al-Babayn, a village near the Nile, a combined Franco-Egyptian army faced the Syrian force under the wily Shirkuh. Saladin himself commanded the center of the Muslim force, and when the heavy Christian knights charged, he feigned retreat, drawing them into a trap. The allied force was decimated, and the Muslims took Alexandria, a city whose Muslim populace had not welcomed the Christian alliance.

In 1168 a new wave of crusaders appeared, spurred on by the disasters of the previous year, and another round of fighting broke out in Egypt.

Shirkuh's army was out of position, and the first Frankish attack was successful at capturing Bilbeis. But the massacre that followed, in which both Christian and Muslim inhabitants were slaughtered with equal indifference, so horrified the Egyptians, that for the first time a universal reaction emerged against everything Frankish. The wily caliph invited the Syrians into Cairo, and the country was saved.

Although it had been Nur-al-Din's Syrian army, led by his Kurdish general Shirkuh, that had so far thwarted the crusaders' plans in Syria and Egypt, the young Saladin had been present, gaining experience as a military leader. Indeed, Saladin personally resolved the problems in Egypt by murdering the fickle Egyptian Caliph Shawar, on January 18, 1169. This hard act completed the destruction of the pro-Frankish element in Egyptian politics. The young man's great chance came only two months after the occupation of Cairo. Shirkuh ate himself to death, and Nur-al-Din appointed the relative of Ayyub in his place.

By the end of 1169 Nur-al-Din held Syria as one unified nation, and his vassal Saladin held Egypt. This combination should have set the stage for the destruction of the crusader kingdoms. However, the recurring themes of medieval warlordism and Muslim disunity were stronger than the bonds between the two men. It is true that Nur-al-Din had made Saladin king of Egypt. It was also true that Saladin was the ruler, and Egypt was every bit as powerful a nation as Syria. The vassal had become the equal of his master, and thus, in the end, his own master. This came to a head in 1171, when the Syrian ruler, a Sunni, demanded that his "vassal" remove the Shia underpinnings of the Egyptian state. Saladin refused, for to do so would not only cause great distress to his subjects, it would also define him as the lesser of two equals. The situation became tense enough that King Amalric of the crusader kingdom of Jerusalem felt comfortable in offering Saladin an alliance against his Syrian overlord. Fortunately, the last Egyptian Shia caliph soon died and the question became moot. Syria and Egypt did not go to war, and Saladin did not ally with Amalric. Still, the two great Muslim kings were not close allies.

In 1171 and again in 1173 there was talk of a Syrian expedition against Egypt, but nothing came of it. In 1174, Nur-al-Din died and the way was clear for the once vassal Saladin to acquire his master's lands. By the end of 1174, against little opposition from Nur-al-Din's eleven-year-old son, Saladin was the ruler of both Egypt and most of Syria. In 1183 he would enter Aleppo, in northern Syria, completing the conquest. For the first time since the crusaders had arrived, the Muslim world had a united and very astute ruler.

Saladin was a skillful ruler indeed. Schooled in war by Shirkuh, and with politics in his blood, the new king of Egypt and Syria was a thoughtful, generous, and highly intelligent man. Like all of his contemporary warlords, his ultimate goal was personal power. This may be seen as greed, although in the ethic of the time it was not. Certainly Saladin was a wise ruler in all of his lands, and if his personal power grew to be enormous, so did the nobility of his character.

Saladin's early years were spent in consolidating his enormous empire. His chief threats were from Persia and Turkey, and of course there was the ever-present danger of revolt by a subordinate. Slowly and methodically he dealt with the various threats as they arose. It would take several years to completely consolidate his authority, but he had the necessary time. The crusaders failed to respond to his rise other than with their normal bickering and jealousy.

Between 1180 and 1183 Reynauld of Châtillon, a powerful warlord of the Jerusalem kingdom, ordered a number of raids and massacres into Muslim lands. Reynauld was as merciless and murderous a man as any warlord of the day. He was one of those who did not accept that the small crusader states would have to live with their Muslim neighbors to survive. One of his pillaging expeditions went as far as Arabia itself. Saladin tried measured responses, but by 1187 he would no longer be restrained. He attacked the kingdom of Jerusalem, laying siege to the town of Tiberias. The main Christian army filed out of Jerusalem and marched to relieve Tiberias, crossing miles of dusty plains and dry riverbeds. Worn out by fatigue and thirst, they were easily smashed by Saladin's forces on July 4, 1187, at the Battle of Hattin. Saladin personally executed Reynaud, whose depredations had caused the war. The religious order knights were also massacred, as they were the perpetrators of many atrocities.

The Battle of Hattin was one of the decisive battles in world history. Virtually all of the military might of the crusaders had been annihilated. The Christians had stripped their garrisons to provide a field army. Little remained with which to mount a defense of the cities and castles that the crusaders held. Saladin struck swiftly. Jerusalem fell at the beginning of October. Most of the Frankish holdings withered quickly. By the end of the year all of the crusader kingdoms had been reduced to the isolated cities of Tyre, Tripoli, and Antioch.

The news of the great Muslim victories shocked Europe, and as before, waves of reinforcements began swarming into the Middle East. Frederick Barbarossa led a great army of Germans south. This fine and honorable old man died either of sickness or drowning—or both—at a river crossing in Turkey just before his troops might have made an impact, and they returned home. King Richard the Lionheart of England led a brave contingent across the seas in 1191, accompanied by King Phillip Augustus of France. Richard actually defeated Saladin in a pitched battle, one of the few fights that Saladin lost, at Arsuf in September 1191. The European kings, however, could not spend their time in the East away from their homelands. Their influence faded just as quickly, and they themselves went home. They were gone in a year, departing in 1192. Saladin, his great work accomplished, died in 1193.

With the departure of the European kings, and the reoccupation of most of the lands and cities that they had taken, the real power of the Franks was ended. They would linger on for years, but their lands were gone, and with them their wealth and their armies. As late as 1249 a fresh wave of Frenchmen, under King Louis IX of France would launch a futile attack against Egypt, but he would have little assistance from the remnants of the earlier crusader kingdoms. The crusader kingdoms were exhausted and simply did not have the manpower necessary to mobilize meaningful assistance to the French.

In 1292 the Egyptian Mamluk Sultan Khalil captured Acre. It was the last Frankish outpost of the once powerful crusader kingdoms. That it took so long to finish the Christian state would be surprising, had not in 1258 a huge army of Mongols erupted into the Muslim world and occupied its attention as completely as had the Seljuq Turks in the eleventh century. The Mamluk king of Egypt, Qalawun finally dealt with the Mongols in 1281. By then the Christians were no longer a priority, they were more of a historical footnote.

The span of nearly 200 years, from the first crusader attacks until their ultimate defeat, was a momentous time, and one that has done much to shape the modern Muslim world. The perceptions of the era have become so fixed that the reality of the events is no longer of much importance. The perceptions, which are terribly misleading, are in some ways as cruel as the crusaders at their worst.

One of these misconceptions is that Christianity fought Islam. In fact, a much more accurate statement would be that medieval warlord fought medieval warlord. Some were Christian, and some were Muslim. Religion occasionally provided an excuse for an action, but never a reason. The real reasons for the fighting were always the same—the greed for personal power and wealth. If there were truly noble men like Saladin and Zangi, even these fought for self-aggrandizement. Most of their wars were against other Muslims. The Christians rarely if ever presented a united front against their Muslim enemies. They too were more likely to bicker among themselves.

Another perception that is played about today in the Middle East, is that the West attacked the East. The Crusades are seen as a sort of early imperialism, an idea that fit conveniently into the propaganda of the Cold War. In actuality, the Crusades hardly fit the patterns that European imperialists would later form. In the later period, well-organized and technically superior nations would dominate less advanced peoples with vastly superior trade, weapons, and cultures. During the Crusades, it was nearly the reverse—the Muslim states were clearly superior societies by every conceivable measurement. It would be better to liken the crusaders to the barbarians who swept down on the advanced Greek and Western empires—this is a far better analogy than that of imperialism and fits in completely with the actions of the Seljuqs and Mongols.

Another perception is that the Crusades were an appalling act of savagery carried out by the warlike adherents of Christianity against the peaceful followers of Islam. There could be some minor truth to this, without historical context. Actually, if the crusaders were no more attractive as conquerors than most nations, they weren't much worse either. They were certainly warlike, but so were the Muslim states that they confronted. It is possible that the Muslims, who properly considered themselves a superior culture, were most deeply offended by the scorn with which the barbarians treated these superior cultures. If the mighty Byzantines were respectful of Islam and the Arab Middle East, how could the Westerners act so?

The Crusades left few physical marks on the Islamic world other than ruined castles that represent some of the finest examples of medieval military architecture in the world. By way of culture, the invaders were little more than barbarian hordes and had little to offer the more cultured elements of Islamic society. If anything, the Crusades brought much of Islamic culture and learning back to the West where it helped to spur on the birth of the Renaissance. The crusaders were not evangelical and made no effort to convert the populace. Indeed, if their religion had any influence on the Middle East it was to the detriment of the local Christians.

They did have two major influences. First, they crippled the Byzantine Empire by the storming and capture of Constantinople. This so weakened the Byzantines that the Seljuqs were eventually able to overrun and conquer the doddering but resilient old empire. Had the crusaders not irreparably damaged the Byzantines by their greed, the history of the Middle East might have been significantly different.

The second major influence was the emotional impact the crusaders had on the Middle East. The invasion by a force of infidels and their occupation of Islamic lands for nearly 150 years was a tremendous shock to a people who had known nothing but conquest and victory for five centuries. The Crusades shattered the myth of the invincibility of Islamic armies and traumatized a people who saw God as being on the side of the victors. How God could allow the lands of the followers of the one true faith to be invaded, occupied, and pillaged by infidels was incomprehensible to them. It shook the very roots of their faith and produced a hatred for the West that can be seen to this day. In the Middle East it is common to hear Westerners referred to generically as "Franks," and when President George W. Bush referred to his war on terrorism as a "crusade" the Muslim world shuddered as visions of Western armies pouring into the Middle East again appeared before them.

CHRONOLOGY

1071	Seljuq Turk Alp Arslan defeats the Byzantines at Manzikert, and captures Anatolia.
1096	Peter the Hermit's Crusade is crushed outside Nicaea by Kilij Arslan.
1097	First Crusade captures Edessa, Antioch, and Jerusalem in 1099.
1098	Crusader kingdoms expand until about 1144.
1144	Zangi captures Edessa.
1146	Nur-al-Din succeeds Zangi, consolidates power in Syria.
1148	Second Crusade defeated at Damascus.
1167	Nur-al-Din sends Saladin to Egypt. Saladin defeats a Franco-Egyptian army at the Battle of Al-Babayn and occupies Egypt.
1174	Saladin usurps the Syrian throne from Nur-al-Din's minor son.
1174–83	Saladin consolidates his power in Egypt and Syria.
1187	At the Battle of Hattin, Saladin destroys the crusader field armies, breaking the power of the Frankish states. Jerusalem is freed by Saladin.
1191	Third Crusade of Richard and Phillip
1192	Death of Saladin, disintegration of his empire
1249	Seventh Crusade temporarily reoccupies Jerusalem.
1292	Sultan Khalil eliminates Acre, last vestige of the Frankish states.

NOTE

1. See Chapter 12 for a complete history of the Assassin sect.

Chapter 4

THE SWORD AND INDIA: THE MOGHUL CONQUEST

As early as the eighth century, with the conquest of Persia still fresh, Muslim eyes looked to the east, pondering the vast wealth of the Indian subcontinent. This was not a new idea, as the old rulers of Persia had also tried to extend their power east, and it was natural for the Muslim overlords of the old Persian lands to try the same.

In 711 the Ummayaid Persian Empire, only recently taken by Islam, sent eastward a small army commanded by one of the most remarkable generals in history. This was Muhammad bin Qasim, a young man of but seventeen years. His army of just 6,000 horsemen and a few auxiliaries rode against Daibil, the principal port of Brahman-ruled Sind. The young man's genius was sufficient to outweigh his youth, and the small army, supported by a huge fireball-shooting catapult, took the place in short order. Bin Qasim then proceeded not only to reduce the balance of the Brahman kingdom, but also to set up an effective Muslim administration that offered remarkable rights to the Buddhists and Brahmans who made up the bulk of the population, thus ensuring that their talents would remain available to the Muslim conquerors.

Bin Qasim's conquest set the basis for modern Pakistan and Afghanistan and was the first step in Islamic occupation of India. Some of those that followed his lead would be able indeed, but few could match the wisdom and courage of the young commander. Sadly, his life and service were not lengthy. Recalled under charges of corruption, the discredited hero died in 720.

It is worthwhile to consider the Muslim conquests in India in their entirety. Their six-century span and the enormous numbers of participants on all sides tends to obscure the basic patterns of a series of events that clearly overshadowed other Muslim conquests.

Geographic knowledge is not a strength for many modern Westerners, so it is probably useful to describe the pattern of Muslim advances in general terms. The first base of the Muslim attacks took Afghanistan, and from that mountain stronghold raids were launched southwest down the Ganges River valley. The raids eventually became conquests, and the Delhi Sultanate roughly followed the river in a broad patch from the Punjab in the northwest to Bengal in the southeast where the Ganges Delta meets the Indian Ocean. Additional early gains were made in Sind on the northwestern coast and down the western coast. The central and southern parts of the subcontinent were the last to be conquered, and by the end of the Moghul Empire, the land still held Hindu principalities.

Clear patterns in the conquests should be held in mind as one looks at the details. The most obvious fact is that no one conquest occurred. During the 600-year period of the invasions, no "One India" waited to be conquered—it was an array of princely states that rose and fell with bewildering rapidity. Nor was there any one conqueror—but rather a constantly changing cast of various warlords and their generally short-lived dynasties. Finally, it was not merely a conquest of Hindu states by Muslim warlords—fresh waves of Muslims attacked each other with the same fervor with which native princes had warred for centuries, and would continue to do so during the conquests.

In fact, the conquests in India well illustrate the difficulties and advantages of medieval Muslim conquest in a foreign culture. In an age in which power was not shared with the population, it was relatively easy to invade a province, defeat the defending army, capture a city, and install a governor. The attackers had to fight a few thousand armed retainers and not an entire nation in arms. With the city in hand, the conqueror then established a governor, or declared it his capital and set up a new administration of his own retainers. The Muslim warlords did all of this with some frequency, aided by their excellent cavalry and the general Hindu acquiescence to government. But to conquer a city is not the same as conquering a continent, particularly one heavily peopled with a population with which the conquerors have little in common.

It is hard to imagine what Muhammad would have made of Hinduism, and how Allah might have revealed scripture to him had he known that his followers would attack India. Islam and Hinduism are dramatically different. Hindus are pantheist, and Muslims are decidedly monotheist.

Hindus look for a succession of reincarnations, and Muslims believe that man has one life in which to serve God. Hindus use music and dance in worship, Muslims do not. Hinduism stresses tolerance of all faiths, Islam does not. Hindus hold to a caste system, Islam is a classless creed. The list could go on, and is probably best illumined by the well-known dietary restrictions of each faith. Hindus keep cattle as sacred beasts, and Muslims keep them as livestock. Hindus care nothing about pork, and to Muslims it is forbidden.

All of these differences were heightened by the Islamic scriptures that allow only slaughter or conversion for people not "of the book"—Jews and Christians. Of course, Islam had ceased to be a reason for conquest by the eleventh century and was hardly even an excuse. Still, the great disparities between the native Hindus and the incoming Muslims made lasting assimilation a slow process and formed the basis for the enmities that exist between Muslim Pakistan and Hindu India today.

The process of conquest was further slowed by the simple fact that medieval warlords had to rely on their offspring to continue the dynasty. It was extremely common for a capable parent to father an incompetent offspring, causing the empire-building process to go astray. Royal succession was frequently accomplished with patricide or fratricide—probably better practices than civil war—but stable and long-lasting administrations of conquered areas do not quickly grow from such erratic methods. Finally, the Muslim raids, which became conquests, were themselves the targets of several waves of destructive raids from the steppe peoples, culminating in Tamerlane's horrific sixteenth-century destruction of Delhi. And so the Muslim conquests were neither rapid nor complete. But with the first foothold in Sind, they came with the consistency of the tides.

The origin of the second wave of Muslim attacks on India came from the Turkish general Alptigin, who was the governor of Transoxania, a province of the old Persian Empire. The good general had made a subtle attempt on the Iranian throne in 961 when Emir Abu al-Hasan had died. Following his unsuccessful attempt at the crown, removing himself from the dangerous intrigues of the capital, Alptigin moved his family and forces east from Khurasan in northeastern Iran to Ghazni in modern Afghanistan, thus looking east rather than west. He had picked a wise time to do so, for neither northern India disrupted by the continual struggles of its warring Rajput chiefs nor southern India torn by its rival Dravidian principalities could offer resistance. Thus, all semblance of unity in the subcontinent had vanished before the Islamic armies launched their invasions. Warnings of the growing threat from the West passed unheeded.

In the century following Muhammad's death, the Muslims had ravaged the Punjab and conquered the Sind. These were mere raids, and the conquest of Sind was but a sliver of the great subcontinent. Subaktagin, emir of Ghazni, and son-in-law of Alptigin launched the first major invasion of India. The old general's plans were coming to fruition.

The invasion spurred a hurried Indian effort to unite the Rajput states, but it was too late, and Subaktagin, at the head of the Muslim army, was upon them.

There is a story that Jaipal, Hindu king of Lahore, infuriated by Afghan raids into his territory, sent an army to punish the raiders. Subaktagin met and defeated them and demanded a ransom for the release of the captured Hindus. Jaipal agreed, offering fifty elephants and a vast sum of gold, to be paid as he returned home. However, his nobles chided him, one saying that it was wrong to give ransom to a barbarian and another saying that it was wrong to break his word, even if given to a foreigner. King Jaipal listened to neither, nor did he send the ransom. In due course, Subaktagin's vengeful army descended upon his kingdom and began the first of the great Ghaznavid conquests. It is such a good story that it really should be true.

The Peshwar quickly became the advanced base of the Islamic army as it moved east into historically Indian territory. This base would serve the Ghaznavids well over the years to come.

It was Subaktagin's son, Mahmud—known as Mahmud of Ghazni— who pushed the eastern boundary of his father's kingdom from Persia in the west to the Ganges on the east. He led Islamic armies no less than seventeen times into India. Thirteen of these campaigns subdued the Punjab, one the Kashmir valley, and one each against the three great cities— Kanauj, Gwalior, and Somnath. In A.D. 1001 he defeated Raja Jaipal and took him prisoner. Not willing to submit peacefully, Anangpal, son of Jaipal, raised an army to free his country from Muslim control. He built his great force with a coalition of Rajput allies from the farthest corners of Hindustan. A decisive battle fought in the valley of Peshawar was won by Mahmud and his Turkish horsemen. The Punjab has, since that day, been Muslim, except for a short period when it fell under the Sikh rule.

The Sultan Mahmud was a masterful tactician and strategist, as was the norm among the warlords of the time. In 1008, he was confronted by a league of Hindu princes led by Anangpal, the son of his old foe King Jaipal. So large was the enemy force, that Mahmud felt it best to erect defensive positions, although the great strength of his army was in the ferocious charge of its cavalry. The sultan realized that it would be best to let the enemy tire itself on his works before the counterstroke. Equally, if the Hindus were reluctant to attack the defensive positions, then so much the better. The sultan well understood that such a vast and unwieldy array must attack quickly or be swept aside by disunity, suspicion, and the logistics of attempting to feed such a large force. Eventually Anangpal's forces did attack, wasting their strength on Mahmud's powerful defensive position. When the Hindu prince's elephant was frightened by a fireball, the Muslims launched their own counterattack, and the vast enemy horde was brushed aside. This was a notable display of military prowess.

The most famous of Mahmud's invasions of India ran from 1025 to 1026 and was against Gujarat. The goal of this invasion was the fabulously wealthy temple dedicated to Shiva at Somnath. Tradition tells that Mahmud marched through Ajmere to avoid the Sind desert. He encountered the Hindu army gathered on the neck of the peninsula of Somnath in defense of their holy city. The battle lasted for two days, but in the end the Rajput warriors fled to their boats and the Brahman priests withdrew into the innermost shrine. Mahmud's forces surrounded the shrine and rejected the pleas of the Brahman priests to spare their idol as well as their offers of ransom. When the temple was taken he smote it with his club and, as the story goes, a stream of precious gems gushed out. Mahmud's club would be preserved, along with the wooden doors of Somnath, at his tomb until the British invasion of Afghanistan in 1839. The club has disappeared, and the gates were returned to India. Sadly, the redeemed gates were subsequently recognized as a clumsy forgery.

The Ghazni dynasty was a short one. Military governments imposed by a tiny feudal class tend to be unstable. The Afghans of Ghor rose and brushed the Ghaznis aside.

An early leader of this new dynasty, Muhammad Ghori, or Shahub-ad-din, was the second great Muslim conqueror of India. In 1175 he took Multan and Uchch. In 1186 he conquered Lahore, and in 1191 he was repulsed in a desperate battle at Tiruri, near Delhi.

Some details of his 1191 Battle of Tiruri against the Rajputs remain, and they make a remarkable record of the fighting of the day. The Muslim tactic was to charge upon their enemy, shoot arrows, and then withdraw as another line of horsemen repeated the tactic. When the enemy was worn down, the mounted troops would ride right over them. The Hindu tactic was to accept enemy action in the center, but to outflank on both wings hoping to surround the foe. On the day of Tiruri, the Hindus were closing on the Muslim rear, and Muhammad raced at them with his household guards, temporarily restoring the situation. But the Rajput prince also intervened on his great elephant, and the two came to blows. Muhammad, realizing that he could not stand against the huge beast, charged in, twirled his horse to retreat, and with a dexterous move, drove his lance into the rajah's face, knocking out several teeth. At the same time, the sultan was himself struck in the eye by an arrow and would have perished, had his guards not pulled him away. The battle ended as a narrow but costly Muslim defeat.

Not deterred, Muhammad Ghori extended his conquests as far east as Benares in 1193 and drove the defeated Rajputs to the hills and deserts now known as Rajputana. In 1199, one of his lieutenants named Bakhtiyar, led an army into Bengal and by clever stratagem expelled the last Hindu raja of Nadia. This put the entire northern plain of India, from the Indus to the Brahmaputra, under Muslim control.

Muhammad Ghori was murdered in A.D. 1206 (refreshingly, not by his family) and Kutb-ud-din, his Mamluk successor, abandoned the title of viceroy, proclaiming himself "Sultan of Delhi." He had been trusted as sole administrator by Muhammad, and upon his sovereign's death, the Mamluk slave became king. So widely was he admired, and so capable was he, that he had no opposition. He founded what would be known as the "slave dynasty," which lasted from 1206 to 1288, so known because Kutb-ud-din, himself a slave, married a slave, gave his sister to marry a slave, and married his daughter to a slave—who succeeded him. The greatest accomplishment of the Ghoris was the defeat of a major Mongol raid in 1286. Just as the Mamluks of Egypt staved off the steppe horsemen, so did the Mamluks of India. Sadly, this was only a raid, and in another century India would feel the wrath of another, and much heavier Mongol incursion.

In 1294, Ala-ud-din Khilji, the third great Muslim conqueror of India, ascended the throne of Delhi by the treacherous assassination of his uncle Feroz II, who had himself supplanted the last of the "slave dynasty." He sent an army to Gujarat to conquer and expel the last Rajput king of Anhalwar. Leading another army in person, the sultan marched into the heart of Rajputana and stormed the rock-fortress of Chittur.

A wonderful story about the siege of Chittur, one that could not possibly be true, certainly conveys the romance of the period. Bheemsi, regent of Chittur, was married to Padmani, a Ceylonese princess of such exquisite beauty that she is said to have driven men mad. As Ala-ud-din arrived with his army, he determined to have her and offered to call off the siege if she was given to him. Bheemsi refused, and the siege proceeded. Ala-ud-din relented and offered to lift the siege if he were only allowed to view the woman. To do so, he entered Chittur, trusting in Rajput honor, and, with an arrangement of mirrors and reflecting pools, was able to admire the girl. Awed, he invited Bheemsi to his camp to congratulate him, but once the regent was in his hands, captured him. Now, so the story goes, Ala-ud-din demanded the girl in exchange for the regent Bheemsi. Nobly, the girl complied and had herself drawn out to the sultan's camp accompanied by a hundred masked serving ladies drawn on a hundred litters, each carried by six stout slaves. The serving ladies were, of course, army officers, and the slaves had weapons concealed in the litters. Once in the sultan's camp, they created enough confusion for the royal couple to escape. In reality, Chittur fell to the sultan in 1295 during a second siege.

Yet another army, commanded by Malik Kafur, a Hindu renegade, penetrated to the extreme south of the Indian peninsula, scattering the unwarlike Dravidian races, stripping the Hindu temples, and sending large quantities of gold and jewels to his master.

Ala-ud-din died in 1316 having brought the Deccan and Gujarat under Muslim rule. His three successors reigned for only five years, the last falling to a revolt headed by Ghiyas-ud-din Tughlak, the governor of the Punjab. His short dynasty had added vast tracts to the Muslim control of India.

Ghiyas-ud-din is said to have been of Turkish origin. He and his son reigned from 1325 to 1351. During his reign he moved the seat of government from Delhi to Deccan, forcing its inhabitants to move 700 miles to Deogiri or Daulatabad. The next in the line was Feroz, who also moved the capital, this time to a point a few miles north of Delhi. This attention to the capital, however, resulted in the controls over the distant provinces growing slack, and those same provinces began to throw off their Muslim overlords. The independence of the Afghan kings of Bengal dates from 1336, when Muhammad Tughlak was on the throne.

The year 1398 was a year of devastation, as the Mongol Khan Timur (or Tamerlane) raided into India. He encountered little organized resistance, sacking Delhi and massacring its inhabitants. As destructive as the Mongol foray was, it is fair to consider it a raid rather than an invasion. Timur had interests closer to his heart than the vast subcontinent, and soon he marched back to Samarkand via Kabul.

There followed a period when various families attempted to rule the Moghul Empire, but their power was consistently interrupted by new Mongol incursions. Mahmud Tughlak was one of these, and the Dayyid dynasty another. After forty years, the Dayyids were replaced by Bahlol, an Afghan of the Lodi tribe, and his successors moved the seat of government to Agra. In 1526, Babur, fifth in descent from Timur, and also the fifth Muslim conqueror of India, invaded India at the instigation of the governor of the Punjab. He won a major victory at Panipat over Ibrahim, the last of the Lodi dynasty, and founded the Moghul Empire, which lasted, at least in name, until 1857.

The conquest of India began anew with the invasion led by Babur, the young king of Kabul. A Mongol in descent, he differed from his ancestors in that he came as a conqueror, not a raider. His army was almost insignificant in number, but it was supported by the first field artillery to be seen in India, and his leadership was brilliant. On April 21, 1526, he fought the battle of Panipat against Sultan Ibrahim Lodi, the ruler of the sultanate of Delhi. Babur's 15,000 men, well supplied with artillery and muskets, confronted the 100,000-strong defending array and in a short morning blasted it apart. His new artillery blasted the old walls of the Indian cities as easily as it had the walls of the old castles of Europe.

Delhi and Agra were easily occupied. Babur then turned to the subjugation of Hindu India with the help of his new Moghul conquests. A Rajput confederacy had been established under Rana of Udaipur. Babur met them in battle at Sikri, near Agra. Before the battle was joined, Babur swore off alcohol, his principal sin, and then led his forces to victory. By the time he died in 1530 his dominions extended from the Oxus to the frontier of Bengal and from the Himalayas to Gwalior. Babur was succeeded, in 1530, by his son Humayun, and then more effectively by Akbar, who would continue his work.

For the first seven years of his reign, Akbar was constantly at war. In 1567 he stormed the Rajput stronghold of Chittur and conquered Ajmere. In 1570 he conquered Oudh and Gwalior. In 1572 he marched into Gujarat, defeated the last of the independent sultans of Ahmedabad, and formed the province into a Moghul viceroyalty or *subah*. That same year his generals drove out the Afghans from Bengal and reunited the lower valley of the Ganges to Hindustan. This gave Akbar control of the largest unified part of India that had ever stood under the rule of a single man. During the remainder of his life he continued to extend the boundaries of his empire, annexing Orissa to Bengal in 1578. Akbar died in 1605, and the kingdom passed to Jahangir, his son. His was a glorious reign, and he was not only a conqueror, but also a supporter of the arts and sciences. It is interesting that in 1576, at Shiraz, an inventor presented him with a repeating matchlock—a gun that fired twelve times in succession!

Jahangir was succeeded by his son Shah Jahan, who rebelled against his own father, just as his father had rebelled against his grandfather. It was Shah Jahan who erected the peacock throne in Delhi and built the Taj Mahal as a mausoleum for his favorite wife, Mumtaz Mahal. He lies beside her in the famous memorial.

Of Shah Jahan's four sons, the third, Aurangzeb would succeed to the throne by the preferred method of treachery and violence. He declared himself emperor in 1658, while Shah Jahan was still alive. Sultan Aurangzeb was a remarkable man—modest, capable, ascetic, honest, and an excellent battlefield commander. He was also a near perfect model of intolerant and extreme Islam. He removed non-Muslims from all positions of authority, reimposed the hated *jizya*—the tax on unbelievers—destroyed hundreds or thousands of Hindu temples and dictated a strict public morality based upon the ideals—not the practices—of the ruling Muslim minority. He was well hated and well feared.

Aurangzeb led his armies against the sultans of the Deccan and conquered them in hard-fought campaigns, pushing his authority to the extreme south. The resistance was led by Sivaji, founder of the Mahratta confederacy. He conceived and organized a uniquely powerful guerrilla force based on masses of light horsemen. Their mobility and fighting power frustrated the Muslim generals. He successfully outfought the Muslim armies with their own weapons and carved a kingdom out of their territory. His memory is revered to this day as the acme of Hindu patriotism. He died in 1680, and his son and successor, Sambhaji, was betrayed to Aurangzeb and put to death. The rising Mahratta power was checked, and the Moghul armies once again began operating freely in eastern Deccan. In 1686 the Muslims took the city of Bijapur, and Golconda fell the next year. No independent power remained in southern India.

Aurangzeb died in 1707, and the Moghul Empire, rent by intolerant policies and resulting guerrilla strife, immediately began its decline. Like the empires of most warlords, the decline would be as rapid as the rise. Thirty-two years and ten Moghul emperors produced no achievement worthy of the name. In 1739 Persian Nadir Shah led the sixth and last Muslim conquest of India through Hindustan to conquer the imperial city of Delhi. After that, the Great Moghul Empire became only a name. Internal strife and the resurrection of the Mahrattas continued the weaken the empire, though when the Muslim and Mahratta forces met at Panipat on January 7, 1761, the Muslims under Nadir Shah won a useful victory. Following the battle, Nadir Shah led his army back to Kabul in Afghanistan. With his authority placed at a distance, the southern Moghul puppets returned to their independent ways.

By the seventeenth century, British and French ships began appearing in Indian waters in significant numbers and the trading companies and their colonies followed soon after. European colonialism came into contact with the Muslim states of India at this time, and the Muslims played their parts in the extended European rivalries that reached across the globe.

The French meddled in the politics and intervened in the disputed suc-
cessions of Hyderabad and Arcot. The French and English naturally supported rival candidates, which led to the defense of Arcot by the English
General Clive in 1751. The French and British, each with their Indian
allies, began a struggle for the possession of India. In 1760, Coote won
the decisive victory of Wandiwash over the French General Lally and then
starved Pondicherry into capitulation in January 1761.

After the successful surprise attack by the Mahrattas, which led to the
legendary horror, the Black Hole of Calcutta,[1] Clive and Admiral Watson
pulled together their forces. Clive, leading some 900 Europeans and 2,000
sepoys (cavalrymen), supported by 8 guns, faced a Muslim army said to
have consisted of 35,000 foot, 15,000 horse, and 50 cannons in the Battle
of Plassey (fought July 23, 1757).

At daybreak the Muslim army left its camp and moved against Clive's
tiny force. At six, the Muslims began to attack with heavy cannon supported by their whole army, firing on the British for several hours. The
British, who were positioned in a large grove fronted with thick mud
banks, stood the fire easily from such a strong position. The Muslims'
artillery proved ineffective; their guns were poorly placed and their bombardment not concentrated. The British stood behind their defenses waiting to attack the enemy camp at night.

Around noon the Muslim artillery was withdrawn to their camp. The
British sent forward two guns supported by two companies to seize a
position 300 yards from the point from which the Muslim artillery had
directed much fire on them. The British move provoked a renewed advance by the Muslims, but they made so little serious effort, that the British
resumed their advance and took possession of two further rises much
closer to the Muslim camp.

The Muslim army responded strongly to this, but the well-directed British
artillery wrought much havoc on their ill-organized attacks. So successful
was the British fire that the Muslims were thrown into confusion and the
British stormed the corner of the Muslim camp, provoking a general rout.
The British pursued the Muslim army about six miles, capturing upwards
of forty pieces of cannon and a multitude of abandoned baggage wagons.
The nineteen-year-old Suraj-ud-Dowlah escaped on a camel, and upon
reaching Moorshedabad early the next morning, sent away what jewels and
treasure he could and then followed them with only two or three attendants.
The battle cost the Muslim army about 500 killed and the British 21 dead
and 50 wounded, mostly among the sepoys. The Battle of Plassey was short,
but decisive. The British took control of Bengal and the British Empire in
India was solidly settled, built on the ruins of the Moghul Empire.

With the consolidation of British commercial, political, and military power, the independent Muslim military history of India came to an end. The Muslim conquests of India struck the subcontinent at a time before much unity was present. Despite significant resistance, in the end, a small feudal military class of Turkish horsemen subjugated a vast population. Much of this is because Islamic culture offered a great deal to the Indian peoples, but it is also true that Hindu India offered much to Islam. Had the sultans obeyed their religious instruction—and starting with bin Qasim, they did not—the Hindu people would have been annihilated. They were not, largely because their destruction might well have been beyond the physical capacity of the Moghul rulers and because their lives and labors provided the wealth that made conquest inviting. There was never much doubt about the victor, when practical self-interest conflicted with Koranic scripture!

It is interesting that the eighth-century conquests of the regions that would become Afghanistan and Pakistan brought in an Islamic culture that has been the dominant religion for 1,200 years. On the other hand, although Islam was introduced to India, it did not become the dominant religious or cultural force. India is one of few lands that turned its back on the Prophet's religion. This suggests that the military conquest of the great Indian states may have been of less importance than most other campaigns waged by the sultans and caliphs.

CHRONOLOGY

711	Qasim occupies Daibil in Sind.
961	Alptigin establishes Gaznavid state in Afghanistan.
960s	Subaktagin begins raiding into India from Gaznavid Afghanistan.
1000	(approximate date) Mahmud of Gazni launches seventeen attacks on India, the first great wave of conquests.
1175	(approximate date) Muhammad Ghori, the second great invader continues the advances into India.
1199	Muhammad Ghori's lieutenant Bakhtiyar occupies Nadia, completing Muslim conquest of Northern India—the Delhi sultanate.
1206–88	The Slave Dynasty in Delhi
1294	Ala-ud-din-Khilji, the third great conqueror, ascends the Delhi throne, taking the Deccan and Gujarat during his reign.

1225–1351	Ghiyas-ud-Din moves the capital from Delhi to the Deccan.
1398	Tamerlane's great raid
1526	Babur attacks the sultanate of Delhi, founding the Moghul Empire.
1560	Akbar, last great Moghul conqueror, comes to power.
1658	Aurangzeb reigns until 1707, extending military rule to the south.
1739	Nadir Shah of Persia leads the last Moghul conquest.
1757	Battle of Plassey signifies the end of Moghul military and political dominance and the advent of British India.

NOTE

1. The Black Hole of Calcutta has a special place in history. The story goes that a total of 146 British soldiers taken prisoner at Fort William in Calcutta, during a revolt were locked in a cell 24 by 18 feet (some suggest 18.5 by 14), on June 21, 1756, the height of the scorching Indian summer. Only one small window allowed ventilation. Left overnight without food or water, of the 146 locked in the cell only 23 survived. The room was so small that when the door was opened in the morning even the dead were still standing. Historical evidence suggests that the story has been embellished, and that no more than sixty-nine were held and no more than forty-three died.

Chapter 5

EGYPT IN THE WORLD OF ISLAM

During the Crusades, when Saladin became sultan of Egypt, one of his early projects was to organize an army to defend his new lands. Among his army was a personal bodyguard of 500 yellow-clad Mamluks. These were mercenaries: Kurds, Turks, and Arabs or Bedouin nomads.

The word *mamluk* in Arabic is the past participle of the word to "own," that is, "owned." The use of mercenaries, particularly of Turks as mercenaries, had started under Khalif Mutasim, more than 400 years earlier. The Mamluk system was a variation of the common system of hiring foreign mercenaries, supported by a special class of merchants. These merchants traveled through the Asian steppes, buying boys ages 10–12 from their parents. The youths of the steppes were preferred because they were natural riders, born to the saddle, and already trained in the basics of the bow and sword.

The arrangement differed from simple slavery, as we would understand the English word. The boys came of their own will and were not chained or otherwise bound. The promise of a life in Egypt, to these boys, was the promise of life in the adventurous center of civilization—what we in the west call "the big city"!

Once in Egypt, they were sold to prominent men and trained in the use of the bow, lance, sword, and mace on horseback. They also received whatever other education their owner thought appropriate. When they were old enough to fight in battle, they were freed and armed. However, because of the tradition of Arab countries, these freedmen were under a moral obligation to remain as loyal retainers to their patrons, with whom they had a blood obligation. Upon this bond of honor the Mamluk system was founded.

This obligation to serve, however, did not necessarily transfer to the son of the patron. Should the patron die, the Mamluk was free to sell his services elsewhere. Nor did, once hired, this depth of loyalty transfer to his new patron.

The numbers of Mamluks in Egypt grew from Saladin's reign (1169–1193) through the six successive successors to his Ayoubid Empire. In 1249 the French crusader army under Louis IX landed at Damietta and, because of its military incompetence, found itself compelled to surrender to the Mamluk army defending Egypt.

On February 28, 1250, Turan Shah, the last of the Ayoubid, arrived to succeed his father as sultan of Egypt. His brash behavior and arrogance soon cost him his life at the hands of enraged Mamluks. Emir Aibek, by marrying the favorite wife of Al-Salih Ayoub, Turan Shah's predecessor, was proclaimed the first Mamluk sultan, establishing the Mamluk rule of Egypt. In what would become a common process of succession, Emir Aibek was murdered. He had been a prudent leader, brave in battle, but addicted to bloodshed. He had assured a smooth transition to Mamluk rule by maintaining the Ayoubid civil service in the hands of the educated Egyptians and Syrians who had run the bureaucracies for many years. This was doubly important, as the Mamluks spoke Turkish and would otherwise have been unable to communicate with their Arabic-speaking subjects.

On February 13, 1258, the Mongols capped their invasion of the Middle East with the capture of Baghdad. The city was utterly destroyed and its citizenry slaughtered or enslaved. Damascus was next on their list of targets and, knowing this, the city rulers called on the Mamluks of Egypt for help. The Mongols besieged and broke into the city on March 1, 1260, treating it in the same manner as they had Baghdad.

While Damascus was under siege, the Mamluks, under the Sultan Qutuz, mobilized their army and advanced into Syria. They met the enemy force on the morning of September 3, 1260, near Ain Jaloot (the Spring of Goliath). The battlefield topography was such that the Mamluks would ride downhill and the Mongols uphill.

The initial Mongol charge was so furious that the Mamluk advance guard was swept aside and their left flank overrun. However, the well-trained and disciplined Mamluks did not panic, so their center and right flank stood firm. The Mamluks worked around the Mongols' flanks, pressing the nomadic horsemen. At the decisive moment, the Sultan Qutuz rode to the front of his army, took off his helmet so he could be recognized, and cried, "Oh Muslims! Oh Muslims! Oh Muslims!" He then moved forward, surrounded by his escort and followed by the Mamluk army. Qutuz plunged recklessly into the Mongol ranks, slashing at his enemy with his own sword. The impetus of the Mamluk charge was irresistible, and the nomadic army was swept from the field.

The Mongol leader, Kitbugha, had his horse killed underneath him, was taken prisoner, and decapitated. The rest of the Mongol army was utterly routed. Qutuz, with General Baybars at his side, was in the heart of the battle.

Chased from the field at Ain Jaloot, the Mongols turned briefly at Beisan and the hand-to-hand battle was renewed briefly. Qutuz once more led, crying, "Oh God, give us victory!" The Mongol army finally collapsed and scattered. Kitbugha's severed head was then dispatched to the Mamluk capital, Cairo, as proof of the victory. This significant victory spared the Arab Middle East from Mongol domination. It is interesting that the Mongols were rarely defeated by any nation, and Ain Jaloot stands as a real testament to Mamluk military efficiency.

Qutuz did not live long to enjoy his victory but was murdered by Baybars on October 24, 1260. Murder would remain a common form of death for the sultans of the Mamluk empire that Baybars would found.

Baybars consolidated his control over the Mamluk empire and began a steady push against the remaining crusader states in Palestine. In 1264 the Mongols returned, only to be defeated and driven back into Persia. By 1266 he captured Hebron and when the crusaders surrendered the sultan had them slaughtered. In 1268 Baybars took Jaffa, and in 1273 he wiped out the Assassin sect.[1] Troubles continued with a Mongol resurgence in 1277, but they were driven back yet again.

Enough cannot be said of the success of the Mamluks in defeating the Mongols. The Mongol armies had been considered nearly invincible, and there is justification in speculating that the Mamluk victory at Ain Jaloot saved the West from destruction at the hands of the Mongol hordes. It certainly saved the Arab world.

Baybars died on June 20, 1277. However, he left behind him a powerful empire built on and around the Mamluk army. His army had actually struck fear into the Mongols such that they never invaded Syria again during his reign. He also fortified Alexandria and rebuilt the Egyptian navy, giving it forty new war galleys. The astute horselord understood the value of more than just his cavalry, for ships were useful to any Mediterranean power.

When Baybars died, the succession passed through a series of weak, and sometimes juvenile, sultans often controlled by others. The empire would periodically have a strong and capable sultan who would rule for some years, but invariably, upon his death, the Mamluk empire would plunge deeper into chaos as the centuries rolled on.

The next important Mamluk sultan was Qalaoon and he, too, would be challenged by the Mongols. On October 31, 1281, Qalaoon stood with the Mamluk army facing the Mongols in what would be known as the Battle of Hims. When the battle was engaged the Mongols fell on the Mamluk right wing but were driven back into their center. On their right, however, the enemy was successful and routed the Mamluk left. The Mamluk left fled to the gates of Hims with the Mongols on their heels. The gates were closed, and the Mongols slaughtered everyone they caught outside the walls.

However, back on the main battlefield, the fight went against the Asiatic horsemen. The Mamluk right flank penetrated almost to the center of the Mongol army, which began to advance against Qalaoon's position. As the Mamluk drums sounded to recall the stragglers, Azdemir al Haj, a senior Mamluk emir, galloped across to the Mongols with a few men, calling out that they were deserters and wished to speak with the Mongol general, Mangu Timur. They were escorted to the Mongol commander, who they promptly cut down. As the Mongols rushed to their leader's assistance, chaos erupted in their leaderless center.

Seeing this disorder, perhaps knowing what Azdemir al Haj had done, the Mamluks charged. Though Mangu Timur was only wounded, he was quickly removed from the battlefield. Azdemir al Haj and his fellows had been cut down, sacrificing themselves in a valiant attempt to give the Mamluks the edge they needed for victory. Their sacrifice was successful, and the charging Egyptians broke and scattered the steppe army.

Meanwhile, the Mongol right was amusing itself by slaughtering the people of Hims and was unaware of the results of the battle. Sated with blood, they turned back to rejoin the main body. Anticipating this, Qalaoon had held back about 1,000 men who laid in ambush awaiting the enemy's return. When the Mongols had ridden past his position, the Mamluks erupted from their rear, smashing them into panic-stricken flight across the plain.

That night, the sun set on an exhausted but victorious Mamluk army. The disastrous retreat had cost the Mongols more men than had the battle. They were so demoralized by their defeat that many fell prey to the angry survivors of the local peasantry who had plenty of scores to settle with them. Unaware of the Mamluk victory, the citizens of Damascus had panicked and begun fleeing until a day later when word of the overwhelming victory arrived. Syria had been saved yet again.

Sultan Qalaoon brought in the first Circassian Mamluks. Prior to this, they had all been Qipchaq Turks. As time passed, the tribal mixture would change, and eventually the Mamluks would cease being a homogeneous ethnic organization. For the moment, however, their army consisted of 29,000 of the finest cavalry the world had ever known.

The string of victories continued as Sultan Qalaoon made use of his superb fighting machine. In 1291 Acre was taken, and the last crusader possession on the mainland was forever lost. Only the island base of Cyprus remained of the crusader conquests. In 1292 Aleppo was taken from the Mongols and the Mongol residents received the same treatment they had given its earlier occupants: the only survivors, the women and children, were taken into slavery.

However, the Mongols remained the main enemy of the Mamluks, and once again the two premier mounted armies of the world faced each other on December 22, 1299, at the Battle of Wadi al Khaznadar. Five hundred Mamluks, specifically trained as artificers, took positions in front of the Mamluk army. On horseback and armed with flaming bombs of naphtha, they charged the Mongols with liquid fire.

Ghazan, the commander of the Mongols then brought forward a mass of foot archers, estimated to number 10,000, who poured a cloud of arrows into the Mamluks. The arrows fell most heavily on the lightly armored Bedouin allies, who fell back in confusion. The Mamluk left then charged and broke the Mongol right, chasing them from the field.

The Mongols made one final effort and Khan Ghazan, their commander, personally led a charge against the Egyptian center, which broke. The Mamluk army routed and fled the field, deserting the child sultan and leaving him on the field with only twelve soldiers as his escort.

Glutted with the loot of the Mamluk camp, Ghazan then moved against Damascus. On December 29, the religious leaders of the city brokered a deal with the khan whereby the Mongols would enter the city peacefully. Ghazan promised that no soldier of his would commit any crime against man or woman and that all religious rights would be respected. Once inside the city though, his troops went wild, and on January 11, 1300, the nomads savaged the place, inflicting great loss on the inhabitants.

Torn by internal dissent, the Mamluks had not performed well at Wadi al Khaznadar. The endless streams of infighting and struggles for the sultanship had begun to tear at the fabric of their cohesiveness. When the crucial moments came, their discipline and order were insufficient to fight a foe as dangerous as the Mongols. They were heavily defeated as a result.

The Mamluk army was based on the feudal system with various emirs receiving fiefs of land in exchange for service. In 1313 the sultan began to reallocate the fiefs among his followers, while taking the bulk of them for his own use. Those fiefs he retained served his personal needs and supported the Royal Mamluks. The latter would eventually evolve into an utterly uncontrolled palace guard, whose demands for bribes would ruin the finances of the empire. The sultan had controlled the nobility with the army, but there was no controlling the army.

As time progressed and the power of the Royal Mamluks grew, they steadily abandoned their martial training and focused more and more on politics. Their interests as a privileged foreign class were not those of the nation. The core of the empire would literally rot out. The army lost their services, and they ruined the court with terrible corruption and venality.

While the Mamluk empire struggled with internal disorders in 1394, the great Tamerlane appeared. Born in Samarkand in 1336, in 1381 he led his army into Persia, imitating Genghis Khan by slaughtering every man, woman, and child in each town that he captured. He took Baghdad in October 1393 and then Tabriz. In February 1394 he sent a long dispatch full of threats to the Mamluks in Cairo. The Mamluks responded by mobilizing and marching to war.

On December 31, 1400, the Mamluks met Tamerlane outside of Damascus in battle. The Mamluk left was defeated, but their right forced back Tamerlane's left. The battle was a draw, and despite the chaotic rivalries that divided the Mamluk emirs, they were still able to hold their own in a "soldiers' battle."

Tamerlane sent a message requesting a truce, but it was rejected. The Mamluk emirs, instead of planning strategy, quarreled over fiefs and appointments, and some abandoned the Mamluk army, taking their men with them. The rumor spread that they were planning a coup d'état. The sultan's leading supporters, alarmed for their privileges back in Cairo, swept up their puppet and on January 8 rode posthaste to Cairo, abandoning the field and their army to Tamerlane. The remaining Mamluks, seeing themselves abandoned, immediately decamped. The army that had held off a ferocious foe literally disintegrated of its own ineptitude.

Damascus, abandoned by the Mamluk army, was then attacked by Tamerlane's host, but the citizens defeated the first effort. The Mongol warlord then entered into negotiations with the principal religious leaders, professing that he had accepted Islam. True or not, the imams believed him— apparently forgetting their recent experiences with Ghazan—and signed an agreement with Tamerlane to spare their city for a bribe of one million gold dinars. However, once inside the city, Tamerlane repudiated his agreement and Damascus was once again obliterated and its people murdered in the most horrendous manners. After eighty days of looting, murder, and rape, Tamerlane left Damascus a pile of smoking ruins and returned to Samarkand.

The Mamluk empire continued in its steady decline. A few military successes ensued, such as the naval operations in 1426 that led to the conquest of Cyprus, making it a tributary state. However, a similar expedition against Rhodes failed. The Black Sheep and White Sheep Turkmen tribes in Persia would replace the Mongols as major sources of border problems, but few major battles erupted. The disintegration of the Mamluks cost them many of these border clashes and the few pitched battles. Egyptian frontiers in Syria were pushed back west. Eventually the growing power of the Italian city-states and the Portuguese would drive the Mamluk navy from the seas and take Cyprus away from them as well.

A major problem arose when the Portuguese discovered how to sail around the Cape of Good Hope and penetrate the Indian Ocean. They would eventually drive the Mamluk southern fleet from the seas, destroying it in battle in February 1509. This naval dominance allowed the Europeans to establish colonies in India that would give them control of the spice trade. This utterly destroyed the finances of the Mamluk empire, whose revenues depended heavily on the taxation of the overland traffic in goods from the Far East.

Financially crippled, the sultans were no longer able to bribe the Royal Mamluks, whose ranks were kept filled by the importation of more and more slave boys to replenish the ranks. On August 23, 1514, fate began knocking at the Mamluks' doors. On that day the Ottomans, under Sultan Selim, known as Selim the Grim for his brutality, defeated the Persians in the Battle of Chaldiron. Sultan Selim then moved against the Mamluks and engaged them in the Battle of Marj Dabig on August 24, 1515. The cavalry-based Mamluk army faced a relatively modern Ottoman army equipped with cannons and highly trained musket-armed infantry.

The Mamluks opened the battle with a headlong cavalry charge in fine old medieval style, led by the commander-in-chief, Sudoon al Ajami, and Emir Sibay, the viceroy of Damascus. The Ottoman left was overrun and fled, abandoning seven colors and numerous guns to the Mamluks. It is alleged that Selim was on the verge of flight when the Mamluk left, under Khairbeg, viceroy of Aleppo, withdrew from the field for no apparent reason. It later transpired that Khairbeg had betrayed the Mamluk cause to the Ottomans.

Selim's victorious army began an easy advance against now defenseless Cairo, occupying it on January 26, 1517. The Mamluk empire was thus extinguished and the land became a province of the rising Ottoman empire. However, the great distance from the Ottoman capital in Constantinople would begin to tell. In 1586 the Janissary garrison of Cairo mutinied and arrested the Ottoman viceroy. Further military mutinies occurred in 1589, 1591, and 1601.

When the garrison was disloyal, the Ottoman viceroy was obliged to call on the leading Mamluk families for support. In 1605 the viceroy, after trying to discipline the Janissary garrison, was murdered, and in January 1609 the Spahis mutinied, fighting a battle with the Mamluks outside Cairo. The Mamluk beys (formerly emirs) now controlled Egypt once again. In 1631 they suspended the viceroy and took over. They soon returned to their practices of political corruption, as each family struggled to dominate the others and rule the country. By 1711 the Ottoman viceroys were reduced to utter impotence and the feud between the Qasimiya and Faqariya Mamluk families dominated Egyptian politics. It was the old story of Nur-Al-Din and Saladin over again. Egypt, technically a vassal state of a greater power, was actually independent in all but name. The independence fostered corruption unchecked by competent authority, and the cycle continued.

This internecine feuding continued throughout the eighteenth century. Egypt became a backwater suffering equally from Turkish indifference, internal feuding, and lack of revenue. The great events of the outside world would catch up to her by the end of the century, though.

The rising star of the French army, Napoleon Bonaparte, saw an opportunity for greater glory, and the French government saw in Napoleon's planned attack on Egypt a way to get him out of Europe. A fleet was organized, an army drawn together, and after a harrowing trip across the Mediterranean, the French landed 5,000 troops outside Alexandria. The landing was unopposed and incurred only a few minor engagements with Mamluk forces before the French arrived at the gates of the ancient port city.

The Sherif Seyd Muhammad el-Kortaim, a descendant of the family of the Prophet, was governor of Alexandria, which he ruled with extortions and tyrannies. He was a representative of the Turkish pasha, but had been secretly bought off by the Mamluks, with whom he split the spoils that they stripped out of his tributes. At the first news of the invasion, he made preparations for the defense. The citadel received munitions, the militia was armed, and a cloud of Bedouins was drawn out of the desert and encamped near Alexandria.

Having no artillery, Napoleon was reduced to launching an assault on as many points as possible. The population of Alexandria manned the walls and fired on the advancing French infantry, but it did not last particularly long. The French stormed up the walls and into the city. The Rosetta gate was cut open with axes, and the French troops poured in.

If a few Janissaries, supported by their militia, had stood in defense at the moment of the escalade, the story might have been different, but they did not. The defenders fled in confusion behind the Sarrasin Wall and sought refuge in the new town, and finally in the triangular fort (also known as the Pharaohs' Fortress).

The initial attack, however, did not assure victory. As the French troops rallied, Napoleon had the commander of a Turkish caravel—a merchant ship—brought to him. He told the Turk that all resistance was useless. He went on to say that he would allow Alexandria to be pillaged by his army if it continued to resist and that he would have the inhabitants slaughtered. He repeated that his intentions were friendly, that he was a friend of the sultan, but an enemy of the Mamluks, and asked that he take to the Alexandrians his hopeful words.

The Turkish captain went into the city, repeated everything that he had heard and added that the French general had promised to respect the religion and property of the faithful. The populace, hearing this and reassured by Napoleon's promises, asked their leaders to submit.

An hour after the Turkish captain went into the city a group of imams, sheiks, and sherifs was seen coming out. They sought personal assurances from Napoleon and asked to view the forces facing them. New promises were exchanged and confidence began to be established.

Sherif Kortaïm alone continued to resist. He closed himself up in the Pharaohs' Fortress with a few Mamluks. He refused to surrender until later that afternoon when it became obvious that any further resistance was impossible. A generous Napoleon comforted Kortaïm for his defeat and reassured him that he would continue to govern Alexandria.

On July 1 the city of Alexandria, its gates, and fortifications, were entirely in the hands of the French. Toward evening, the city had calmed down. Napoleon ordered that the Muslim prayers and ceremonies continue as usual, and soon the Alexandrians began to wonder if they had actually changed masters.

Once his full army was ashore and secure in Alexandria, Napoleon immediately set about organizing his forces for the march on Cairo. The march south began on July 6 and for the French soldiers, the march through the desert was a tremendous hardship.

The Mamluks had begun to respond to the French invasion and gathered their forces. A force of 4,000 mounted Mamluks and 12,000 *fellahin* militia remained under Murad to defend Cairo, while a force of around 100,000 advanced north to engage the French.

The first minor engagement occurred on July 10. Mamluk cavalry charged the French infantry, who formed a square and drove them away with disciplined musketry. Further small fights continued until July 21, when the French army marched onto the plain at Giza and into the shadows of the Pyramids and the Sphinx.

Murad Bey assumed command of the defending army. He probably should have stayed on the east bank of the Nile, but it was not the Mamluk way to avoid combat. He led his army across the Nile and established a primitive fortified camp surrounded by rough trenches and protected by forty immobile guns.

The 25,000-man-strong French army found itself confronted by the 8,000-man Mamluk cavalry army supported by a large force of Egyptian infantry, whose military value was slight. The French formed themselves into great hollow squares with their artillery at the corners and their cavalry in the middle of the squares. A small flotilla of French gunboats floated on the Nile to support the French flank.

The Mamluks charged forward in their ferocious battle formation, but the French squares stood firm and raked the oncoming squadrons with disciplined musketry and canister-fire from their supporting cannons. Despite the murderous fire, the Mamluks swept around and through the line of squares, firing their pistols at close range, but their effort was overwhelmed by that of the French. Empty saddles multiplied in the Mamluk ranks at a tremendous rate.

The fire of a battery of Mamluk cannons came from a village, but the French infantry overran them and slaughtered the gunners. This maneuver cut off the Mamluks' retreat and they panicked. Turning toward the Nile, they plunged into it and tried to swim away. At least 1,000 drowned and a further 600 were shot down. When the battle ended, Murad Bey and his 3,000 surviving cavalry withdrew to Cairo. Egypt was lost and gained. Napoleon's victory had cost him 29 killed and less than 300 wounded. Murad Bey had lost more than 2,000 Mamluks and thousands of *fellahin* militia.

More than just Egypt was won on the fields at Giza—loot was abundant. The Mamluks had a tradition of carrying large quantities of gold and jewels with them into battle. Many a French soldier grew rich picking the bodies of the dead Mamluks. In this vein, a soldier of the 32nd Demi-Brigade was the first to go fishing in the Nile. The Mamluks that had drowned or been shot in the river were floating treasuries just waiting to be looted by an industrious angler. This soldier discovered that the poorly tempered French bayonets could be bent into quite acceptable fishing hooks and made his fortune fishing in the Nile for Mamluks.

The French went on to occupy Cairo. They failed, however, to subdue the upper Nile and expeditions into that region found themselves chasing the wind as the Mamluk cavalry simply danced away from the lumbering French infantry. Napoleon even launched an attack into Palestine, but fortune and the British navy destroyed his siege train, and the great fortress of Acre proved beyond his ability to subdue. Beaten, he withdrew to Cairo. Political events in France demanded that Napoleon return to his homeland to begin the process that would make him emperor. He left General Kléber in command in Egypt. Kléber was attacked and stabbed to death by a fanatic Muslim named Suliman-el-Halepi on June 18, 1800. General Menou assumed command. After the British victory over the French at Alexandria by General Abercromby, a convention was negotiated and the British agreed to remove the French from Egypt and transport them back to France. With that, the French invasion of Egypt came to an end, and with it the first major invasion of the Muslim heartlands since the Crusades.

In 1805 Mehmet Ali, commander of the Albanian garrison sent to Egypt by the Ottomans, seized power in his own name. The Turks, incapable of removing him, pragmatically appointed him governor. He was not a Mamluk, and the Mamluks were by this time a spent force. In 1811 Mehmet Ali invited the Mamluk leaders to the Cairo citadel, where he murdered them and established an Albanian dynasty that ruled Egypt for the next 140 years. One of Mehmet's most interesting campaigns was to be against Wahabbi religious fundamentalists in Saudi Arabia. The Wahabbi Wars have an influence still felt today.

Muhammad 'Abd al-Wahhab was born in the Najd town of 'Uyainah, (in modern Saudi Arabia) about 1705. When he studied law in Medina his teachers thought they detected signs of heresy in his views, but nothing came of it. After a period of many years as a wandering scholar through Iraq and Persia, he married a rich wife and embraced the mystic system of the Sufis. In Qum (modern Iran) he returned to the orthodox teachings of the Hanbali School of Law. Two decades later he began to preach a return to the practice and beliefs of the time of Muhammad and the first generation of his successors, that is, fundamentalism. He declared that all knowledge not based on the Koran or the sunna—traditions of Muhammad—was suspect. He declared the veneration of saints forbidden because he thought it detracted from the "oneness" of God. He forbade the faithful to invoke the names of saints (associates of Muhammad during the Prophet's lifetime) in prayer, to make vows to them, or to visit their tombs.

The mystic beliefs of the Sufis were also forbidden. He preached predestination—the absolute nonexistence of free will—as an article of faith. Public prayers became mandatory; tobacco, alcohol, music, coffee, and the wearing of silk and gold were forbidden. All Muslims who did not subscribe to his beliefs were declared idolaters and were liable to whipping or, in extreme cases, death.

Like Muhammad, al-Wahhab and his family were driven from his home in ʿUyainah and was taken in at Darʿiyah, where Muhammad ibn Saʿud ruled. Al-Wahhab's Unitarian creed took root and began spreading.

Armed with a new dogma, Muhammad ibn Saʿud trained his men in the use of firearms and built up a small army to spread the new creed. The old traditions of the desert were sharpened by the edge of faith as they had been 1,000 years earlier. As each tribe was defeated, the Wahhabis built a fort and garrisoned it with a force of faithful soldiers. They then installed a mufti and a qadi to instruct the people in Unitarianism.

In 1766 the religious authorities of Mecca became concerned and summoned a Wahhabi delegation to Mecca that it might be examined for heresy. The Wahhabis were exonerated and continued to expand. After thirty years of conquest and proselytizing, they had the greater part of the interior of Arabia under their control.

One of the mechanisms that they employed to expand their control was to prey on the natural proclivity of the desert people to highway robbery. Saʿud gave them license to rob and pillage any traveler who was not a Unitarian. This resulted in tremendous pressures on the caravan trade into Arabia. The Wahhabis also made two or three raids a year to plunder the borderlands of their richer neighbors in Iraq and Syria. These raids, which interfered with the pilgrim caravans to Mecca, forced the Sublime Porte Selim III to take action, and in 1790 he ordered the sharif of Mecca to take the field against the Wahhabis. The Meccan army, a motley force of mercenary Moors and Negroes was quickly slaughtered and the gates of Mecca were opened to the Wahhabis, who initially came in peace. The fundamentalist Wahhabis soon found the sights that greeted them in Mecca offensive to their sense of Islam. The city had, essentially, become a den of iniquity, with open prostitution, use of alcohol, and other proscribed behavior brazenly displayed.

In 1802 the Wahhabis went on a raid into central Iraq and sacked the city of Karbala. Their actions, including the destruction of the dome over Husain's tomb and the graves of other Shiite saints, shocked the Muslim world. The Sublime Porte again ordered action against them, but it came to nothing. In 1802 a Wahhabi raid attacked and sacked the town of Tayif, brutally slaughtering everyone. This was a prelude to the attack by Muhammad ibn Sa'ud against Mecca.

Mecca was besieged and taken in 1803. Medina was taken in 1804. Sa'ud ordered his men to strip the Prophet's Mosque of its treasures and to tear down the dome over it. The destruction of the dome was stopped, however, after several Wahhabis were injured in falls. They contented themselves with the wrecking of the tombs of Muhammad's family and companions. Sa'udi soldiers then roamed the streets with staves, forcing the male population into the mosques where a roll was called of all the citizens. All Turks were ordered to leave the city, and those who were slow to obey had their beards cut off.

Initially the Turkish sultan accepted the transfer of power in Mecca, but this soon changed and he ordered Mehmet Ali, sultan of Egypt, to send a military expedition to recover the holy cities. The first attempts were complete failures, but by 1817 Mehmet Ali launched a campaign well supplied with artillery. At the wells of Mawiyah the Wahhabi cameleers were no match for the Turks under Mehmet Ali's general, Auzun Ali. In the following year the Turks steadily slaughtered the armies the Wahhabis sent against them, ravaging their heartland and destroying Dar'iyah in September. The Turkish forces pillaged the city and a particular vengeance was directed against the religious leaders of the town. The qadi had his teeth pulled out before he was killed, and the grandson of Muhammad 'Abd al-Wahhab was forced to listen to the hated music of a guitar before he was executed.

The power of the Wahhabis was broken for the time, but the House of Sa'ud remained a power within the tribal structure of Arabia. Its principal rival for dominance of all of Arabia was the family of Ibn Rashid. The Rashids took dominance when the House of Sa'ud fell and would dominate the Arabian peninsula until World War I, when they were ousted, along with the Turks.

Abd al-Aziz ibn 'Abd ar-Rahman Al Faysal Al Sa'ud, better known as Ibn Sa'ud, the leader of the House of Sa'ud at the time, led a force of forty friends and relatives into the desert. With this tiny force he suddenly appeared at the gates of Riyadh and in a brilliant military feat captured the castle and killed Ibn Rashid's governor on January 16, 1902. With this act Ibn Sa'ud began the march of his family to the throne of Saudi Arabia. The British signed a treaty with Ibn Sa'ud at the beginning of World War I, seeking to use his forces to further discommode the Turks.

A battlefield success by the Sa'uds in 1919 caused the British to attempt to reconcile the two sides in 1923 without success. When the Republic of Turkey was formed, the office of the caliphate was abolished and Husain

Ibn Rashid declared himself Caliph of all Islam. The Saʿuds and the Wahhabis considered this a sacrilege and began a renewed military campaign. In December 1925 Ibn Saʿud completed the military defeat of the Rashids and of the Arabian peninsula. He was declared King of the Hijaz in the Holy Mosque of Mecca on 18 January 1928. Founded in the fundamentalism of Wahhabism and the sword, thus began the rule of the House of Saʿud, which continues to this day.

Thus Mehmet Ali had an interesting part in the beginnings of modern Saudi Arabia, and also at the birth of modern Greece. In this sense, Egyptian forces were used as the Ottoman "fire brigade," shifting from one emergency to the next. Fortunately for both countries, the able Egyptian lacked the weight to decisively hinder either of the new nations.

In 1821 a revolution broke out in Greece. Much of the instigation for this revolution was traceable to Russia, which had a policy of inciting Greek Christians to revolt against their Ottoman oppressors. This policy was traceable back to the reign of Czarina Anna, but Catherine II brought it forward with a passion. Her "favorite," Admiral Orlov, moved into the Aegean Sea with a fleet of Russian ships in 1769, landed in the Morea, and organized a revolt. This revolt failed, Orlov reembarked, and the Greeks he left behind were subjected to terrible massacres at Tripolitza, Lemnos, and elsewhere. The Albanians, also Muslims, completed what the Turks began in the way of savage repressions. The Treaty of Kutchuk-Kainarj (1744) granted Russia a vaguely defined protectorate over the Ottomans' Orthodox Greek subjects and gave Greek traders the right to sail under the Russian flag.

Like oppressed people in many parts of the world, the ideals of the French Revolution inspired the Greeks to seek relief from their oppressors. Revolutionary groups were organized and once again received support from the Russians.

In 1820 Ali Pasha of Yannina, the Muslim governor of Greece, revolted against the authority of the sultan. Earlier Ali Pasha had ruthlessly oppressed and slaughtered Greeks by the hundreds, but now he declared himself their friend and joined "The Friendly Society." In March 1821 Alexander Ypsilanti led an abortive attack by an armed band in an effort to liberate Greece. That same month, Archbishop Germanos of Patras raised the standard of revolt in Hagia Lavra, near Kalavryta, in Morea. The Greek Revolution had begun, and soon it was going badly for the Sublime Porte.

When the revolution began the Ottomans had plenty of warning, but were entirely unprepared. The bulk of the Ottoman army had been fully occupied in crushing Ali Pasha in Iannina. The Greeks, with their history of piratical seafaring, outfitted a horde of corsairs and quickly outclassed the Ottomans in the Aegean and cut off the Turkish lines of communication, capturing vessels of every nation that entered the Aegean.

When the Greeks took Tripolitza, the capital of the Vilayet, the Greek commander Kolokotrones rode in triumph to the citadel over streets carpeted with the dead. More than 10,000 Turks were murdered. The large number of documented massacres of Turks by Greeks and the savagery with which they were executed is hard for modern readers to comprehend. Such massacres occurred at the hands of the Ottomans as well. The war was not without Greek reverses and setbacks, but overall the early part of the fighting was successful for the revolutionaries.

As the war progressed, it became one of mutual extermination. Both sides acted with great barbarity. In the spring of 1822 two Ottoman armies advanced into the Morea. One, under Omar Vrioni, moved along the coast of western Hellas and the other, under Ali, Pasha of Drama (Dramali), moved through Boeotia and Attica. Omar was stopped by the mud ramparts at Missolonghi, but Dramali crossed the Isthmus and, smugly confident, marched to relieve the Ottoman garrison of Nauplia. However, as he came to the acropolis of ancient Argos, he found the Larissa Castle garrisoned by a band of 100 determined Greeks under the command of Demetrios Ypsilanti. Dramali's advance was stalled, and Kolokotrones collected an army. Lacking a fleet to support them, Dramali's Ottoman army was forced to retreat. The Greeks waited for Dramali's undisciplined army at the pass of Dervenaki. After rolling boulders down on them, the Greeks swooped down on the dazed Turks and annihilated them.

This victory went to the heads of the Greek leaders, and in 1823 they fell into a civil war as each faction struggled to establish dominance. This allowed the Turks to rebuild and reorganize for their next thrust back into Greece.

The Sultan Mahmud summoned Mehmet Ali, Pasha of Egypt, to assist. His army had subdued Crete the year before and had also worked in Arabia. It now marched against the Greeks. His moves were decisive and destructive. The Greeks, stuck in their petty squabbles, fell easy prey to his disciplined troops.

Surprisingly, many Greeks looked favorably on Mehmet Ali's success. The peasants in the open country looked upon the restoration of order by the Ottomans with relief from the chaos that had existed under the revolutionaries.

At this point Western Europe intervened. The European powers deployed their fleets into the Aegean and forced an armistice on both parties. They were determined to compel Ibrahim to evacuate Morea and attempted to do so with the Treaty of London, July 6, 1827. However Ibrahim refused to comply with Western demands without special instructions from the sultan. This led to the movement of the combined British, French, and Russian fleets into the Navarino harbor and the naval battle of Navarino, fought on October 20, 1827. The Turkish-Egyptian fleet was destroyed.

This and the two campaigns of the Russo-Turkish War of 1828–29 decided the issue and Greece became an independent nation. Some observations to be taken from this apply to today's circumstances in the Balkans. The Greeks have never forgotten how the Ottomans turned the Muslim Albanians loose in Greece to slaughter and reinforce Ottoman rule. Also, both the Greeks and the Ottomans ruthlessly slaughtered each other, the Greeks because of the outrages the Ottomans had perpetrated against them, and the Ottomans to attempt by terror to reestablish their oppression of the Greeks. The fruits of these seeds would be seen again in the Balkan Wars in 1912–13 and, the post–World War I invasion of Turkey by the Greeks and the subsequent slaughter of thousands of Turks, and the ongoing Greco-Turkish hostility over Cyprus.

The Egyptian Mamluks were not unique in the Muslim world. The Ottomans raised a similar force known as the Janissaries. Mercenary forces were a useful tool to the Egyptians, and other Muslim governments as well. The drawback to both Egyptian Mamluk and Ottoman Janissary is that they slowed the growth of a modern army in each nation.

There would be other Egyptian parallels with the Ottomans. The early Mamluk sultans fought their way through the ranks and to the throne, and the early Ottoman sultans were also battle-hardened veterans, though they generally succeeded their fathers to the throne. However, both dynasties also clearly demonstrated that the sons who ascended their respective thrones were often poor rulers who were either marginalized or supplanted by stronger men.

It is fortunate for the world that the Mamluk system existed and that they had control of Egypt when they did, as the Mongol invasion of the Middle East and West would have surely resulted had they not been defeated by the Mamluks at Ain Jaloot. The primitive western kingdoms would have had no hope of stopping the Mongol invasion, and our history would have been irreparably altered.

Similarly, it is interesting to speculate on what might have happened had Mehmet Ali, successor to the Mamluks, not defeated the fundamentalist Wahhabis in 1817. The absence of a strong, fundamentalist group in the Middle East facilitated the penetration of the Middle East by the imperial Western countries in the nineteenth and twentieth centuries and also allowed the Ottomans to continue their control much longer than might have otherwise occurred.

CHRONOLOGY

1169–93	Saladin's reign in Egypt and the beginning of Mamluk influence
1250	Turan Shah, last Ayoubid caliph, is murdered by the Mamluks, their first great political act.
1260	(date approximate) Mamluks under Sultan Baybars (and others) defeat Mongol attacks on Syria.
1280s	Sultan Qalaoon defeats more Mongols and eliminates Acre, the last crusader outpost.
1300s	The Mamluk system is solidified and the Mamluk army becomes the political master of the sultans.
1400	Mongols defeat the Mamluks and destroy Damascus.
1400s	Mamluk effectiveness degrades as they become more political and less military.
1515	The Ottomans defeat the Egyptians at the Battle of Marj Dabiq, thus bringing Egypt under the Turkish throne.
1580s	Mamluks reassert authority by mutinies against the Ottoman viceroys.
1600–1700	Egypt is actually independent, although nominally a Turkish province.
1799	French defeat the Mamluks at the Battle of the Pyramids.
1805	Mehmet Ali takes control of Egypt and is tacitly recognized in Constantinople.
1817	Mehmet campaigns in Arabia against the Wahhabis.
1821	Mehmet campaigns in Greece during the Greek civil wars.
1827	A Western fleet destroys Mehmet's fleet at Navarino Bay.

NOTE

1. See Chapter 8 for a complete history of the Assassin sect.

Chapter 6

THE MUSLIM CONQUEST AND LOSS OF SPAIN

The fiery Islamic storm that blew through Egypt expanded westward and threw sparks into the North African Bedouins, igniting them to yet another jihad that would push across the deserts of North Africa to Morocco. In numerous engagements the raiders pillaged the decaying fringes of the Byzantine Empire, capturing the few imperial outposts scattered along the southern coast of the Mediterranean. As always, conversion and conquest went hand in hand. These newly converted Muslims pushed to Ceuta, on the Moroccan shore of the Strait of Gibraltar, by A.D. 618.

Count Julian, a vassal of King Roderick, repulsed the Muslim assault on Ceuta, led by Musa ibn Nusair. However, Count Julian was a treacherous warlord who then made an alliance with Musa against King Roderick, last of the Visigoth kings of Spain. The Visigoths themselves were the last of a series of barbaric German tribes who had swept the old Western Roman Empire away. They had held Spain since the sixth century. Julian, having no real loyalty except to himself, promised to assist Musa in the conquest of Spain and spiced it with promises of rich booty and beautiful women. The raiding party was organized under Abu Zora Tarik, who led a reconnaissance in force to the Algeciras region of southern Spain in July 710.

The first battle in Spain against the Muslims was fought on the banks of the Guadelete River, to the northwest of Gibraltar. Known as the Battle of Merida, the Spanish army fielded 40,000 or more men, including a large contingent led by the treacherous, but still unmasked Count Julian.

The overall leader of the Visigoths was King Roderick. The Muslim forces were an estimated 12,000 men. The battle lasted several days, and at least one severe assault by Tarik's forces was repulsed. What might have been can only be imagined, for Count Julian took his contingent over to the Muslim side, and Roderick's army disintegrated. Roderick fled the battlefield and drowned while attempting to cross the Guadalquivir.

With the Christian king dead, Count Julian convinced Abu Zora Tarik to advance north and seize Toledo before its defenses could be organized. When Musa, Tarik's overlord, arrived with reinforcements, he was furious with Tarik, but it was difficult to argue with success. By 718 the Muslim army had completely subjugated Spain, pushing the surviving Spanish Christian and Visigothic lords into the mountains of the north and west. Musa returned to Damascus, loaded with booty and accompanied by 3,000 beautiful Spanish virgins for Caliph al-Walid's harem.

With the richest parts of the peninsula under their control, the Moors looked across the Pyrenees. Between 718 and 732 the Muslim army in Spain found employment by raiding north into what is today France. At the time the French kingdom had not yet solidified, and the collection of disorganized states was exceptionally tempting. The Franks, however, would not make it easy for the Muslims to raid with impunity. Their first major invasion in 721 captured Narbonne, which the Moors used as a base for further raids. When Al-Semah captured Narbonne in 721 he had every male inhabitant killed and the women and children sold into slavery. From there he pushed west to Toulouse and was killed in battle against Eudo, duke of Aquitaine.

Command of the army fell to Abd er-Rahman, who withdrew his forces back to Spain, though he maintained the garrison in Narbonne. A new Muslim army came in 724 under Ambissa, which captured Carcassone and Nîmes, sacking monasteries and churches along the way. The Muslims pushed their armies up the Rhone, plundering Lyon, Mâcon, Châlons, Beaune, and Dijon.

One of the most significant battles in history would follow as Abd er-Rahman's army moved once again over the Pyrenees in 732. The storied wealth of the Basilica of St. Martin in Tours had caught the attention of the Moors. In October 732, however, somewhere between the modern cities of Tours and Poitiers, the Muslim army encountered the Christian army under Charles Martel. The Moors had been besieging Tours, but when they learned that the combined armies of Charles Martel and Eudo were striking at their lines of communication, they broke the siege and turned south in an effort to cover the retreat of the train of booty. Charles pressed the Moorish retreat as hard as he could and forced Abd er-Rahman to fight a major battle somewhere near Cenon, on the Vienne River.

Charles's army of Franks may have been of a similar size to that of the Moors—some estimate that each side may have fielded 50,000 men. The Moors would certainly have contained a large contingent of the famous Berber light cavalry, and Charles's army would almost certainly have been the solid Frankish infantry, probably supported by a few mounted retainers. Certainly Charles formed his men into a solid block and advanced toward the enemy camp. Abd er-Rahman led his troops in a headlong charge against the Frankish host, but the lighter horsemen could not break the deep ranks of foot soldiers. Sometime, probably toward the end of the first day, the valiant emir fell at the head of his men, and the spirit of the Muslim host was crushed. During the night they made off with such of the treasure as would not slow their flight. In the morning, the Frankish pursuit overtook the stragglers and regained much of the loot. Christian casualties are said to have been about 1,500, and that of the Moors about 7,500.

With the Moorish army defeated, the Franks began a steady process of recapturing the cities they'd lost, and about 741, when the citizens of Narbonne revolted and killed their Moorish masters, the last vestige of the Muslim invasion of France vanished. Modern Muslim history suggests that the Battle of Tours was an unimportant event—merely a raid repulsed. In the West it is viewed as one of the decisive battles of history. Probably it was both. Abd er-Rahman was not out to conquer the Franks on that day, but it was typical of Arab conquests that after a successful raid had defeated the local forces, a garrison would be installed in some important place, and before long the Saracens would control a province by default. Tours convinced the Muslims that the Franks could not be easily defeated and thus ended the threat of both raid and invasion.

Within the Iberian Peninsula matters were less than completely peaceful. The Moors never subdued some parts of the peninsula, and from these dark corners the resistance stiffened as the local nobles came together, first in mutual defense, and eventually in counterattack. Even without the reconquest, Spain would have not been a peaceful place, as the Moors themselves were disunified and constant struggles erupted between the Moorish warlords.

At age thirty-two, Emir Abd er-Rahman II (912–61) attempted to bring some stability to Moorish Spain. His first move was to bring Cordoba under control. A rebellion was crushed in 928 with the death of the leading rebel. Abd er-Rahman II proceeded to subdue the mutinous cities of Seville, Algeciras, Sidonia, and Carmona. By 929 he had expanded his emirate into a caliphate with himself as caliph. From there he turned against the Christian kingdom of Leon, under King Ordono II. Ordono had taken

Talavera, sacked it and put its Muslim population to the sword. Er-Rahman responded with an attack on the fortress of San Estevan de Gormanz, but the attack was a failure and his army was decimated during the retreat. In 920 the combined armies of Leon and Navarre attacked and sacked Pamplona. Er-Rahman responded with raids and incursions, but in the one major battle his army was again destroyed, his general killed, and the viceroy of Saragossa was taken prisoner. Er-Rahman was present at the battle and barely escaped. Simancas was the first important victory of the Christians over the Moors in what would be a 460-year campaign to recapture Spain.

The war, however, was not to be a string of Christian victories, and in 981 Zamora was captured by the Moors. Worse, at the end of the tenth century the great warlord Almansur (938–1002) awoke the real possibility of total Moorish domination of the peninsula, with an empire based on Cordoba. During his time, the Christian ambassadors of Leon, Navarre, Barcelona, and Castile made homage to Cordoba to deliver tribute. In 997 his forces plundered the greatest Christian shrine on the peninsula, the shrine of Santiago of Compostela. Almansur's death in 1002 resulted in the splintering of his empire, and his Christian subjects were as quick as his co-religionists to pick up as many pieces as possible.

When the Umayyad dynasty in Spain finally fell apart in 1031 it was replaced for fifty-five years by a collection of thirty little Muslim states, each with its own king perched in some well-defended city. The shock of the Christian successes prompted these kings to invite the Almoravids of Morocco—a successful sect of Berber zealots—to establish a dynasty.

This introduction of a foreign military/religious order into the Iberian Peninsula makes an interesting parallel with the crusades that would shortly erupt into the Holy Lands. In both cases the newcomers were initially successful. In both cases their success ended about the time that they acquired wealth and position, and in both cases the zealots—Berber fundamentalists and ignorant Frankish knights—caused fatal damage to their causes by destroying any real hope for a mingling of the cultures. The Almoravid replacement by Almohads did nothing to better the process.

Around this time, the kingdoms of Navarre and Castile again joined forces and conquered Leon. In A.D. 1009 one of those Moors, Sulaiman, called on Sanco, the count of Castile, to support him. In return, the Muslims gave Castile 200 fortresses that they had taken from Castile over the years. At the battle of Cantich, 10,000 Moors were killed or drowned attempting to escape from the Castilians. Later, Sulaiman, supported by 9,000 Catalan Christians, engaged a Moorish army of 30,000 men and defeated them. This episode is merely symbolic of the frequent shifts in alliance between the warlords of both Christian and Moorish religions. Until near the end, the wars of the *Reconquista*[1] would not see the sides defined by religion. Self-interest would trump Christian or Moorish principles in almost every case.

In 1085 Alfonso VI of Castile captured Toledo, a shock that awoke the Moorish kings. Their anxiety grew as he began his siege of Saragossa. A combined Moorish force came to meet the Christian forces at the Battle of Zalaca or Sagrajas, fought in 1086. The initial attack by Alfonso VI, who had a combined force of Castilian and Aragonese troops supported by a body of French knights, drove off the first Moorish line. As Alfonso's soldiers cut down the Andalusian Muslims, the leader of the Almoravid Muslims watched them go.

Alfonso then launched his attack against the Almoravids who stood their ground. While engaging the Spanish to the front, the Almoravid leader, Yusuf, led a force of Saharan desert nomads to the rear and struck the Spaniards in the flank. The Spanish army was utterly destroyed, and Alfonso escaped with only a guard of 500 men.

At this time the Spanish hero, El Cid, waged war against the Moors. El Cid, though a Christian hero, like any medieval warlord served his own interests first. After a falling-out with Alfonso IV he actually allied with the Moors.

When Alfonso was defeated at Zalaca he called on El Cid to support him, because Yusuf was on a rampage through Castilian territory. El Cid moved against the Muslim city of Valencia and besieged it for twenty months, one of the longest sieges in the Reconquest of Spain. It fell in 904, and El Cid became a king in his own right. The wars continued, and in 1094 the Christians won their first victory over the Almoravid Moors at the battle of Cuarte. El Cid played a pivotal role in the battle, launching an attack into the rear of the enemy army. Three years after El Cid's death in 1099, Valencia fell to the Almoravid leader, Yusuf's nephew, known to the Spanish as King Bucar.

As the Crusades were declared by the various popes and Christian armies moved to Palestine, others went to Spain to fight the Muslims—who were much more geographically convenient. By 1114 large numbers of French knights from Provence, Gascony, Bearn, and Languedoc, and others from Normandy, Burgundy, and the north of France joined the crusade in Spain.

The Almoravids provided a useful block to the Christian resurgence, but by 1118, after the fall of Saragossa, they lost their following. There simply weren't enough Moroccan Berbers available to provide a constant military presence in Spain, nor were they universally successful. When their armies were no longer victorious, the native Saracens grumbled against the Berber dynasty, and in 1122 open rebellion broke out. By 1147, after a quarter century of fighting, the Almohads, yet another Moroccan sect, had completely suppressed the Almoravids. Again, the Christian warlords were quick to take advantage of the civil wars, and captured Lisbon, Almeria, Lerida, and Tortosa. These acquisitions were halted only when the new Almohad dynasty unified Moorish resistance.

In 1195 the Castilians, under Alfonso VIII, met the combined armies of the Muslims at Alarcos, south of the city of Toledo. Details of the battle indicate just how hard it was fought. The initial Castilian charge was successful and drove back the Muslims, breaking their line, and killing the general, Abu Hafas, who died trying to rally the broken Muslim infantry. The tribe of Henteta, Muslims from North Africa, was surrounded and cut to pieces. However, the battle suddenly turned when the Muslims of al-Andalus charged striking where Alfonso VIII stood with his bodyguard. The Spaniards broke and fled, losing thousands. The battle of Alarcos, near Ciudad Real, was thus an overwhelming Muslim victory. It was also the beginning of the end for Muslim Spain. Castile's defeat at Alarcos made the various Christian states understand that only cooperative action would defeat the newly unified Muslim power. They began to forget their jealousies and concentrate on the reconquest. Following up on their victory, the Moors invaded Castile, but Alfonso VIII repulsed them.

By 1212, the Christians were ready to strike in force. Under Alfonso VIII they marched into the heart of Moorish Spain and offered battle at Las Navas de Tolosa. Alfonso's army of 2,000 French knights, 10,000 Spanish horse, and 50,000 infantry advanced south and was confronted by the Almohad Muhammad I, with perhaps 200,000 men. Shortly before the battle, however, the French abandoned Alfonso VIII, complaining of the effect of the heat and their armor. When Muhammad I learned of the French departure, he moved briskly north to intercept the now weakened Christian army. The two armies met with the Moors massed in the narrow entrance of the Losa canyon. In a repetition of the events at Thermopylae, where the Spartans faced the Persians, a Spanish shepherd led the Christian army through an otherwise unknown mountain path that brought them into the Moorish rear. The stunned Moors found Alfonso VIII's army deployed behind them on the plain of Mesa Del Rey, and blocking their front at the narrows of the pass. Both sides rested their armies until July 16, when the battle was joined. The Spaniards attacked and overwhelmed the Muslim light infantry forming the first line. The heavily armored Christian knights pushed back the two wings of the Almohad Moorish army, but the Moorish center, mostly cavalry, held fast and launched repeated counterattacks. The end came when these failed and the whole army suddenly broke and fled the field. Muhammad I fled all the way to Jaen as the Moorish cavalry and infantry became thoroughly mixed and confused. A massacre followed, and 150,000 Muslim warriors are reputed to have died that day. The Moorish defeat gave Alfonso VIII control of central Spain.

The Battle of Las Navas de Tolosa can fairly be considered among the most important in history. It was not the end of Moorish Spain, but it marked the defeat of the last great Muslim army, and the occupation of the heart of the Peninsula by the Christians. If it was not the end, it was certainly the beginning of the end.

The war continued until 1235, when Ferdinand III of Castile recaptured Cordoba. Seville was taken in 1248 and Jaen in 1246. Valencia fell to King Jaime I of Aragon. Though infighting troubled both sides, it was far worse among the Moors. Fractured by internal dissent, they were steadily driven back by the Spanish.

In 1340 Alfonso XI of Castile, supported by Alfonso IV of Portugal, routed a considerably larger Moorish force at Rio Salado, near Tarika. The Moorish army was formed of warriors who had recently arrived from Morocco where the general idea of a holy war against the Christians provided the Marinid Moorish armies of Spain with a constant supply of Berber and Arab recruits. Despite this, all that remained of Muslim Spain was a region along the Mediterranean coast extending from near Gibraltar to the northeast near, but not including, Cartagena. This last Granadan stronghold would not last long.

In 1487 the Christians captured the city of Malaga, in the province of Granada. They then pushed against and laid siege to the capital, Granada itself. No major assaults were made, as both sides knew that a Muslim surrender was inevitable. No relief could be hoped for from North Africa. A capitulation signed in November 1491 set the date of surrender at January 2, 1492. When January 2 arrived, the gates were opened and the Muslim occupation of Spain ended.

In the end, Muslims occupied Spain, in whole or part, for nearly 800 years. When they arrived and broke the relatively fragile Visigothic grip on the country, it seemed that the peninsula would be just one more entry in the enormous list of Arab conquests. Certainly Islam took hold as it had elsewhere, and certainly the Moorish civilization was enlightened by European standards. The ongoing native resistance, while undeniably fierce, was probably no fiercer than in many other lands occupied by the Arabs and their adherents. Yet at the end, Spain proved to be the only major nation retaken from its Islamic conquerors. From Africa to India the new religion came in on the standards of the invading warlords. Muslim princes, powers, and dynasties rose and fell like all others, but in the entire world except Spain, Islam survived independent of local politics. Only in Iberia did Christian princes permanently turn back the spread of the Arabian religion. Their success may have had an astonishing impact on world history. Consider that when Muslim Spain was extinguished in 1492, Columbus was only months away from his discovery of the New World. Western Christians, not Muslims, would discover North and South America and the great ocean routes that bind the world. There would never be a caliphate of New York. Had it not been for the *Reconquista* in the only nation ever lost to Islam, who can say what might have been?

CHRONOLOGY

681	Muslim armies reach Ceuta across from Gibraltar.
711	Battle of Merida, the beginning of the Islamic conquest of Spain
718	Occupation of central Spain complete.
718–32	Muslim raids into France finally checked in 732 at Tours.
800s	Competing Moorish cities in Spain
928	Caliph Abd-er-Rahman consolidates power in Cordoba.
950s	(date approximate) Abd-er-Rahman makes war on surviving Christian states.
1000	(date approximate) Reign of Almansur, who expanded Cordoban authority.
1050s	(date approximate) Ummayad dynasty splinters.
1100	Almoravids from North Africa control Cordoba.
1085	Alfonso VI of Castile captures Toledo but is defeated at the Battle of Zalaca by the Almoravids.
1094	El Cid wins a battle at Cuarte, the first Almoravid defeat.
1100s	Almoravids increasingly dominant in Spain, as Spanish Christian resistance flares up.
1147	Almohads from North Africa replace the Almoravids as the ruling group in Muslim Spain.
1195	Muslim victory at Alarcos alarms Spanish Christians and convinces them to unite.

1212   Battle of Las Navas de Tolosa gives Christians control of central Spain and marks the beginning of the end of Muslim rule in Spain.

1235   Cordoba captured. Seville follows in 1248.

1340   At the Battle of Rio Salado, Alfonso XI routs a Marinid contingent, the last wave of African tribes to move into Spain.

1492   Granada, the last Muslim bastion in Spain, falls.

NOTE

1. *Reconquista* is the Spanish term referring to the reconquest of Spain from the Moors.

Chapter 7

THE RISE OF THE OTTOMAN EMPIRE

The Ottomans descended from the nomadic tribes originating in the region of the Altai Mountains in Outer Mongolia, a region east of the Eurasian Steppes and south of the Yenisei River and Lake Baikal. Like most steppe nomads, they lived as herdsmen and raiders, taking what they could from their weaker neighbors. Sometime around the second century they began moving to the west, and those that moved toward the Middle East called themselves Oguz; those they attacked called them Turkomans or Turks. Blocked by the mountain ranges of the Hindu Kush, they moved into the lands between the Hindu Kush and the Aral Sea, known as Transoxania. Here a natural road leads from the steppes into Iran and the Middle East.

These Turks established the Gokturk Empire, which lasted from A.D. 552 to 744 and stretched between the Black Sea along the northern borders of Mongolia and China almost to the Pacific Ocean. Though called an empire, it was really a confederation of nomadic tribes with no significant level of civilization, no capitals or cities, and leaving little mark of its existence. When the Gokturk Empire collapsed, its peoples continued their pressures on the borders of modern Iran, eventually penetrating into that land. The Seljuq dynasty rose from those migrants, formed around a group of mercenary Oguz warriors that had been organized for the service of the Karahanids of Persia. In 1055 Tugrul Bey, leader of the Islamicized Seljuqs and founder of the Seljuq Empire, forced the Abbasid caliph of Baghdad to make him the protector of orthodox Islam and to recognize him as the sultan, or temporal ruler of northern Iran. With the Seljuq leader as sultan, he assumed the caliph's authority to legislate and rule on all matters, including military questions that were not directly regulated by Muslim law.

The movement of Seljuqs into the Middle East continued and soon had all of northern Iran and Iraq professing submission, which presented them with the problem of restoring order to the region while simultaneously providing their nomadic vassals with booty and grazing lands. This forced them to press ever farther westward until they began pushing into Armenia. The harsh policies of Sultan Alp Arslan (1063–72) forced more Turkomans to flee Seljuq rule in Iran, and these flowed into Anatolia. These refugee Turkomans accepted service as mercenaries under the Armenian and Byzantine feudal nobles in their internecine struggles.

In 1065, as Alp Arslan consolidated his position in Iraq, he launched a campaign into eastern Anatolia to consolidate his control over the frontier Turkomans as well as the Christian princes in the region. Byzantine raids into Syria designed to stop these penetrations were driven back. Alp Arslan then sought a truce with the Byzantines so that he could concentrate on the Fatimids. Upon learning that the Emperor Romanus Diogenus was sending a new army against him, however, he moved north to confront the Byzantines in open battle. The two armies met at Manzikert, north of Lake Van, on August 19, 1071. The Byzantines were overwhelmed and destroyed by the Turks' bow-wielding light cavalry. The Byzantine emperor was captured and killed.

Fortunately for the Byzantines, Alp Arslan was still focusing on the Fatimids and did not avail himself of his victory to push farther into Anatolia. Unfortunately for the Byzantines, their old system of border defenses had been destroyed and the path into Anatolia was open for a constant stream of raids that devastated agriculture and trade. The Byzantines sought to deal with the Turks by recognizing their rule of south central Anatolia, an area that would eventually form the basis of the Seljuq empire of Rum.

As Anatolia was slowly converted into a Turkish domain, the Great Seljuq Empire, now centered at Isfahan, reached its peak. Alp Arslan was killed in battle fighting the Karahanids, another Turkish clan not subservient to the Seljuqs. Maliksah, his son, succeeded him and with active cooperation of the Byzantines he extended his power into Anatolia, building a force to counter the Rum Empire.

All did not go well for the Seljuqs, as the Fatimids, who remained active in Egypt and southern Syria, sent disruptive Shia missionaries throughout the Seljuq territories. The Ismaili Assassins[1] were founded during this period, and their campaign of assassination and terror against political and religious leaders of the Seljuq state further undercut Seljuq stability and strength. Added to this was the practice of dividing up possessions among all members of the family, which led to large provinces being carved into small ones. These soon evolved into new states with their own armies and treasuries. A feudal process was established to support Maliksah's senior Mamluk army officers, further breaking up the unity of the empire.

In 1092 Maliksah and his minister died and the empire began to dissolve, being replaced by small Turkoman states ruled by tribal chiefs with nomadic armies. It was into this weak stew that the crusader armies were injected. The decay continued until the Baghdad caliph al-Nasir (1180–1225) rose to power. He suppressed the independent Turkomans in Iraq and reestablished a direct caliphal rule. He even brought a degree of control over the Assassins, stopping their killings in exchange for recognition of their autonomy. In 1242, after al-Nasir's death, the Mongols invaded and defeated the Seljuqs of Rum and then swept into Iraq, destroying the last of the Abbasid caliphs. Continuing into Syria, the Mongols were defeated by the Mamluks.

In 1284 Yavlak Arslan ruled the small principality of Ilhanid in Anatolia. He was astute enough to cooperate with the combined Mongol and Seljuq armies by defeating some of their enemies and thus maintained his independence. Yavlak's son, Ali, succeeded his father and began to penetrate into Byzantine territories as far as the Sakarya River. Ali was succeeded by Osman Bey (1280–1324), the founder of the Ottoman dynasty. After a series of smaller victories and conquests, his real achievement began around 1300 as the Seljuq collapse allowed him to occupy several key forts that commanded the passes between the central Anatolian plateau and the plains of Bithynia. His first significant victory was the capture of Yenisehr, which became his capital. Osman and his warriors swept across the plains eastward to the Sakarya river, taking two more forts and severing communications between Constantinople and the cities of Bithynia and Nicaea. The Byzantine city Bursa was slowly enveloped and cut off from the rest of the Byzantine Empire. The Ottomans put it under loose siege in 1317, and it fell in 1326.

The Byzantines finally launched a major expedition against the Ottomans, now ruled by Orhan. This expedition was personally commanded by the Emperor Andronicus III (1328–41). In 1328 the Byzantines met the Ottomans at Maltepe (Pelecanon) and were routed. The emperor fled to Constantinople and the empire abandoned all further efforts to regain Anatolia. Nicaea itself, only a few days' march from Constantinople, fell in 1331. The combination of political quarrels within the Byzantine Empire and steady pressure allowed the Ottomans to slowly push farther and farther toward the ultimate goal of Constantinople. Sultan Orhan meddled in the Byzantine infighting and recruited some Byzantine renegades who would become major leaders of his army.

With the death of Emperor Andronicus III (1341), Orhan could push into Europe. The Byzantine fight for succession was such that John VI Cantacuzene hired Turkish and Serbian mercenaries to support his claim. This force ravaged Macedonia and opened the Ottomans' eyes to what stood to the west.

In 1346 Orhan led 5,500 soldiers into Thrace and conquered the coastal region of the Black Sea north of Constantinople. By 1349 the Ottomans began a process of permanent conquests. The Emperor Cantacuzene protested these conquests by Suleiman, Orhan's son, but to no avail. Cantacuzene enlisted support of the Serbs against his rebellious Ottoman allies, but this effort allowed his rivals to throw him out of power, raising John V Palaeologus to the throne.

In 1349 the Byzantines again asked for Ottoman assistance against the Serbian Stefan Duscan (1331–55), who had taken Salonika from the crumbling empire. The struggles between Cantacuzene and John V continued with Orhan routing the combined force of Bulgarians and Serbians organized by John at the battle of Dimotica. In return, Cantacuzene gave Orhan control of the fort of Cimpe (Tzympe) on the Dardanelles to serve as a base for such future expeditions. In 1353, from this fort, Suleiman Pasha advanced north to raid Thrace and establish Ottoman rule as far as Rodosto. In 1354 Orhan was assisted by the Genoese, who sought to use the Ottomans to break the dominance of the Venetians in commerce with the Byzantine Empire.

Cantacuzene again protested Orhan's conquests, but Orhan refused to abandon his new territories. An Ottoman tradition relates that the Byzantine forces in Gallipoli, including Cimpe, were destroyed by an earthquake on March 2, 1354. Suleiman then told the emperor that he could not abandon those territories because the earthquake was a sign of God's will that the Turks should remain. Gallipoli became a permanent Ottoman foothold in Europe.

Originally all the soldiers in the Ottoman army were Turkoman light horsemen. They were organized by clans and tribes under the command of tribal chiefs and religious leaders and were almost entirely horse archers. Those assigned to border areas or deployed in raids against Christian areas were paid by being allowed to pillage, but this discouraged the formation of the disciplined troops necessary for siege operations against fortresses and walled cities. Although such irregular cavalry, formed mostly of nomads, were useful in overwhelming enemy field armies and pursuing beaten enemies, their nature ran contrary to the Ottoman desire to establish settlements in conquered areas—raiders are more likely to loot and destroy than to occupy and build. These disruptive nomads, who would continue to prove troublesome until as recently as 1918, were sent to the frontiers where their depredations would fall more on neighbors than on their friends.

Unfortunately, the Ottomans needed a suitable replacement before they could dispense with the services of this irregular force. As a result, Orhan Gazi, the Ottoman ruler from 1324 to 1359, began the process of organizing regular, salaried bodies of soldiers. His Ottoman standing army consisted of infantry or *yaya* and cavalry known as *müsellems.* This army included both Christian and Muslim Turks, but as the Ottomans moved into the Balkans under Sultan Murat I (1326–89) the emphasis shifted to Muslim troops. As the army grew, the Turkomans were moved to the frontiers for use as shock troops and known as *akinci* (raider) or *deli* (fanatic).

Orhan's eldest son, Suleiman, died before Orhan, so Murat I (1360–89) succeeded the great leader, and ascended the Ottoman throne. Under Murat I the *yayas* and *müsellems* remained the permanent army paid in provincial fiefs rather than cash. In order to gain greater control of the mercenary troops raised by the provincial commanders, Murat began to organize a new military force composed of the "slaves of the Porte" *(kapiskullari).* These men came to the sultan's service as young men. They were educated in the Turkish language and Ottoman culture. The "New Force" or Janissary corps was given military training and organized as infantry or as cavalry known as *"Spahis."* The Janissaries received salaries paid directly by the sultan and were under the direct control of the central government. The Spahis, however, were supported by a series of fiefs, known as *timars,* controlled by the old Turkish nobility. This process pushed the *yayas* and *müsellems* into rear-line duties. The New Force and other salaried forces became the primary instrument of conquests.

Once on the throne, Murat I began extending Ottoman control in central Anatolia. Completing his occupation of central Anatolia, he turned on Europe. He bypassed Constantinople and made his first target Edirne, which commanded the pass between the Balkan and Rhodope Mountains. With his lines of communication secure, he began a steady push into the Balkans.

On June 15, 1389, the Ottoman forces under Murat I found themselves at Kosovo, facing a Christian army. Some suggest that the Ottoman army had 60,000 men and the Christian army under King Lazar of Serbia had 100,000 men. The Ottoman army right was formed by Murat's European vassals and his center was formed by the Janissaries. The Anatolia Ottomans held the left.

The initial rush of the two armies severely pressed the Muslim line. Murat's son Prince Bajazet charged into the ranks of Serbian knights, inspiring the Ottomans and saving the day. The Ottomans began pushing the Christians back when a Serbian knight rode forward, calling out he was a friend. The knight, Milosch Kabilovich, King Lazar's son-in-law, rode to within a few feet of the sultan, dismounted and knelt in homage. When the sultan approached, he sprang forward with a dagger, stabbing Murat through the belly. He leapt toward his horse to escape but was overtaken and torn to pieces by the Janissaries. The wound was fatal.

As he lay dying, Murat I ordered that his reserves be committed to the battle. Their well-timed attack brought the Muslims victory. When the Ottomans surged forward, King Lazar's nephew, Yuk Banovich, fled the battlefield in panic and reputedly provoked a general rout of King Lazar's army. King Lazar was captured and dragged before the dying sultan, who ordered him executed.

King Lazar was the first of many Serbs to be executed that day. But defeated Christians were not the only ones to suffer. As soon as the sultan breathed his last, his eldest son, Bayezit, still standing before Murat's lifeless body, ordered his brother Yakup seized and strangled with a bowstring. Bayezit feared Yakup's popularity would threaten his ascension to the throne. He thus instituted what would become a regular Ottoman practice—fratricide, until only one heir remained, thus eliminating any potential rivals.

The Battle of Kosovo was an utter disaster for the Serbs. The slaughter made it known as the Field of Blackbirds, for the ravens that feasted on the dead. More significantly, it subjugated Serbia to five centuries of Turkish occupation. What remained was a vassal state under Stephen Lazarevich, Lazar's son. His position was not an enviable one, and he sought only survival, permitted at the Porte's whim. He even married off his sister, Dispoina, to Bayezit, his father's murderer.

Serbia would extract revenge of sorts. Dispoina became Bayezit's favorite wife and taught him the pleasures of wine. Though the Koran strictly forbade wine, Bayezit ignored the commandment and Dispoina eventually turned him into a drunken sot.

Despite his looming alcoholism, Bayezit completed his conquest of the Macedonian highlands by taking Skopje and settling thousands of Turkomans in the Vardar valley. He also conquered farther lands in the Balkans, but his major accomplishment was ringing Constantinople with a series of forts that ended all Byzantine rule outside the city's walls.

Eventually, most of Greece was occupied and raids were sent as far north as Bosnia and Hungary.

In 1396 a force of 10,000 French knights responded to calls of assistance from King Sigismund of Hungary. By September they arrived in Hungary and had captured the Ottoman-held fortress of Rachowa. Unable to spare the men to guard their Turkish prisoners, they slaughtered them. Then on September 12, they moved against Nicopolis (modern Bulgaria), the objective of their crusade. The French surrounded Nicopolis, but lacking any siege equipment, they could only blockade it. Three weeks later the Ottoman army, under Sultan Bayezit, appeared. The Ottoman advance guard was surprised by 1,000 French knights and overwhelmed.

The main Ottoman army arrived before the French camp on September 25. Bayezit had lifted his siege of Constantinople to face this new enemy. The arrogant French foolishly refused Sigismund's advice on how to deal with the Turks and, devoid of all reason, galloped out to strike their foe. Initially the French, more heavily armored and mounted on larger horses, overwhelmed and scattered the first Turkish line. This line, however, was only light cavalry and had no intention of standing. In effect, the light cavalry evaded the opening French assault and pulled it forward into a highly disordered charge toward the solid core of Janissaries waiting behind a light palisade.

The French found themselves showered with arrows and facing lines of infantry behind barricades of sharpened stakes. The French dismounted to pass the stakes. At this point Bayezit and his Spahis, concealed behind a hill, charged their now dismounted and disordered foe with crushingly superior numbers and at the most opportune moment. Sigismund, realizing the battle was over, discretely withdrew his army.

Six thousand French knights were to die in the battle and 3,000 surrendered. Because the French had murdered their captives from Rachowa, Bayezit ordered his prisoners decapitated. The next morning they were paraded before him, naked and in groups of three or four. The mass beheading began early in the morning and continued through the day. Only twenty-four knights, those expected to produce large ransoms, were spared. The sadistic and drunken Bayezit forced them to watch the deaths of their comrades. The French might have listened to Sigismund, or they might have heeded the lessons of Crecy and Poitiers, where similar charges had led to disaster. At Nicopolis their foes did not observe even the rude niceties of European warfare.

The Ottoman threat to Hungary, however, ended abruptly at the appearance of Tamerlane, who struck hard on the Ottoman eastern flank. Bayezit immediately moved his army to eastern Anatolia to defend his territories. A decisive battle finally occurred on July 27, 1402, at Cubuk, outside Ankara. The battle lasted for fourteen hours, and initially Bayezit's Turks did well. However, some of the sultan's allied troops defected to the Tartars, and this turned the battle into a Turkish defeat. The record is unclear; some sources indicate a force of Turkoman auxiliaries defected and others indicate the Serbians. Bayezit was taken captive and the Ottoman army was routed. Tamerlane would remain in Anatolia for eight months, ravaging, pillaging, and murdering as he saw fit. Bayezit and his sons Musa and Mustafa remained captives until Tamerlane died in 1405.

Bayezit was in captivity, but only the Ottoman field army had been destroyed. The bulk of the Ottoman garrisons remained intact and under control of Ottoman princes who struggled for ascendancy. The old sultan's grandson, Murat II, succeeded in 1421 but would find himself facing a further challenge from the West. This time the threat would be subtler than the charge of European nobility, and in the end much more dangerous.

The first challenge occurred in 1425 when the Venetians sought to undermine Ottoman power in Macedonia by setting up a false Ottoman prince claiming to be Murat's brother Mustafa. This war would drag on until 1430 because the Ottomans had no naval presence of significance and could not deal with the seagoing Venetians. However, Murat eventually succeeded establishing his control over all of the Macedonian ports, and forced Venice to accept this at the Treaty of Lapseki.

With the Venetian defeat, agitation arose in Europe for a new crusade against the rising Turkish power. The Hungarian hero, John Hunyadi, the *voivode,* or war leader, of Transylvania, who had risen to prominence because of a series of victories over Turks in 1442, sparked the movement. The West believed he was the leader who would end the Muslim threat, and groups of crusaders flowed east to join the Hungarian army under King Ladislas. Hunyadi organized his crusade at Ofen and marched into Moravia, confident that with the sultan absent in Anatolia, he would be victorious. He pushed into southern Serbia, brushing aside the local Ottoman garrisons and frontier troops, eventually reaching over the Balkan Mountains into Bulgaria, taking Sofia by winter.

Upon learning of the invasion, Murat reacted sharply. He rapidly marched what he could of his army, the Janissary corps, to the west. Unable to match the crusaders in numbers, he chose to hold the Trayan gate, through which the enemy must pass to reach the lowlands. The crusaders were initially successful, but when the weather closed in, Hunyadi was forced to abandon the expedition for the year. He slaughtered thousands of Muslim prisoners and returned to Hungary for the winter.

Word of Hunyadi's victories brought more and more western crusaders. The Albanian revolt spread, and the Byzantine despot of Morea moved back into central Greece and reoccupied Athens and Thebes. The Ottoman treasury was empty. A short negotiated peace did not last long. The crusader army moved south on September 1, 1444, and was joined by Hunyadi's force of Transylvanian knights at Orsova. The Ottomans advanced and met the Christians near Varna on November 10, 1444. At first, the battle went for the crusaders. A Christian victory seemed so sure that Murat looked to flee, but he was convinced to remain. In the renewed fighting that broke out, the horse of King Ladislas of Hungary was killed under him, throwing the king to the ground in the middle of the melee. A Janissary brought his scimitar down on the hapless king's neck, decapitating him. The head was quickly put on a pike and displayed to the Hungarians, who panicked and fled.

The battle was bloody, but without significant fruits. Four years later Hunyadi was still fighting with a new army of 24,000 men. He engaged the Turks at Kosovo (October 17–20, 1448) near the site of the earlier battle, and again the fighting was touch-and-go until the Wallachians deserted Hunyadi in favor of the sultan. This was too much for the hard-pressed Hunyadi, and his forces broke after three days of fighting.

Murat died in 1451 and was succeeded by Mehmet II "The Conqueror" (1451–81). Mehmet's crowning military achievement was the capture of Constantinople. Though not calm, the Balkans became settled enough that Mehmet could focus on the ultimate prize, and he began his siege in February 1453. A cry for help went out from Byzantium to the West, but only a few hundred foreign volunteers, mainly Genoese, actually came to help the besieged city. The first major attack came on April 6, with a heavy bombardment against Theodosius's Wall, on the landward side of the city. Storming attempts followed this, but the small imperial garrison beat these off. A great chain boom lay across the Golden Horn and prevented enemy ships from approaching from the seaward side.

On May 31, 1453, a Genoese fleet of three galleasses and an imperial grain ship arrived in the Bosporus to bring relief to Constantinople. Attacked by the Ottomans, the Genoese defeated their attempts to board while the galleasses cut their way through the low-slung galleys of the Ottoman fleet. Using Greek fire and swivel guns they pushed into the inner harbor, leaving a swath of destruction behind them.

Mehmet was furious at the failure of his fleet and ordered his admiral impaled. His generals prevailed upon him to spare the poor admiral's life, so Mehmet beat him senseless with a stick as four slaves held him.

The Ottoman fleet would be the key to victory. The admiral's beating must have done him some good, for he conceived a clever plan. His crews began physically dragging some of their ships over the peninsula and relaunching them beyond the boom that had frustrated their earlier attempts. In this manner, the seaward flank of Constantinople was laid open. In a combined naval and land assault that began on the night of May 28, the Ottomans attacked in full force. Huge cannon from the world's most powerful and advanced siege train tore gaps in the walls, and the attackers flowed into the city as the fleet landed Ottoman soldiers on the poorly manned seaward defenses. Constantinople fell, and for two days the enraged Turks looted, burned, murdered, and raped. Once sated with blood, the destruction stopped. The survivors were left to pick up what they could, and Mehmet began the process of establishing his capital in his new possession—now to be called Istanbul.

The Siege of Constantinople was one of the great turning points in human history. Mehmet's guns broke down not just the fabled walls of a proud city, but also the last vestiges of 2,000 years of Roman imperial history. The Eastern Empire, which had more than its share of disasters, and seemingly more lives than a cat, would not rebound from this blow. After 800 years of battering, Islam had finally broken down the guardian of the Christian west.

Mehmet set about reconstructing his now largely devastated capital. It had between 60,000 and 70,000 inhabitants. Most were killed or sold into slavery, leaving only 10,000 in the city by the time Mehmet began rebuilding it. He repopulated the city by giving gifts of property and tax concessions to all who would come. Steadily, the city was rebuilt to a new glory under the Ottomans.

After his conquest of Constantinople, Mehmet turned his attention to the northern shore of the Black Sea and in 1454 moved into Moldavia. Here he forced Vlad "the Impaler," generally considered the historical basis for the Dracula vampire stories, to submit to Ottoman suzerainty.

Mehmet continued his conquests in the Balkans and in 1456 stood before the walls of Belgrade in Serbia. His guns crushed the defending walls, and on July 21 the Janissaries launched a general attack against the city. The Christian inhabitants of Belgrade called on God to defend them just as the Muslim attackers called on Allah. The Ottoman General Hassan, commanding the Janissaries, was killed in the battle that reportedly cost 25,000 Turkish casualties. A Serbian counterattack under John Hunyadi drove the Janissaries back and captured their 300 supporting cannon and stores. It was John Hunyadi's last victory over his ancient enemy. His acts would keep the Ottomans out of Hungary for the next seventy years. When they finally came, they would not stay long.

Undiscouraged by his defeat, Mehmet continued with further expeditions. In 1456 he undertook a third Serbian campaign. Later in the same year, in response to attacks by pirates, he moved against the Genoese islands in the Aegean. By 1461 Greece and Serbia were under his control.

The next major campaign came in April 1480 when the Ottomans attacked the island of Rhodes, held by the Knights of Saint John, an order of religious knights founded during the Crusades. After the Ottoman guns had broken the walls and everything was set for the final assault, the Janissaries went on strike and refused to attack. Their commanding general had forbidden them the right to pillage the city. Refused the booty that had historically been theirs, the Ottoman army reboarded its ships and sailed back to Istanbul. The Knights of Saint John had their first great turn of luck since the Crusades. They would be lucky again.

Later in the same year the Ottomans landed in Italy, near the city of Otranto. After taking the city, they pillaged it, murdered half the population, and shipped the rest back to slavery.

Mehmet II died shortly after this expedition, on May 3, 1481. Mehmet had made significant changes to the Turkish forces. Under him the Ottoman army developed a massive artillery train, but this was not favored for field operations because it was slow and restricted the traditional rapid movements of the Ottoman cavalry. The defeats suffered by Bayezit II under the Mamluks in eastern Anatolia had taught the Ottomans the value of handheld firearms, and arquebuses were introduced, as were some few mobile cannon. The armorer corps, which handled these weapons, numbered no more than 625 men in 1574 but began to rapidly expand.

Mehmet II also organized the cannon corps to manufacture and use cannons. It came to its full strength under Bayezit II's reforms. In 1574 it had a total strength of about 1,100 men and by the seventeenth century it had grown to about 5,000. Siege warfare had become more sophisticated, and the Ottomans developed a pioneer corps charged with digging the mines and trenches used in attacking fortresses. In addition, the specialized gun known as the mortar came into use and corps of mortar crews was also organized. Some of these were attached to the Janissaries and others to the Spahis.

When Mehmet II died, the Janissaries became involved in the struggle for succession because of several defeats that they had suffered under Ahmet, Mehmet's eldest son. As a result of the struggles, Bayezit (1481–1512) rose to the Peacock Throne. Bayezit's assumption of the throne was contested when Cem, another of Mehmet II's sons, demanded that the empire be divided and that he be given Anatolia. A decisive battle occurred on June 20, 1481, and Bayezit's numerically superior army won a decisive victory. Cem and his surviving followers fled to Egypt and took refuge with the Mamluks. This was one of the rare occurrences in which the succession was decided by civil war, and not the strangler's silk.

Bayezit's first military operations made some territorial gains in Moldavia. A short war with the Mamluks was little more than a series of skirmishes. A major war began brewing in 1496 when Ottoman ports were closed to Venetian grain merchants. In 1497 a Venetian ship filled with Christian pilgrims for the Holy Land was captured and its passengers sold into slavery. Venice responded by building up its fleet, which forced a similar response from the Ottomans. On July 4, 1499, the Ottomans seized Lepanto, in western Greece, inflicting a major blow on Venetian naval power in the Adriatic and Aegean. Venetian ports were taken in Morea (modern Greece) and raids devastated Venetian holdings in Croatia and Dalmatia, penetrating to the gates of Venice and capturing Durazzo on August 14, 1501. Later in the year, a crusader fleet moved into the Aegean with the goal of taking Lesbos, but it was dispersed by a storm and failed in its endeavors. Venice sued for peace.

When Bayezit abdicated in 1512 he had doubled the size of the Ottoman Empire. A worthy successor to the great Mehmet, Bayezit was succeeded by Selim I, sometimes known as "Selim the Grim." He received that title because of his sadistic streak and the endless stream of carnage that occurred in his reign. On his succession he had his five nephews and two brothers strangled. As a devout Sunni, he considered the Shiites as heretics, and in order to deal with their heresy, he had a census taken. When 70,000 were identified, he sent out special teams of executioners that murdered 40,000 of them. In 1514 Selim began a campaign against the Safavids in Persia. He defeated the Persian army before the gates of Tabriz and, upon his victory, ordered the Muslims that he had taken prisoner, executed. After Persia he brought renegade parts of Anatolia back under control. From there, in 1516, he moved against Syria. In 1517 he moved against Cairo and defeated the Mamluks in battle. After defeating the Mamluks, several hundred Mamluk prisoners were executed on the spot despite promises that if they surrendered they would be spared. Fully 25,000 of the defenders of Cairo were killed in the battle. Another 50,000 of the city's inhabitants were also killed in the pillage that followed.

In the last days of his reign, Selim decided that all Christians in the empire should be put to death, but the wise intervention of the mufti prevented the implementation of his plans. Selim's desire to murder the Christians was based on the same religious fervor that had earlier caused him to slaughter the Shiites, whom he had also seen as heretics and apostates. Selim clearly believed in and practiced murder for purely religious reasons.

During his reign, Selim I sought to strengthen his control over the Janissaries by conciliating them and enlarging their numbers to 35,000 men. Selim's conciliatory efforts did not last long and in 1514, as he began his war against the Safavids, he had already started implementing a much stricter program of discipline. The struggle of the sultans for dominance over the Janissaries and the Janissaries for independence from the sultans would be an ongoing problem in Ottoman politics until the Janissaries were finally destroyed.

When Selim died in 1520 he was succeeded by Suleiman I (1520–66). The Ottoman Empire reached its peak under Suleiman, who would earn the title, "the Magnificent." The Janissary corps served as his instrument of power to control all elements of the Ottoman ruling class. This control reached a level never seen before or since. Suleiman, however, was a military man and would become one of the greatest Ottoman military leaders.

Under Suleiman, the Janissary corps rose to a strength of 101 battalions *(orta)*. Its officers were known as *corbacis* (literally "soup-ladlers"). The Janissaries were supposed to maintain themselves on a war basis at all times and ready for instant action. They were not allowed to marry and remained in barracks, training regularly. Though they numbered about 30,000, their organization, training, and discipline, and their muskets, made them the most important part of the Ottoman army until well into the seventeenth century. When not on military operations in the field, they were responsible for the security of key points throughout the empire. In Istanbul they guarded the Imperial Council as well as serving as the city's police and fire department.

Suleiman launched his first major campaign against Rhodes and the Knights of St. John. Pirates from Rhodes were an endless problem for Muslim commerce in the eastern Mediterranean and needed to be removed. In 1522 he sent a massive force against the fortified island and its garrison of 60,000 soldiers. Assault after assault failed until agents among the Jews and Muslim women enslaved by the Knights enabled the Ottomans to force entry and capture the fortress. By the terms of the subsequent surrender, all who wished to leave the islands were permitted to go, and the Knights were permitted to take their weapons and belongings. Those that chose to remain were to be exempted from taxes for five years and given the freedom of religion found elsewhere in the Ottoman Empire. The Knights left in papal ships, first for Cyprus, and then for Malta, which they fortified as a new base against Islam. These terms were surprisingly lenient, given that the Ottomans appear to have lost 60,000 men taking the island.

After dealing with a revolt in Egypt, Suleiman turned his attention to Hungary. Initially he moved to eliminate the last few Christian enclaves in the Balkans along the southern banks of the Drava and Danube, in Serbia and Bosnia. On August 8, 1520, he took Belgrade, and its garrison died to a man in the massacre that followed. The advance into Hungary was delayed until 1526, but when it began it overwhelmed the forces thrown against it. The major battle occurred on August 29, 1526, on the plain of Mohacs, on the right bank of the Danube south of Buda.

The Ottoman army departed Istanbul with 300,000 men and at Mohacs confronted a force of 22,000 men under King Louis II of Hungary. Wiser men advised Louis to wait for the Ottoman assault, but young, impetuous, and stupid, he chose to attack. Obviously he had not learned the lesson of Nicopolis—that the Turks could deal with feudal cavalry. As his army charged forward they were first disordered by the light cavalry screen and then cut down by the guns and musketry of the Janissaries. After two hours the Hungarians were destroyed and King Louis, attempting to escape, fell into a stream and drowned, weighed down by his heavy armor. Sixteen thousand Hungarians died in the battle. The 2,000 prisoners had their heads used as decorative ornaments around Suleiman's tent.

After their victory, the Ottomans roamed through the Hungarian countryside, hunting the peasants as if they were game. Within a few months, 100,000 Hungarians were sent to the slave markets at Istanbul and eventually some 2,000,000 Hungarians were enslaved.

From Mohacs, the Ottomans turned south, returning to their homeland and choosing only to leave a few scattered garrisons in Hungary. The Hungarian nobles sought support from the Hapsburgs and Poles to recover what they had lost. At the battle of Tokay, the Hapsburg forces defeated the Ottoman provincial commander of Hungary on September 26, 1527, and much of the kingdom was recovered. In 1528 the Ottoman response arrived in the form of a new army, which recaptured Buda on September 3, 1529, and the remainder of the country thereafter with little difficulty. On September 23 the sultan's army of 250,000 appeared before the gates of Vienna in the first siege of that great city. The siege would last only six weeks, for the defense was stout and the season was late. Suleiman wisely broke off and on October 16 turned his army south. However, as they withdrew they committed a wide variety of outrages against the peasants and others that they captured, leaving a legacy of hatred that would continue for centuries.

Suleiman's third Hungarian expedition occurred in 1532. The Hapsburgs had reinvaded Hungary and besieged Buda in 1530. Suleiman led 300,000 men north and ravaged much of the Hapsburgs' lands in order to force them to withdraw from Hungary to protect their own holdings. The sultan hoped, but failed, to force the Hapsburg main army to battle and, with his objective missed and the season once again late, withdrew from Austria to winter over in Hungary.

Realizing that large-scale operations would not likely succeed, in 1533 Suleiman negotiated a peace treaty with the Hapsburgs. Peace, however, was not in the cards for Suleiman. Now that his western frontier was secure and calm, he could turn to his long-held ambitions against the Persians and begin the conquest of Mesopotamia. The Persians, though, simply surrendered territory and refused battle. Frustrated and concerned about overextending his army, Suleiman turned on Iraq and captured Baghdad. During his approach, the Sunni leaders of Baghdad led the population in a revolt that butchered the local Shiite population. By 1538 Ottoman rule extended to the Persian Gulf.

Campaigns were frequent in the Balkans and Transylvania. Treaties meant little to either the sultan or the Hapsburgs, and so warfare was fairly constant. In 1566 the Hapsburgs and Ottomans were once again at war, the reason being constant raiding by the Hapsburgs (and no doubt the Ottomans as well) across their mutual borders in Transylvania. Revolts occurred and the Ottoman army moved into action to squelch the disturbances. The major event of this campaign was the Siege of Sziget on August 7.

The citadel at Sziget was occupied by 2,500 Magyars. This small and relatively unimportant place had a ferocious soldier, Count Miklos Zrinyi, to defend it. After a month of fighting, Zrinyi knew the end was upon him and prepared a bitter reception for the attackers. The Ottomans assailed the citadel, striking at the gate where a cannon stood loaded and ready to fire. Count Zrinyi fired it point blank as the Turks broke through the gate, slaughtering dozens of them, but it was not enough to stop their rush. He then advanced with his sword, slashing his enemies, dying under their blows and bullets. This was but a prelude, for Count Zrinyi's death was followed by the explosion of a huge magazine deep in the citadel. As the count fell, a further 3,000 Ottoman soldiers were slain by the blast.

When Suleiman learned of his victory he died of a heart attack. The explosion at Sziget in 1566 blasted apart the long unbroken chain of capable sultans. Shorn of its leader, the Ottoman army turned around and marched south to Istanbul for a new struggle for succession. In the event, however, Suleiman's son, Selim, ascended with little effort. Like Suleiman the Magnificent, his son Selim would also have a sobriquet. Selim was known as "Selim the Sot," for he was an alcoholic and quite addicted to Cypriot wine. Selim's ascent began the gradual decline of the Ottoman Empire.

The accomplishments of the great Ottoman sultans are impossible to overstate. They descended upon the Arab Middle East that had enjoyed 600 years of uninterrupted rule by one people and displaced them with little effort. They survived the crusaders and Mongols, and not even Tamerlane had their full measure. It was the Ottomans who finally toppled the decrepit old Byzantine Empire. And it was the great line of capable sultans who very nearly broke out of the Balkans and into Christian Europe. Few peoples have had more glorious eras in history.

CHRONOLOGY

1055	Seljuq Turk Tugrul Bey seizes power in northern Iran.
1063–72	Seljuq Sultan Alp Arslan in power
1071	Alp Arslan wins the Battle of Manzikert against the Byzantines.
1092–1180	Seljuq power dissipates between minor states.
1180–1225	Caliph al-Nasir of Baghdad reasserts central authority.
1280–1324	Osman Bey establishes the Ottoman dynasty.
1331	Nicaea falls to the Ottomans.
1346–50s	Sultan Ohran occupies Thrace and squeezes remaining Byzantine territory.
1360–89	Sultan Murat expands into the Balkans, winning the Battle of Kosovo.
1396	Sultan Bayezit rings Constantinople with forts and wins the Battle of Nicopolis.
1402–05	Tamerlane's Mongols intrude into Anatolia.
1421–30	Sultan Murat II fights with Venice.
1442–56	John Hunyadi attacks the Turkish Balkans.
1453	Sultan Mehmet II captures Constantinople, finishing the last spark of the Byzantine Empire.
1454	Mehmet II moves into Moldavia.
1455	John Hunyadi defends Belgrade.
1461	Greece and Serbia are brought under Ottoman control.
1481–1512	Reign of Bayezit, expansion into Greece, war with Venice

1512–20	Reign of Selim the Grim. Persia and Egypt become Ottoman provinces.
1520–66	Reign of Suleiman the Magnificent
1520–26	War with Hungary decided at the Battle of Mohacs on August 29, 1526.
1521	Knights of St. John evicted from Rhodes.
1529	Buda captured.
1529	Vienna is attacked but defended.
1530–32	War with the Hapsburgs in Austria.
1538	Turkish rule extended to Baghdad.
1566	Suleiman dies and is succeeded by Selim the Sot.

NOTE

1. See Chapter 12 for the history of the Ismaili Assassins.

Chapter 8

THE SICK MAN OF EUROPE: THE BALKANS AND THE FALL OF THE OTTOMAN EMPIRE

When Suleiman's army was driven back from Vienna in 1529, the Turks suffered a significant defeat. Nevertheless, that battle signaled neither the end of the Ottoman Empire, nor even its high-water mark. The Turks were and would remain the most significant European and Asian power for many decades. The great strength of the Ottomans was of course their magnificent army. In 1529 it was certainly the largest, and at its core also the finest in the Eurasian world.

The Ottoman army underwent few changes from its setback at the gates of Vienna in 1529 until the early nineteenth century. Much of the force was little more than a conscripted levy, without drill or discipline. Fire-arms had slowly spread through the ranks, but many soldiers continued to carry swords until almost the twentieth century. They were formidable in their own way, but for the most part bore little resemblance to an organized, disciplined European army—they remained very much a feudal levy with a small professional core of Janissaries. Their tactics, particularly those of the cavalry, changed little over the centuries. Thus, although in 1529 the numerous feudal levies of the Empire were militarily useful, by 1700 the unchanged Ottoman military giant ran into more sophisticated European discipline and technology. But for many years, the Ottoman army held the Empire together.

Until the middle of the nineteenth century the Ottoman land forces were composed of two types of soldiers—those who received pay and feudal levies who served without pay. The latter was, by far, the largest portion of the Ottoman army until about 1900. The army had a wide variety of troops, including the Janissaries, a large body of disciplined infantry, and a substantial force of highly disciplined and powerful heavy cavalry. Another force, the Spahis, or light cavalry, was among the best cavalry ever. In addition, hordes of conscripted rabble subsisted, if they could, on loot. Artillery had existed before the time of Suleiman the Magnificent, as had specialized military engineers.

This reliance on irregular forces was both the greatest weakness and the primary strength of the Ottoman military system. Some drawbacks are obvious: the lack of discipline, coordination, and command control of such an army. A less than obvious problem was that the irregular forces were tied to the land, and when planting season or the harvest arrived, they returned to their fields to tend to the business of agriculture.

As time progressed, the Ottoman military traditions became increasingly antiquated and produced fewer and fewer successes. Still, they were good raw material, and in the right circumstances, Turkish soldiers were as good as any in the world. At the siege of Acre in 1799, a few hundred of them held off the elite of Napoleon's army. British General John Moore, who was sent to evaluate the Ottoman army in 1801, reached the same conclusion. However, he reported that under the existing Ottoman administration the army was "a wild, ungovernable mob."

This would become apparent again in World War I. In a most unusual admission of military incompetence, the Ottoman government made General Liman von Sanders, a German general who was head of the German military mission in Turkey, Turkey's commander-in-chief. Similarly, German Feldmarschal von der Goltz was given supreme command of the Turkish forces in Mesopotamia.

It was most evident in World War I that the Turks were individually ferocious soldiers, but the Ottoman army failed on an organizational level. The Ottomans were utterly incapable of managing the logistics necessary to maintain an army, be it in the seventeenth century or the twentieth century. Because of this lack of administrative ability their pre-twentieth century armies tended to live off the land and were a plague on both their enemies and their own citizens.

The most famous of the corps of the old Turkish army were the Janissaries. These slave-soldiers were the elite corps of the standing army of the old Ottoman Empire, of the Sublime Porte. They were first organized in 1330 and annually received 1,000 twelve-year-old Christian boys from the Balkans as a slave tribute to fill their ranks. Service in the Janissaries brought with it great privilege, and parents actually begged to have their children enrolled, even though they were converted to Islam. The strength of the force grew to 20,000 by around 1575 and to 48,688 by 1591. Under Ibrahim (1640–48) they were reduced to 17,000, but began to increase again and had risen to 135,000 by the time they were finally destroyed in 1826.

By the seventeenth century the Janissary corps had become a praetorian guard in the worst sense of the word. When Sultan Selim III attempted to organize and establish a properly disciplined force to take their place, they revolted and forced him to abdicate. In the role of kingmakers they flourished, becoming an important part of the Turkish government and a recognized part of Ottoman society. This was acceptable for the long centuries that Turkey was a great power, but as their military power declined—the result of their soft life in the capital—so did their ability to control the government. Under Bairakdar Pasha of Widdin a new modern military force was raised and drilled. This competition was unacceptable to the Janissaries, and in 1806 they rose in revolt. They were repulsed and the uprising crushed, but the new troops were soon disbanded. The Janissaries returned to their old ways and again became so violent and demanding of the sultan that in 1825 Sultan Mahmud II decided to raise yet another force. He had a *fatwah* issued that stated it was the duty of all Muslims to serve in the military and established this new model army along modern lines. On June 10, 1826, the Janissaries revolted in Et Meidan Square in Constantinople and attacked and pillaged much of the city. The government drew together its forces, and when the Janissaries refused to surrender, they were slaughtered. Those who escaped the fighting were taken before the grand vizier and hanged. This was the end of the honorable old Janissary corps, which for centuries had been such a power on the battlefield and in the court of the greatest of European powers.

The second famous formation of the Ottoman army was the Mamluks. The Mamluks were originally slaves introduced into Egypt as troops to aid the local ruler. As mentioned earlier, they followed the course of the Roman praetorian guards and eventually came to rule Egypt for themselves. Istanbul could not challenge them militarily, and as long as the Mamluks paid the taxes and recognized the nominal authority of the Ottoman governor appointed by Istanbul, they were left alone.

As time passed from their founding sometime before the twelfth century to the end of the eighteenth century, they still replenished their numbers by importing fresh supplies of slave boys from the Caucasus. In this way they created and maintained a superior warrior caste that exercised absolute power over the native Egyptian population. Approximately 12,000 Mamluks served in Egypt at the time of the French invasion that would crush their power forever.

The Mamluks lavished great sums on their clothing and on that of their horses. They carried gold and jewels on their persons at all times, which made their corpses rich pickings for the French in 1799. When describing the Mamluks in 1799, French General Antoine Jomini said, "Nothing can compare with the beauty of the *coup d'oeil* presented by this African cavalry; the elegant forms of the Arabian horses, relieved by the richest trappings; the martial air of the riders; the variegated brilliancy of their costume; the superb turbans enriched with their plumes of office; altogether presented to us a spectacle new and peculiar."

From 1529 until 1683 the Ottomans were involved in innumerable wars on every frontier of the Empire. The recounting of them all would be difficult in the extreme, but a partial list of the major Ottoman campaigns in the last quarter of the sixteenth century is illuminating. In 1567 an expedition was sent to bring Yemen under control. In 1570 the Persians were ousted from the Caucasus. Naval fighting continued throughout the whole era against virtually every Mediterranean naval power. A major expedition sought to recover Iran in the 1570s. Aside from other more minor expeditions, the major theaters of war for the Ottoman Empire would increasingly be the Balkans and the lands surrounding the Black Sea. Here they would run into the emerging powers of Austria and Russia. Literally dozens of major battles would mark an era of unceasing warfare. Probably most significant about these wars is that during the sixteenth and seventeenth centuries the Ottoman Empire's Western opponents became less and less susceptible to the old style of warfare that had been the Turkish forte for 500 years. It is useful for the modern reader to understand that the constant fighting in the Balkans—most of it by brutal irregular forces and much of it against civilians—forms the basis for the modern-day racial hatreds that exist in the area. These hatreds provided the spark that ignited World War I and has recently involved the United States of America in a campaign to protect Muslim interests. It is interesting to imagine what Suleiman the Magnificent would think to know that a great national—and notionally Christian—power would come from around the world to protect his Balkan subjects.

These wars seem distant to the modern reader. We do not much use the names anymore—the princes are long forgotten—the causes are so long lost that we don't understand them. However, it is probably fair to illustrate a tiny portion of one campaign in one war in this period.

In 1598 the Hapsburg Austrians captured Raab and in 1599 Prince Michael of Wallachia brought Transylvania to assist the Hapsburgs. The Ottoman army was unable to respond because of political disputes in Constantinople. Prince Michael took advantage of this to capture Moldavia, but this caused him to split with the Hapsburg emperor, who had sought Moldavia for himself. Now facing a divided enemy, a joint campaign by the Ottomans and Poles allowed the Sultan Mehmet III to recapture both Wallachia and Moldavia. Once occupied, he put both of them under native princes loyal to the Empire. In 1603 Mehmet III died, and his son, Ahmet I (1603–17) assumed the title of sultan.

In a sad cycle that would be often repeated until the twentieth century, the Catholic Hapsburgs were absolutely intolerant of the Protestants living in Hungary and Transylvania. Every time these lands would pass from Ottoman to Hapsburg control, the repressive, anti-Protestant measures of the Hapsburgs would soon turn the local populations against them. Memories of the tolerance they'd experienced under the Ottomans quickly led to active support of Ottoman military campaigns against the Hapsburgs. The combined effect of the Sublime Porte's counterattack and local support for the Turks forced the Hapsburgs to evacuate Transylvania and peace was restored. Many modern readers find this catalog of unfamiliar princes, provinces, and problems dizzying. But these ancient affairs fuel the antipathy of many Balkans to this day.

By the middle of the seventeenth century, the Ottoman state was beginning to show the strain of constant warfare. Where there was not fighting, there was likely to be revolt in protest of the taxation and conscription that fed the fighting front. When local Ottoman governors became too powerful and ignored the central government, essentially becoming independent, the government rarely had the resources to deal with them. Sultans could still be a powerful force in the Empire, but increasingly they fell under the influence of the Janissaries or became the puppets of the grand viziers. It became the business of a major national effort to capture Crete in the 1640s. That this small island, so close to the heart of the Turkish navy, should prove a significant obstacle, is an indication of the difficulties beginning to hamper the Empire.

By 1663 the grand vizier Fazil set the stage for a decisive event in modern European history. Not surprisingly, the context was a war with Austria. It is worth a look in some detail.

All through the 1660s, bandits in Hapsburg employ had raided Turkish territory in the Balkans. Fazil demanded an end of the Hapsburg border raids, recognition of the sultan's suzerainty in Transylvania, and increased tribute from northern Hungary. When these were refused in 1663, he prepared for war. That summer of 1663 saw Tartar raiders moving through Transylvania into Moravia and Silesia, which provoked a general rising in Western Europe to support the Austrians. Fazil personally led the Ottoman army against the Christian army under Montecuccoli. Montecuccoli had deployed his army on the right bank of the Raab River, and on August 1, 1664, a decisive battle occurred at St. Gotthart, a small village that commanded the routes to Graz and Vienna. Though they battled to a draw, the Ottomans were prevented from crossing the river, which in Europe counted as a spectacular success. Overall, the Ottoman losses were greater than those of the Christians. The Ottomans had lost all their equipment and cannon, but the army was intact and capable of inflicting great damage on the Christians. Knowing this, Montecuccoli quickly accepted the sultan's offer to negotiate a peace, which was signed in 1664. By this treaty the Austrians agreed to evacuate all the territories they had occupied in Transylvania and to recognize the sultan's appointed prince. This campaign was but the prelude to the great attack on Vienna that would come in a few years. Fazil died in 1676 and was succeeded by Kara Mustafa Pasha.

Kara Mustafa Pasha would bring the Ottomans to the gates of Vienna for a second great siege. First, however, he had to resolve the dispute with the Russians as to who would rule the Cossacks. The war was actually started by the Russians, and they eventually compelled the grand vizier to accept peace. By this agreement, the Ottomans abandoned their claims to the region north of the Dnieper, which became the northernmost boundary of the Ottoman Empire. This treaty was forced as much by the lack of Ottoman success on the battlefield as by the Hungarians' renewed push to establish their independence. The sultan recognized Thokoly as king of Hungary, and Thokoly quickly conquered all of upper Hungary in the summer of 1682. The Hapsburgs, meanwhile, were involved in a war with the French, and French agents convinced Kara Mustafa that it was time to attack Vienna.

The existing peace treaty between the Ottomans and Hapsburgs was due to end in 1684. The war party in Istanbul, eager to take advantage of both Thokoly's successes in Hungary and the pending end of peace with the Hapsburgs to begin another campaign against Austria, pressured the sultan into accepting a preemptive strike in the year before the treaty would end. The Turks began calling their army together and advanced into the Balkans.

Seeing the attack coming, the Holy Roman Emperor, Leopold of Austria, worked desperately to organize a coalition to defend the eastern border of Christendom. His most important ally was Jan Sobieski of Poland, but Saxony, Bavaria, and Franconia would also send troops. The Ottomans pushed to the gates of Vienna and began the siege in July 1683. Upon their arrival they called upon the garrison to surrender, their herald saying, "Accept Islam and live in peace under the sultan! Or deliver up the fortress and live in peace under the sultan as Christians; and if any may prefer, let him depart peaceably, taking his goods with him! But if you resist, then death or spoilation or slavery shall be the fate of you all!"

The Ottomans, led by Kara Mustafa Pasha, focused their attention on the siege of Vienna, while their light cavalry, the Tartars and Hungarians, dispersed across the Austrian countryside, spreading fear and fire. The siege progressed steadily. The Turkish soldiery were encouraged by Kara Mustafa, who gave solemn warnings to them all and ordered each one of them to do his utmost to bring the enterprise to a successful conclusion, expending life and property for the true faith.

Kara Mustafa focused too much on the siege and failed to take elementary precautions such as sealing off the passes through the Wiener Wald and mountains to the west. Instead, he concentrated his forces around Vienna. In addition, the bad roads in the Balkans had prevented him from bringing his heavy artillery. Thus his siege efforts concentrated on tunneling under the walls of the city, filling the caverns with gunpowder, and detonating the charges to bring down the walls to permit an immediate assault by his infantry.

The combination of heavy fortifications, staunch defense, and the timely arrival of Leopold's army prevented the Ottomans from taking the city, although the Western European army arrived at almost the last possible minute. As Kara Mustafa had not blocked the approaches to Vienna, the coalition army cleared the rough terrain and deployed on the plain to the west of Vienna, driving off the small detachments of Ottomans sent to face it.

Kara Mustafa badly mismanaged the following battle, sending his forces to meet the Western alliance in a piecemeal fashion. He had not mastered the concept of mustering a covering force large enough to defend his siege works from outside attack. Though the battle was hard fought, the coalition forces broke the Ottomans and scattered their army. The Turkish retreat was chaotic; their heavy equipment was abandoned and their camps left to be pillaged.

The Christian pursuit of the defeated Ottomans was, by the standard of the day, aggressive. Kara Mustafa sought scapegoats to cover his failure and started a series of executions that began with Ibraham, the Turkish governor of Buda, and ended with an additional series of Ottoman officers. The Tartar khan was deposed and replaced. In spite of these measures, or because of them, the sultan's coalition began to disintegrate. Thokoly's Hungarians and the Tartars stood by as the advancing Christian army caught and destroyed elements of the Turkish army. Even within the Ottoman ranks, dissent arose. Some wished to continue their flight, while others remained loyal to Kara Mustafa's orders. A revolt erupted and the loyal troops triumphed, but Ottomans killing Ottomans in a power struggle only brought greater success to the Christian armies.

The Ottomans attempted a stand at Gand on November 1, but they were overwhelmed. The Ottoman defensive system for their northern borders was smashed and the road was open for the European powers to drive the Ottomans out of the Balkans. Kara Mustafa's enemies in Constantinople correctly convinced Mehmet IV that he was responsible for the failure. Kara Mustafa was dismissed from office and executed by strangulation in Belgrade on December 15, 1683. Its leader gone, the army promptly fell into an even greater state of disorganization and confusion.

The Turkish defeat at the gates of Vienna was another of the decisive battles of world history. Had the ancient Hapsburg city fallen to the Muslim east at the very dawn of the modern world, the cultural and political ramifications would have been enormous. As it was, 1683 might conveniently be described as the turning point for the Ottoman Empire. Their feudal hosts were no longer a match for the disciplined infantry of the European powers. The splendid Turkish and Asiatic cavalry was almost irrelevant on a battlefield increasingly dominated by firepower. The Ottomans no longer had a monopoly in artillery, and were, indeed, falling behind in that decisive arm.

Most telling, though, was that the Western European nations were moving beyond their feudal roots. Modern financial and administrative ideas would organize them far better than the Sublime Porte was organized. In the West, the rise of national rather than tribal monarchies was giving the European populations an identity unavailable to the sprawling collection of clans, tribes, and peoples ruled by the Ottomans.

The war between the Holy Roman Empire, ruled by the Hapsburgs, and the Ottoman Empire was at a critical point. As was typical for the era, Louis XIV used the Ottoman attack on Vienna to cover his invasion of the Spanish Netherlands. However, as soon as the French achieved their goals they abandoned their Ottoman allies. The Hapsburgs soon found themselves reinforced by forces from Poland, Malta, Venice, Tuscany, and the Papacy. Russia would join as soon as Poland promised concessions in the Ukraine. The Ottomans would spend the next two decades fighting on several fronts simultaneously: against the Hapsburgs in Hungary, Bosnia, and Serbia; against Poland in the Ukraine; against Venice in Dalmatia, Albania, and Morea; and against the Russians in the Crimea and the principalities of Wallachia and Moldavia. These strains, which her defeat at Vienna in 1683 might have avoided, merely hastened her decline.

Between 1683 and 1687 the disasters that befell the Ottomans caused a tremendous internal disintegration. The Empire's agricultural base suffered from heavy conscription of men for the army. Serious shortages of food resulted. Thousands of demoralized soldiers, fleeing the battlefields to the north, turned to banditry. The losses of Hungary and Transylvania stripped the Empire of much tribute. The occasional wise sultan, like Suleiman II, could slow the disintegration, but not halt it.

At the same time that the Austrians were inflicting these disasters in the northwest, the Russian threat was surfacing in the northeast. Peter the Great (1689–1725) had built the Russian military into a coherent force and marched south, taking Azov in 1696. The Russians had begun the process of turning the Sea of Azov into a Russian lake. Before the century had passed, the Russians would be trying to do the same to the Black Sea.

After years of short, disastrous reigns, in 1703 Ahmet III ascended the Ottoman throne and would remain there until 1730. This might have been an opportunity for an Ottoman recovery. The capable Ahmet faced a Europe tangled in the War of the Spanish Succession and the Great Northern War, which gave his Empire a chance to sit back, reorganize, and rebuild. The peace was short-lived however. A new and aggressive Russia joined the Austrians as enemies of the Ottomans.

Peter the Great ended the Swedish threat to his kingdom at Poltava, and on December 20, 1710, declared war on Turkey with promises of support from the princes of Moldavia and Wallachia. The opposing armies met at the Pruth River in Moldavia, and the Ottomans caught the Russian army in a bad tactical and logistical situation. Peter the Great offered a negotiated peace. The Ottomans, in equally precarious logistical straits, accepted this offer to negotiate on the basis of a return of conquered territories and the surrender of their cannons as a prerequisite for talks. The Treaty of Pruth, signed on July 23, 1711, returned the conquered territories to the Ottomans and had the Russians destroy their frontier forts and promise to abstain from further intervention in Ottoman affairs.

Having defeated the Russians, the Ottoman war party pushed to engage Venice and recover Morea, a part of modern Greece. War was declared on December 8, 1714. Morea was taken with little effort, but this Ottoman success provoked Austria to renew its alliance with Venice and demand full Ottoman withdrawal from their latest conquests. Thinking themselves strong enough to deal with the Hapsburgs and reconquer Hungary, the Ottomans expanded the war to new frontiers and quickly encountered new disasters. The grand vizier, leading 100,000 men, was attacked and routed by Eugene of Savoy at Peterwardin on August 5, 1715. Serbia was opened up to Austrian invasion.

The year 1717 saw one disaster after another, with the Austrians occupying Belgrade in August, and while doing so capturing all the Ottoman artillery and ammunition, plus thousands of prisoners. Meanwhile, the Venetians, supported by the pope and the Knights of Malta, attacked the Ottoman rear, capturing Preveze and landing troops in Dalmatia. The only Ottoman successes were a naval engagement off Cape Matapan in July 1717 and the defeat of a Venetian effort to recapture Morea. A disastrous peace was signed in 1718, and the early promise of Ahmet's reign ended in catastrophe.

Peace was restored on the northwest frontier, but in the east wars continued. A few years of peace in the west ensued, but in the 1720s, Ottoman armies were fairly constantly engaged suppressing rebellion and religious strife in Iraq and Persia.

In 1736 a new war broke out, as both Austria and Russia combined to strike the tottering Turkish Empire. The Russian goal was to make the Black Sea into a Russian lake by occupying the Crimea and mouths of the major rivers that emptied into the Black Sea and by destroying the Tartars, who had caused much damage to the southern Russian provinces. The Austrians wanted to keep pushing to extend their frontiers farther to the south. The Ottoman Empire faced both the Austrians and Russians simultaneously.

The Ottomans, caught by surprise, actually staved off first the Russian and then the Austrian advance, inflicting several sharp defeats on both. This was too much for the Hapsburgs, who sued for peace in September 1739. Russia quickly followed suit, accepting French mediation. This victory was to prove a short-term blessing for the Empire, for in 1768 the same two powers again advanced against the weary Turks. This time, the improved Russian and Austrian forces were too powerful. The Crimean Peninsula was swept clean of Ottoman influence and the Austrians finally acquired complete control of the Balkans, laying open the possibility of an advance on Istanbul itself. All that saved the sultan was a combination of circumstances—Pugachev's rebellion diverted the Russians, and Prussia applied pressure to both European powers to limit their conquests. Peace was signed in 1774, but vast lands had fallen to Russia, and the vital approaches to the capital were now in Austrian hands.

This crushing defeat was followed in 1787, when the two European powers again helped themselves to slices of Ottoman territory. This might have been the end of the ancient, and by now decrepit Empire. Salvation for the last of the ancient autocrats came in the unlikely form of the French Revolution, and by 1792 the Europeans were too focused on their own problems to interfere in the south. More disasters and few bright days would follow, but the revolutionary fever in Europe bought the Empire another 100 years of existence.

If the Empire was to be spared the hammer blows of her more advanced neighbors, there were still misadventures aplenty. In 1799 the French—Turkey's most reliable European ally—invaded Egypt, sending a fleet and army ample to break Mamluk power, but insufficient to form a permanent foothold. In the Balkans, bandits and murderers took advantage of Turkish weakness to terrorize the Muslim populations as efficiently as generations of Ottoman-supported bandits had terrorized Christian populations in the past. In the early nineteenth century no imperial troops restrained them.

On July 21, 1799, Mamluk general Ibrahim Bey and nearly 100,000 Mamluks and militia confronted the much smaller French army at Giza, in the shadow of the Pyramids. The battle was a contest between two traditions. On one hand was the 2,000-year-old heritage of the eastern horse warrior that the Mamluks brought with them, undeniably the finest battlefield light cavalry in the world. On the other hand were the disciplined conscripts of the west who brought firepower instead of tradition to the battlefield. In a short battle the new ideas destroyed the old, and Mamluk valor was shattered by the volley fire of the modern world. The brief French occupation of Egypt would end in 1801, not because of Ottoman force of arms, but because of the arrival of a British army.

Between 1806 and 1811, yet another Russian War erupted, but the intense pressure of Napoleonic France held Russian power in check in the north, and for once, the sultan's levies held on long enough for a negotiated treaty to return the status quo ante. This defensive victory was nearly the only bright Ottoman moment in a long and gloomy nineteenth century. In the 1820s the Greeks revolted, spurred on by post-Napoleonic romantic movements in Western Europe, Russian gold, and guns from Eastern Europe. What might have been just an untidy revolt became complicated when the local Turkish governor rebelled against the sultan in Istanbul in support of the rebels. If the Greek Revolution is to be noted for anything, it must be for the absolute savagery with which each side dealt with the other. Atrocity and massacre were commonplace on both sides. The hatred that erupted between these two nations continues to this day and takes physical form on the island of Cyprus.

Repeated losses on land and a covert European naval presence were enough to break Greece free from the Empire by 1822. But in the Balkans freedom frequently means little more than the freedom to kill one's neighbor, and soon the Greeks were fighting among themselves. The sultan, in despair, asked his Egyptian vassal Mehmet Ali to crush the rebellion, but the Europeans, caught up in the romantic mythology of Greek independence, smashed Ali's fleet at the Battle of Navarino in 1827. It is interesting that Turkey, heir of the landlocked Asiatic steppe peoples, participated in this last great battle of the sailing ship era.

With the Greeks in revolt and the Turkish armies distracted, Russia thought the time propitious to renew its attacks into the Ottoman-held Balkans. On April 28, 1828, Russia formally declared war on the Ottoman Empire yet again. After a seesaw campaign, the Russian infantry again prevailed, and in 1829 Moldavia and Wallachia were finally and irretrievably lost to the Ottomans. As the distant provinces fell, the way to the Turkish homelands began to open. The next blow was to be a major rebellion. Not for the first time the Turks would receive substantial European assistance. This time, however, the western powers were more concerned with maintaining a weak Turkey and containing a strong Russia. The balance of power would never again pivot on the sultan's throne.

With the end of the most recent war with Russia and the settlement of the Greek question in 1830, the Ottomans looked forward to a period of peace, but such was not to be the case. Muhammad Ali, the ruler of Egypt, had come out of the Greek Revolution with tremendous prestige, but few rewards. Greek independence had deprived him of the territories he had expected to rule as a reward for his efforts, so he asked for compensation in Syria, but Mahmut, the Ottoman sultan, refused and quietly ordered Syria to prepare for an attack. Muhammad Ali intercepted this message and realized that his request had been rejected, so he sought an excuse for war. Claiming that the Ottomans had failed to return some 6,000 *fellahin* who had fled to Syria during the war and that the governor of Acre had neglected to pay funds due him, he launched a successful invasion of Syria under the command of Ibrahim Pasha. By June 18, 1832, all of Syria was under his control.

The Ottomans reacted slowly. In March 1832 Mahmut officially declared Muhammad Ali and his son Ibrahim Pasha as rebels, dismissed them from their posts, and designated a replacement. Ibrahim, however, had taken advantage of the slow Ottoman reaction and established himself defensively and built local support by promising Arab self-rule. When the Ottoman troops finally entered Syria, they were met by a greatly enlarged and modern Egyptian army. Two battles fought at Homs and Belen went against the Turks.

Mahmut was unable to obtain any support from the European powers and found himself obliged to organize a new army under the command of Grand Vizier Resit Mehmet Pasha. Ibrahim Pasha, however, had not remained idle and had pushed his army through Cilicia onto the Anatolian plateau where he gained support from the many groups in Anatolia that opposed the sultan. Resit Mehmet attempted to cut the Egyptians' lines of communications to Syria but was routed at Konya on December 21. The way to the conquest of Anatolia by the Egyptians was wide open.

The sultan's defeat at Konya provoked Czar Nicholas of Russia to intervene. He preferred the Ottomans weak and he feared the formation of a powerful new state able to resist Russian penetration into the region. Mahmut requested Russian assistance, and a Russian military mission soon arrived in Istanbul to prepare the way for the arrival of Russian troops. This startled France and Britain, who sent emissaries to Cairo and obliged Muhammad Ali to agree to accept mediation that would assure his rule of Syria. Despite that agreement, his forces, under Ibrahim Pasha, resumed their advance on Istanbul and on February 2, 1833, occupied Cathy. They then prepared to winter over in Bursa, only fifty miles from the capital. Mahmut panicked and granted permission for a Russian fleet to enter the Bosporus and a Russian army to march through the Balkans to defend the city. The fleet arrived in the Bosporus on February 20 and the Russian troops were slated to arrive later.

The British and French, now thoroughly alarmed, forced the sultan to agree to remove the Russians and surrender Syria to Muhammad Ali as the basis for a settlement with threats of a blockade and the withdrawal of French military assistance if he refused.

Emboldened, Muhammad Ali demanded even more. The Russians now admitted that they could not deliver troops to Istanbul in time to defend it if Ibrahim resumed his offensive. Mahmut caved in and granted all the Egyptian demands on the conditions that their army be withdrawn. Simultaneously, the Russians were invited to land their troops at Buyukdere, on the European side of the Bosporus and to put them into a position to defend Istanbul if Ibrahim should prove treacherous and attack. The Russians landed on April 5, to the great dismay of the citizenry. They opposed the use of infidels against Muslims, no matter how threatening the latter might be, and their presence within an Islamic nation.[1] In practical terms, the Russian presence convinced Ibrahim to negotiate, and an agreement was reached in which Ibrahim received the governorships of Damascus and Aleppo as well as that of Cidde. This put him a position to control much of the Arab world. Muhammad Ali was confirmed as governor of Egypt and Crete. The war ended when Ibrahim withdrew from Anatolia.

This new friendship with the Western Europeans proved useful in the next few decades. However, now Russian expansionism would be checked and Turkey would see European armies aiding her again. The age-old religious differences between Islam and Christianity would play a curious part in the operations that culminated in the Crimean War.

The holy sites in Palestine have been a source of constant conflict not only between the East and West, but within the Middle East. In 1850 both France and Russia began demanding of the Ottomans greater influence in Jerusalem as well as protection for their priests at the holy sites. As early as 1829 Russia had been championing the rights of the Orthodox priests against those of the Latins, and in 1843 the Orthodox patriarch obtained Ottoman assent for his separation from the Patriarch of Constantinople. This allowed him to begin building his own power base with the help of the Czar.

France responded in 1850, demanding new privileges, and initially she prevailed. The Czar demanded balancing concessions, and the entire situation began spiraling out of control. Religion, national prestige, and the intransigence of the Czar, Louis Napoleon, and the helplessness of the sultan would soon lead to war.

Emboldened by the developing diplomatic situation, the Ottoman commander at Sumla presented an ultimatum to the Russian commander in the principalities (of the Balkans) on October 4, 1853, demanding that he evacuate them under the threat of war. When no reply was received, the Ottoman army crossed the Danube and attacked the Russian positions between October 27 and November 3, 1853. At the same time, an Ottoman army in eastern Anatolia moved into the southern Caucasus, attacking the Russian troops stationed there.

The Ottoman fleet under Osman Pasha also mobilized and moved into the Black Sea, probably because it feared a Russian attack on the Bosporus. Not finding the Russian fleet and encountering a powerful storm, the Turkish fleet moved into Sinope to seek shelter.

In early November 1853, the Russian squadron of Vice-Admiral Pavel Nakhimov found them riding at anchor at Sinope. The Russian fleet, which included new steam frigates, attacked on November 18 and destroyed the Turkish fleet. The heirs of the steppe had the curious distinction of participating in the first naval battle in which modern steamers figured prominently. During the Battle of Sinope, 266 Russian officers and crewmen died, while the Ottomans suffered more than 3,000 casualties and the wounded Osman Pasha was taken prisoner. European opinion was roused, and the British government sent word to its fleet to protect the Ottoman flag as well as Ottoman territory. They were also to compel the Russian fleet in the Black Sea to return to Sevastopol. War was declared.

Prussia and Austria, the two major European powers not to enter the Crimean War, persuaded the Russians to abandon the Balkan principalities so as to avoid a general war. Thus, all of Europe combined to meet the Ottoman war aims!

The war ended with the signing of the Peace of Paris on March 29, 1856. Although the war emptied the Ottoman treasury and forced it to take on heavy loans, the Russians abandoned their conquests in eastern Anatolia and the Allies left the Crimea and Black Sea. The signatories declared their joint guarantee of the territorial integrity and independence of the Ottoman Empire, promising to mediate jointly any quarrels that might arise. The Strait of Dardanelles was to be closed to warships of all foreign powers, and the Black Sea was to be neutralized, open only to merchant shipping. The Ottomans and Russians would keep only such small warships as needed to defend their coasts. The larger warships would be removed and all naval shipyards on the Black Sea would be closed. The Danube and the Strait were also opened to the merchant shipping of the world. Thus now Europe was the protector of the sultan. The 200 years since the Great Siege of Vienna had wrought wondrous changes indeed.

With the European safeguards in place, the Ottoman Empire might have enjoyed a respite, but revolts sprang up in Montenegro and Crete between 1858 and 1869. These confused affairs merely diverted attention that might have been given to widespread reforms. The Turkish government, however, simply lacked the energy to implement reforms on anything more than a local basis. But some reforms did occur, and the Turkish army was finally modernized to the point that it was once again able to compete with European forces—at least those forces that could be sent into the Ottoman frontiers. This was fortunate, for Russia was not yet satisfied.

The Russians had been pushing back against the Ottomans in southern Russia and the Balkans for centuries. Historically, the czars had sought to extend their hegemony into the Balkans under the guise of pan-Slavism. Provocations occurred on both sides, as well as considerable propaganda where the truth was often lost.

The last Ottoman outpost in the Balkan Peninsula had long been an unstable dominion of the Ottoman Empire and frequent revolts were brutally suppressed. In the summer of 1876 rumors began to flow out of Bulgaria that whispered of unspeakable atrocities committed by the Turks against the Christian Bulgarians. Disraeli, the British prime minister, was anxious to preserve the Near Eastern status quo and to keep Russia from an excuse to intrude, yet again, into the Balkans, so he discounted the stories in the press. He suggested that a few Bulgarian insurgents had been killed, but nothing more. He was probably correct in his judgments. There were certainly murders, but probably no more than normal for those troubled lands.

Inspired and intrigued by the rumors, J. A. MacGahan, an American journalist with the London *Daily News,* was, at that time, working in Istanbul. He decided to go to Bulgaria and investigate these stories. He proceeded to send a series of telegrams from Batak and Philipopolis that struck the world press like a bomb and aroused the horror and indignation of the western world. Gladstone, a former prime minister, declared that the Turks must be thrown out "bag and baggage" from the Bulgarian provinces. His pamphlet on the topic, which sold 50,000 copies—and netted him a neat £12,000—said, "Five million Bulgarians, cowed and beaten down to the ground, hardly venturing to look upwards, even to their Father in Heaven, have extended their hands to you." This was fiery stuff to the straitlaced moralists of the high Victorian era.

In Bulgaria, MacGahan, accompanied by Eugene Schuyler, the American consul-general in Turkey, sent telegrams that described how on approaching a town they found skulls scattered about and a ghastly heap of skeletons. His report, which appeared in the *Daily News* on August 7, 1876, went:

> I counted from the saddle a hundred skulls, picked and licked clean: all of women and children. We entered the town. On every side were skulls and skeletons charred among the ruins, or lying entire where they fell in their clothing. They were skeletons of girls and women with long brown hair hanging to their skulls. We approached the church. There these remains were more frequent, until the ground was literally covered with skeletons, skulls and putrefying bodies in clothing. Between the church and the school there were heaps. The stench was fearful. We entered the churchyard. The sight was more dreadful. The whole churchyard for three feet deep was festering with dead bodies partly covered—hands, legs, arms, and heads projected in ghastly confusion. I saw many little hands, heads and feet of children of three years of age, the girls with heads covered in beautiful hair. The church was still worse. The floor was covered with rotting bodies quite uncovered. I never imagined anything so fearful. There were three thousand bodies in the churchyard and church. . . . In the school, a fine building, two hundred women and children had been burnt alive. All over the town were the same scenes. . . . The man who did all this, Achmed Aga, has been promoted and is still Governor of the district. The newspaper accounts were not exaggerated. They could not be. No crime invented by Turkish ferocity was left uncommitted.

MacGahan went on in further letters describing barbarities, bayoneting of babies tossed into the air, paraded around the streets on the points of bayonets, and so on. However true these stories of MacGahan's may or may not have been, cannot be determined today. Numerous sources, however, are clear that thousands of men, women, and children were slaughtered and scores of villages were destroyed.

It is well known that the Balkans were an unstable region and that the Russians had carefully fostered that unrest. This particular region of Bulgaria, however, had a history of peaceful coexistence prior to 1860 when, for some unknown reason, the Sublime Porte, in a fit of extreme stupidity, imported 60,000 Circassian settlers from Asia Minor into Bulgaria. The Circassians formed a major part of the *bashi-bazouks,* or feudal levy of the Turkish army, and as such were mobilized to quell a minor insurrection of Bulgarian nationalism, probably as a result of the Circassians in 1875–76 being given land taken from Bulgarian peasants. The Circassians proceeded to massacre every Bulgarian they could catch, and the Turkish government was powerless or perhaps disinclined to stop the events. It was left to MacGahan to describe, with whatever literary license he chose to employ, the sights that met his eyes as he explored the region occupied by the Circassian *bashi-bazouks.*

World press screamed for action, and Russia had its excuse to invade yet again, this time with at least tacit Western approval. MacGahan, having created the war with anti-Turkish stories, now reported favorably on the heroism of the Turkish army. In effect he created the war, and then the heroes to people it!

The Russian armies marched forward in 1877 and drove to the focal point of the region, the city of Plevna. They met Osman Pasha, a courageous and modern soldier with the flower of the new Turkish army, at that fortress city commanding the pass through the Black Mountains. Arriving on July 19, he took up positions on the bare hills to the north and east of the city. The Russian General Schilder-Schuldner, who commanded the 5th Division, IX Corps, had completed his capture of Nikopol and had been ordered to march on Plevna. He arrived in front of the fortress shortly after Osman Pasha had taken up positions there. The Russians quickly brought their guns into action and on July 20, without having bothered to reconnoiter the position, Schilder-Schuldner sent his infantry forward in four separate columns.

On the north, the Russians drove back the Turkish right wing. Desperate Turkish counterattacks drove back, breaking the offensive momentum and forcing them to withdraw, leaving 2,800 of the 8,000 attackers dead on the field. The Turks lost about 2,000. Thus ended the first Battle of Plevna. The outnumbered Turks had fought in the open against a modern army and held their ground. Now it was time to dig in.

Osman immediately began the fortification of his positions. Night and day the Turks dug entrenchments and redoubts. A stream of reinforcements flowed into the Turkish lines, swelling their ranks to 20,000. Steadily their hold on their positions around Plevna grew stronger and stronger. On July 30 a new assault, led by General Krudener, was launched. The Russian forces now totaled 40,000 men supported by 176 guns. The second battle of Plevna began at 3:00 P.M. as Russian columns marched against the Turkish positions. The columns striking the north and northeast were repulsed with heavy losses. Russian General Shakovskoi temporarily occupied two Turkish redoubts but was driven out by a counterattack launched by the Turkish reserves. Again the Russians withdrew, leaving 7,300 dead behind them, and the Turks lost another 2,000 men. Though their victory was substantial, Osman failed to pursue the defeated Russians, letting the fruits of his victory slip away. The Russians were dependent upon possession of an undefended bridge over the Danube a mere forty miles away. Capturing it would have spelled the destruction of the Russian army.

Unwilling to stop, the Russians concentrated every soldier they had in the region and called on the Romanians to aid them. By the end of August they had amassed 74,000 infantry, 10,000 cavalry and 440 guns before Plevna. On August 30, Osman moved out of his works and on August 31 he attacked the Russians near Pelishat. The fight was indecisive, and he left 1,300 dead on the field to the 1,000 Russians that lay amongst them. The Russians then moved against Osman's communications, broke them, and turned back on Plevna.

The third battle of Plevna began when the Russians launched an attack during the night of September 6. A heavy bombardment preceded the attack, and parts of the Turkish fortifications were seized and held. On August 12 the Turks recaptured some of the fortifications, but others remained in the hands of Russia's Romanian allies. The Russians' losses in the first six days of the battle exceeded 18,000, and Turkish losses were estimated near 5,000. Using their superior numbers and overwhelming artillery force, the Russians were steadily grinding the Turks into submission. Their losses, however, had convinced the Russians that a siege was preferable to more bloodletting, and their assault ground to a halt. A total investment was completed by October 24. Osman had earlier requested permission to withdraw, but the Sublime Porte had refused. Trapped by Russian guns and the stubbornness of the throne, Osman's fate was sealed and it was only a matter of the clock ticking down. When his supplies were exhausted, Osman attempted one last futile sortie during the night of December 9. When that failed, he and his army capitulated and the 1877 Russo-Turkish war ended. Osman's Turkish army had been beaten, but not humiliated. This was a small ray of hope for the future.

The victorious Russians, finally restrained by the Western Europeans, dictated the Treaty of San Stefano to the Turks on March 3, 1878. This treaty created the Bulgarian nation, but left Macedonia, Albania, and Thrace to the Ottoman Empire. Although the treaty ended the fighting, it was not a success. The West did not want the newly formed Bulgaria to become a Russian client state. The Treaty of Berlin, signed on July 13, 1878, cut Bulgaria's boundaries to the territory between the Danube, excluding the Dobruja, and the rest of the Balkans, with Samokov and Kiustendil. Vranje, Pirot, and Nish were given to Serbia, and Turkey retained nearly all of Macedonia. These transfers of territory were made without any consideration of the nationalities of the people occupying those territories, and large portions of Bulgarian-speaking peoples were cut off from the newly forming state of Bulgaria. Macedonia had many Bulgarians, as did Vranje, Pirot, and Nish, but they eventually became parts of non-Bulgar states. Thus were laid the seeds of 100 years of discontent, border disputes, and war that continue to this day.

The twentieth century saw a continuation of the long decline. In 1911 the Italians gobbled up as much of the North African coastal territories as they chose, and which had not already gone to France. In October 1912, the new Bulgarian government, allied with the Greeks, Serbs, and Montenegrins launched a successful offensive to clip off the exposed Turkish holding north of the Bosporus.

The Turks were ill prepared for such a war. The war with Italy was barely finished, and the Turks had little opportunity to set right the losses inflicted on them there. The Greeks blockaded Turkish ports, while the Bulgarians drove victoriously to within twenty-five miles of Istanbul. The Turks collapsed, defeated in a few weeks. In December a peace conference was convened, but Turkey was unwilling to surrender Adrianople, and Bulgaria insisted on it. The peace conference ended and the war resumed, with the Bulgarians, supported by 60,000 Serbians, pressing the siege of Adrianople. The city was stormed on March 26. The fighting ended April 23 with the surrender of Scutari.

Turkey paid a tremendous price for peace. It lost its territory in Europe except a small enclave on the western bank of the Marmara Sea. Crete was surrendered to Greece, as were most of the Turkish-held Aegean islands.

The Turks might well have taken some pleasure in the events of the next year. Bulgaria, dissatisfied with its portion of the spoils, launched a war against its neighbors. Serbia, Romania, and Greece engaged the Bulgarian army and the war went badly for the aggressor. When it ended, Bulgaria had lost. Southern Dobruja, which had belonged to Bulgaria since 1878, was given to Romania, and Macedonia was divided between Greece and Serbia.

At least the hands grasping the Balkan thorns would no longer be Turkish. It was just as well, for the great cataclysm of World War I was about to immolate most of the Eurasian world. Sadly, Turkey chose to join in the conflagration.

On August 2, 1914, Germany and Turkey signed a secret alliance. When the war initially erupted, Turkey declared its neutrality, but mobilized. The Allies demanded that the Turks expel the crews of the German warships *Goeben* and *Breslau*,[2] which had escaped into the Sea of Marmara and sought refuge from the Allies. At the same time the British seized two Turkish warships then under construction in Britain that were being paid for by "popular subscription" of the Turkish people. The Turkish population became furious. The Germans cleverly offered the two interned vessels to the Turks and in a brilliant coup, by the surrender of the two warships, they brought Turkey into the war on the side of the Central Powers. On September 8, 1914, Turkey declared herself free of the capitulations of 1878.

Turkey was thus at war with the Allies in Mesopotamia (modern Iraq) and on the Caucasian frontier (between the Black and Caspian Seas). The British would soon land a force of Australians on the Dardanelles, the most treasured geographical possession of the Ottoman Empire—the passage from the Mediterranean to the Black Sea.

The Turks successfully defended the Dardanelles, but the Russians advanced steadily south, seizing Trebizond, Erzerum, and Erzinjan, and moving against Sivas. The Turks launched an attack against the Suez Canal, but it failed. The British invaded and occupied Syria and Iraq. They would push an army into Palestine and inflict numerous defeats on the outclassed Turks.

On the Caucasian front, the Armenians created disturbances behind the Turkish lines and threatened to cut their lines of communication. To resolve this issue, the Turkish government began a general deportation of Armenians and horrible atrocities were committed on a large scale. When the Russian general Antranik entered east Anatolia, the Armenian soldiers under his command, the so-called "Christian Army of Revenge," responded with equally horrible atrocities against the ethnic Turks who fell into their hands.

First Lord of the British Admiralty Winston Churchill had conceived of the idea of an Allied attack on Turkey that would be decisive and knock it out of the war. To this end, he proposed that the Allies land a force on the Dardanelles and strike directly into Istanbul, thus removing Turkey from the war, or at least easing the pressure on Russia. The first blow fell on March 18, 1915, when an abortive naval bombardment occurred. During this attack the Turks performed admirably. At Kilid Bahr, on the Gallipoli side of the strait, they were reported to be fighting with wild fanaticism, an Imam chanting prayers to them as they served their guns. The gunners exposed themselves without consideration to the flying shrapnel and bursting shells from the Allied battleships and cruisers. Their defense of the vital strait was such that on March 23, 1915, Vice Admiral Robeck, commander of the fleet, point-blank refused to resume the attack without a preliminary landing by the army.

The Allies had seriously underrated the Turks. Some in the British War Office had actually hoped that when the Turks saw the Commonwealth troops landing, they would flee. Little did the English realize, despite all their experience in the Middle East, that the Turks would view them as alien invaders.

The five-division expeditionary force organized itself in Egypt. Facing them under General Liman von Sanders, a German general who headed the German military mission in Turkey and served as Turkey's commander-in-chief, were six Turkish divisions that were spread along both banks of the Dardanelles as well as up the Aegean side of the Gallipoli peninsula.

The Allied force launched its assault on the Cape Helles region of the tip of the Gallipoli peninsula on April 25. The British forces landed at dawn without undue difficulties, but as they climbed the heights, they encountered withering fire and suffered heavy losses. The Australians and New Zealanders landed at a relatively undefended beach area and established themselves strongly, but could not advance any significant distance inland.

On April 25, as the Anzacs landed, they encountered the Turkish 19th Division under Mustafa Kemal Pasha. The advancing Anzacs were driven back from the critical Chunuk Bair ridge by a ferocious bayonet charge launched by the Turkish 57th Infantry Regiment, supported by an Arab regiment of the same division. When ordering them to attack, Mustafa Kemal was straightforward. He said, "I don't order you to attack, I order you to die. In the time which passes until we die other troops and commanders can take our places." The Turkish 19th Division suffered 2,000 casualties that first day, but had held the elite Anzac Division in check.

General von Sanders responded quickly. On April 26 Ottoman troops launched heavy counterattacks and were beaten off with losses. More Allied troops landed, but a stalemate developed. Both sides dug in and developed elaborate trench systems. The Allies attempted to break this with further landings on April 25 and again on August 6, but the Turks sealed off those landings as well.

During the August 6 operations the Allies launched an attack with thirteen divisions, approximately 120,000 men. That day alone seven Victoria Crosses were won and more than 4,000 Allied soldiers killed. In the crucial Anafarta sector (Chunuk Bair), Mustafa Kemal stood in command. His 19th Division took the first shock of the New Zealanders' attack and demolished the Australian light horse. They then turned on the British 32nd Brigade and all but annihilated it as it attempted to move up to the crest of Tekke Tepe. As the lead company went forward, the Turks broke over the rise above them. The Turks charged and cut the brigade to pieces. Within minutes all British officers were killed, battalion and brigade headquarters overrun, and the British soldiers scattering in wild disorder.

The Allied attack on Gallipoli was a complete failure. Even the confident soldiers of England began to speak respectfully of "Johnny Turk." The Turks had held their heartland, but the sultan's armies faced other theaters.

The war in the region around the Suez Canal had been stagnant from the beginning of the war until September 19, 1918. Because of the critical importance of the canal, the British had amassed a huge force of 95,000 men that included 15,000 cavalry, 80,000 infantry, and 500 guns. On September 19, 70,000 men, supported by 540 guns, advanced eastwards out of Egypt against a force of 20,000 Turks and Germans in Palestine.

Despite the preponderance of strength on the British side, their commander, General Allenby, had made two abortive attempts to seize Amman and Es Salt in early 1918. The British force, in corps strength, was beaten back by a tiny force of Turks and Germans under the command of Jemal Pasha (Kuchuk). To disguise their failure, the British disingenuously called these the First and Second Transjordan Raids.

Grim fighting also occurred in the Arabian Peninsula as the local princes revolted against the hated Turkish foreigners. But even here, in the depths of the desert, the outnumbered Ottomans held on grimly, defending their garrisons and supply lines until forced to withdraw by Allenby's offensive into Palestine in September 1918.

The British had also landed forces at Fao, on the Shatt al'Arab (modern Kuwait) at the head of the Persian Gulf on November 7, 1914, and maintained forces in the region until the end of the war. This foothold was slowly expanded and pushed up the Tigris and Euphrates. The strategic city of Kut-al-Amara was taken in late September 1915. From here General Townshend, the British commander, attempted an advance on Baghdad, but it failed after heavy losses. The Anglo-Indian army then withdrew to Kut where the Turks, under Feldmarschal von der Goltz, who had supreme command of the Ottoman forces in Mesopotamia, surrounded and besieged the Empire forces on December 8, 1915. Despite several attempts to relieve them, the Allied forces in Kut were forced to surrender on April 24, 1916. The garrison of 9,000 British and Indian troops was taken prisoner.

A new British commander, General Maude, arrived and took over the British forces to the south and launched a massive attack on December 13, 1916. He drove the Turks from Kut and pushed farther northward. In December 1916 this Mesopotamian Expeditionary Force, advanced from Sannayiat to Mosul, fighting bitter battles against outnumbered Turkish rear guards the entire length of its advance. Though the Allied advance was eventually successful, the Turks had sold victory to the British at a heavy price. Of the 415,000 troops committed to the Mesopotamian Expeditionary Force, 92,000 were casualties.

Overall, the Turkish army fought the war about as well as could have been asked. They had held their central position at Gallipoli and slowly given ground against larger forces with vastly superior equipment and supplies. Altogether the Turks had tied down 1,200,000 allied troops and had inflicted 340,000 causalities on them in the Dardanelles, Egyptian, and Mesopotamian theaters.

Though the war ended for Germany on November 11, 1918, it did not end for the Turks. A Greek army was landed at Smyrna, under the protection of the British, American, and French fleets. On May 15, 1919, the Greeks began a wave of massacres committed in full view of the combined fleet. The 1917 interallied agreement of St. Jean de Maurienne had allocated Smyrna and Adalia to Italy, and the Italians landed troops in Adalia in April 1918 to take possession of their new territory. The Greek massacres continued in Smyrna and aroused the anger of the Turkish people. The Turkish army was incapable of action, so popular organizations for the national defense sprang up in western Anatolia. In eastern Anatolia they prepared to block any attempt by the Allies to create an Armenian state. The war ground on.

It was then proposed at the Lausanne Peace Conference that self-determination be granted to the Arab provinces south of the armistice line. The strait would open to commerce, and non-Turkish minorities would receive the same rights as they had secured in Europe under various postwar treaties. The pact also demanded, either explicitly or implicitly, that the Turks should retain all territories inhabited by non-Arab Ottoman Muslim majorities, which meant not only Anatolia, but eastern Thrace and the Mosul Vilayet. Istanbul would be given military security, the hated capitulations should be abolished, and public debts would be reasonably settled.

The politics of the region did not go well for the Allies. They occupied the capital, and seized numerous nationalists. The Turkish government, controlled by the Allies, condemned the leading nationalists to death by extraordinary courts and issued a *fatwah* denouncing them as outlaws. The Anatolian government retaliated by issuing its own *fatwahs*. The sultan's government sent forces under the name of the caliphate army and aroused counterrevolutionary outbreaks, but the nationalists succeeded in suppressing them. These nationalist victories greatly embarrassed the Allies, who accepted the offer of President Venizelos that the Greek army should advance beyond the area allotted to it in order to deal with the nationalists. In the months of June and July 1920 the Greek army occupied eastern Thrace and marched on Brusa and Ushak. On August 10, 1920, the Allies concluded the Treaty of Sèvres, with the sultan's government. This treaty was aimed at destroying the independence of Turkey. It assigned eastern Thrace as far as the Chatalja lines, including Gallipoli, to Greece, as well as Smyrna and the surrounding territory, at least provisionally.

To the east, in Cilicia and Aintab, the nationalist forces successfully fought back the French and their Armenian allies. However, the Armenians continued launching raids on Turkish frontier villages. Killings, burnings, and other atrocities were common.

In January the Greeks launched a new offensive against the Turks, but they were twice checked by the Turkish army at Inn-Eunu. On July 10, 1921, the Greeks resumed the offensive and drove the Turkish army east of Sakaria. Mustafa Kemal Pasha was appointed commanding general and after a pitched battle that lasted twenty days, the Greeks were defeated and withdrew behind the Eskishehir River. On March 24, 1922, the Allies intervened and proposed a truce between the Turks and the Greeks. The Turks would not consider it until the Greeks were out of Anatolia. The Greeks refused and demanded to occupy Istanbul, which the Allies wisely refused. On August 25, a major Turkish offensive routed the Greek army. As the Greek army withdrew from Ushak to Smyrna, it burnt to the ground the most prosperous towns in western Turkey and committed large-scale atrocities. When the Turkish army entered Smyrna on September 9, the masses of native Christians fled the town, which was then burned to the ground on September 13. It is reported that in twenty-four hours the Turks burnt 50,000 houses, 24 churches and 28 schools, plus an indeterminate number of other commercial properties.

The Allies had embarrassed themselves by having declared themselves neutral in this Greco-Turkish War. They now intervened and forced the peace of the Treaty of Lausanne, signed on July 24, 1923. To minimize problems, the Greeks in Anatolia were exchanged for Muslim Turks then living in Greek Macedonia. The Greeks in Istanbul and the other Christian minorities were to have the same rights as secured by other minorities in Europe under the postwar treaties. This ended the last real invasion of Anatolian Turkey. The sick man of Europe had mustered the strength necessary to survive the greatest war in human history. The accomplishment cannot be overstated. The long, hard struggles of the Turkish army had at last brought the tired, old Ottoman Empire to the point that a proud modern nation could be built on its shoulders.

During World War I another sad chapter in Middle East history arose that merits some discussion as well. The "Armenian Question" is a highly emotional subject, the history of which is laced with considerable confusion and more than a few willful misrepresentations of fact. However, the fundamental truth of this tragedy is undeniable. Its magnitude is open to debate and makes an accurate analysis almost impossible.

Armenia lies in the southern part of the strip of land that divides the Black Sea from the Caspian Sea, below Azerbaijan and Georgia. Its culture was ancient and predates Christ. Having a Christian prince since 310, Armenia was conquered by the Seljuq Turks in the twelfth century. It was eventually assimilated into the Ottoman Empire in the fifteenth and sixteenth centuries. The Armenians of Anatolia retained a form of unified administration and representation through the theocratic system of government established by the Ottomans, known as the millet system, for the control of their subject peoples.

In 1800 the Armenians were scattered within and beyond the region that now encompasses Armenia, Georgia, Azerbaijan, and Eastern Turkey. Despite this dispersion, a limited sense of national identity continued to exist among the dispersed Armenian subjects of Turkey, Russia, and Persia. In the early nineteenth century Russia began to cast eyes toward Armenia and to expand into the Transcaucasus, the region where the Armenians lived. When the Russians advanced, the Armenians, co-religious Orthodox Christians, sided with and actively supported the Russians. Muslims were displaced from the areas occupied by the Russians, notably the Circassians, some of whom went to Bulgaria and committed the atrocities that resulted in the 1877–78 Russo-Turkish war.

In 1878 the Turko-Armenians did not constitute a clear majority of the total population in any of the six Anatolian provinces where they lived. This was probably sufficient cause to limit any separatists ambitions that might have existed and caused the Armenians to decline into "least favored" status among the various Christian minorities in the Ottoman Empire and among the Western powers.

The influx of Muslims into the Transcaucasus before 1877 had resulted in atrocities committed by both the Kurds and Circassian nomadic tribesmen against the Armenians. The Armenians and Turks, however, continued to coexist with few problems at the village level, despite the second-class citizenship imposed on the Armenians.

Ottoman-imposed limitations on Armenian rights included being forbidden to bear arms, to ride a horse, to hold certain public offices, and to wear certain articles of clothing. Despite this, Armenians prospered greatly in the cities of the empire. Ali Vehbi Bey, a private secretary to Abdul Hamid, claimed that they held one-third of all state positions on the civil list, including those of cabinet minister, provincial governor, ambassador, and principal assistant to Muslim cabinet ministers. In addition, Armenian merchants, entrepreneurs, and bankers controlled shares of imperial trade and industry disproportionate to their numbers. As a result, the upper classes of Armenian society had little interest in revolt or upheaval during the nineteenth century, despite the occasional afflictions visited upon the peasantry. Life was, overall, relatively good and secure until the outbreak of war between Turkey and Russia in 1877.

The 1877–78 war precipitated a general collapse of order. Muslim Circassian and Kurdish nomadic tribesmen fled into the Transcaucasus in great numbers before the advancing Russian armies. This sudden mixture of masses of nomads with the agricultural Armenian peasantry was an utter disaster. The nomads bore arms, which were forbidden to the Armenians. They were unruly and pastured their flocks where they chose, including the fields of the peasants. The Armenians, unable to defend themselves, suffered every sort of outrage. Their crops were stolen or trampled, their women violated or carried off. During the winter, the nomads even drove the Armenians from their homes. Encouraged by the collapse of the local authority, the Circassian and Kurdish tribesmen already living in the region joined in the pillage. Murder, robbery, and rape became commonplace in the villages, and especially on the roads between them.

The Ottoman authorities were occupied with the war and made no effort to stop these outrages. Opposite them, the Russians established an enlightened regime—a genuine rarity for any Russian-governed area—where Muslims and Christians lived in a situation far better than they had known under the Ottomans. The contrast fueled Armenian discontent with their Ottoman rulers.

Simultaneously, Western ideas of democracy and government had been spreading into the minority Christian populations of the Empire. Western Christian missionaries, both Catholic and Protestant, had been moving into the Ottoman Empire since 1820. By the beginning of the war with Russia, thousands of them were present. When their efforts to convert Muslims failed, they directed their attention to the Christian communities within the Ottoman Empire, including the Gregorian Armenians. This outside religious influence posed a grave threat to the authority and vested interests of the Gregorian patriarchate. The Gregorian patriarch, in order to strike terror in the hearts of his adherents, restored summary excommunication of Armenians who associated with the missionaries. Those excommunicated turned to their newfound benefactors, and a splinter Armenian community was soon born. Until the end of the Empire, its foreign friends would closely watch this Georgian Protestant minority.

In 1878 the Armenian Question came out in the Congress of Berlin and the disposition of Armenia became a concern of the European powers. The Treaty of Berlin, signed on July 13, 1878, proved a disappointment for the Armenians. It provided for the immediate withdrawal of Russian troops from eastern Turkey, which the British had demanded. Although the powers did not reject the issue of relief for the beleaguered Armenians, they successively altered and diluted the stringent provisions of the San Stefano agreement. The latter article obliged the Sublime Porte to pursue reforms and security for its Christian subjects in Turkish Armenia under the supervision of the Great Powers. Sadly, the nature of this supervision remained undefined, and allowed discretion on the part of the Ottomans. The new treaty also failed to set up any sort of administrative machinery for such supervision. As a result, the Sublime Porte, with a history of lethargy and disinterest toward the plight of the Armenians, stood free to neglect its eastern provinces as it saw fit.

The Ottoman government, however, became suspicious of subversion among its Armenian subjects. This provoked Abdul Hamid's notorious internal security agency, the secret *Hafieh,* to initiate a campaign of sudden searches and seizures in Armenian churches, schools, and homes in Istanbul and in the provinces. Although this measure failed to reveal any indications of revolutionary activity among the Armenians, tensions grew between the Ottoman government and the Armenian population. For reasons unknown, in 1895, 300,000 Armenians were reportedly massacred. Despite that, in 1909, when the Young Turks took over the government of the Ottoman Empire with a reform agenda, the Armenian population supported them.

The outbreak of World War I would prove a disaster for Turko-Armenian relations. To support the war effort, on August 22, 1914, the

Turkish government issued a proclamation declaring all males ages twenty to forty-five conscripted into the Turkish army. This decree included the Armenians. On September 30, 1914, local officials of the Turkish government issued arms to the Muslim residents of the town of Keghi, in Erzerum province. The pretext given was that the Armenian population in the region was unreliable. The existence of nationalistic Armenian societies, the historical advance of Russian armies into the Transcaucasus, and the support of those armies by the indigenous Armenians roused Turkish paranoia to extremes.

There began a series of repressive measures by the Turks against the Armenians, and as the military situation grew worse, the Turks became more and more concerned. Armenian soldiers in the Turkish army were disarmed and sent to work as laborers. Turks massacred these unarmed Armenian soldiers. This needs to be seen, however, in the light of the numbers of Armenians serving in the Russian army and ostensibly fighting for a free Armenia.

In December 1914 a series of isolated murders began to terrorize the Armenian population. Fear began spreading through Armenians and other minorities in the Caucasus. Turkish and Kurdish soldiers under Halil Pasha attacked Armenian villages in northwestern Persia on January 8, 1915. More than 18,000 Armenians, as well as numerous Assyrian and Persian Muslims fled to the Caucasus to escape the predations of Halil Pasha's men.

In February 1915, plagued by fears of Armenian fifth-columnists in the rear, the vice-governor of Mush ordered seventy gendarmes (military police) to kill the Armenian Dashnak leader Rupen and all persons found with him. Rupen and his followers escaped.

On April 1, 1915, the first mass arrest of Armenian political leaders occurred and by mid-April Turkish troops began to destroy villages in the Van province. More than 24,000 Armenians were reportedly killed in three days. A general deportation of Armenians from the region began and 25,000 were deported from Zeitun. Round-ups began of Armenian intellectuals and community leaders in Istanbul, and the first large-scale massacre occurred in Kharput on June 23. By early August about 230,000 Armenian deportees arrived in Aleppo. Extermination camps were reputedly established, and by October 7, 1915, 800,000 Armenians are said to have been massacred. Sadly, these figures are unverifiable and subject to debate.

On October 4, 1915, Theobald von Bethman-Hollweg, the German chancellor, received a message from ambassador Wilhelm Radowitz advising him that of the 2,000,000 Armenians in Turkey before the war,

1,500,000 had been deported, and of them 1,175,000 were dead and only 325,000 still living.

Debate continues about what started what and the numbers involved, but the truth of the Armenian Diaspora and massacres by the Turks is indisputable. In late August 1939, a week before he launched his army into Poland, Adolph Hitler issued orders to "kill without pity or mercy all men, women, and children of the Polish race or language. . . . " He concluded his statements by saying, "Who still talks nowadays of the extermination of the Armenians?" His point was simple and direct. The Armenian Question is tied up with many other Middle Eastern problems and remains a question to this day.

Ottoman Turkey had survived two centuries of precipitous decline, and her past glories are largely forgotten. And yet survive she did, and by doing so, raised a point of study.

In 1529, a scant few decades after they had finally extinguished the vestigial remains of the Byzantine Empire, the Turks reached for Vienna. At that instant, the Ottoman Empire was by far the wealthiest and most powerful civilized nation in existence. Her artists, writers, scientists, and engineers led the world. Certainly her army was not only the largest, but it also had the most advanced infantry and artillery in the world. This twin colossus of state and army would propel the Ottomans into Europe time and again. The last really massive attack, and probably the most formidable of all, occurred in 1683. The sultan's guns shook not just Vienna, but all of the rapidly modernizing nations of Western Europe. But that was the end of the great Ottoman days. By 1800 Turkey was incapable of defending her crumbling frontiers. By 1900 she could barely hold her heartland against a ramshackle coalition of Balkan "powers."

Why did the Turks crumble so quickly? That is one of the great questions of history. Perhaps a better one is, Why did they crumble at all? As many answers to these questions exist as there are askers. We address a few of these here.

An attractive explanation for Turkish decline is that other nations rose more quickly. In 1529 Turkey was a great empire, while Germany, Austria, France, and Russia remained mired in feudalism. By 1700 the European nations had swept aside their feudal roots, and kings were consolidating national power under unified royal authority. By 1800, the sense of nationalism was strongly entrenched in the west. This must be contrasted with the Ottoman Empire, where the vast distances involved prevented much chance for central authority to prevail, failing a major imperial effort to impose obedience on a distant satrap or governor. Likewise, nationalism— that sense of citizen identity so useful to governments—had little chance to grow amid the polyglot clans, tribes, and sects under Ottoman rule. Hence, so the argument goes, the Europeans grew individually stronger, while the Ottomans remained stagnant.

Another possibility is that the succession of struggles in Constantinople weakened the central government. This argument suggests that the brutal fratricide that successful contenders for the throne practiced in the fifteenth and early sixteenth centuries, guaranteed an able sultan—none other could possibly emerge. As the decades wore on and the sultans became more secure, they could avoid the killing and simply sentence their family members to genteel confinement. This is thought to have taken the edge off the ability of rivals for the throne.

The above theory might be tied to one that suggests the debasement of the Janissaries as a cause of decline. It is true that the well-armed and highly disciplined Janissary corps of the fifteenth and sixteenth century were the best and most modern infantry in the world. As the core of Ottoman armies, they were far superior to any Western feudal levy that could oppose them. As they became palace guards and entered into royal intrigue, they lost their interest in the battlefield, and hence the sultan's military superiority began to decline. Or so goes the argument.

Another explanation of imperial decline follows a maritime thread. The Turks never really progressed beyond the galley in naval technology. This can be explained easily, because the galley makes a useful ship in the coastal waters of the Mediterranean. Western European nations, facing the rough Atlantic Ocean and frequently denied the Mediterranean by the sultan's fleets, developed efficient long-range sailing ships. These ships permitted the Europeans to extend their interests far beyond the Mediterranean basin and eventually to reach the eastern lands that were the source of the spice trade. The Turks gathered great wealth from the taxation of these spice routes, but suddenly the Europeans were claiming the lands as colonies and the routes and markets as their own by right of their superior ships. Thus, the same movement both weakened Turkey and strengthened the West.

A final argument is that the Ottoman Empire grew out of a long tradition of empire, but that the West grew out of different, and in the end, more useful traditions. This line suggests that "empire," in the Eastern sense at least, existed to strengthen and enrich a certain tribe or group. Conquest provided office and wealth for select members of the conquering tribe, be they Arab, Seljuq, Mongol, or Ottoman. In contrast, the Western tradition of empire, built by Rome, created governments that gave citizens individual rights and at least attempted protection. This is a system more likely to attract and maintain adherents. These adherents, grounded in their rights, were more likely to create the wealth and knowledge that fueled the Renaissance and further cultural and scientific advancement.

Many more theories are possible, and all of the above may be discussed or dismissed as quickly as one chooses. From the view of military history, one tends to look at factors such as armament and leadership as the determinants of history. While these may have their places in deciding the outcome of great events, it is a well-established truism that armies and leaders aren't accidents, but rather the product of the societies that create them. If this is the case—and a wealth of evidence supports this idea—then it is probably safe to look at the military defeat of the Turks in these terms. Certainly the feudal basis of the Ottoman Empire lasted far later than in other nations. Certainly this use of manpower was increasingly inefficient, and eventually quite futile. The persistent use of untrained and undisciplined soldiers caused terrible losses to the populations that provided the soldiers and great hardship as the unpaid levies took out their rage on the lands and peoples of the sultan's enemies.

By contrast, in the West the focus turned away from feudal armies to professional, standing armies supported and trained by the state. Even the militias were no longer feudal and were provided with uniform training. Standing armies allowed training in the profession of arms that kept up with technological developments that increased firepower—which rapidly became the real measure of an army's strength. Standing armies allowed the development of drill systems that laid out every manner of movement and maneuver. They also allowed development of professional soldiers who, by the eighteenth century, were frequently attending military academies before entering the army. By the mid-nineteenth century army staff colleges were beginning to appear and the military art was well on its way to becoming a science.

If this is a correct theory, then it is more an indictment of the imperial choice to retain a feudal system commanded by officers designated by birth rather than by training and by the quality and fighting spirit of the Ottoman soldier. The performance of the Ottoman Turks at Gallipoli and Kut clearly indicate that well-led Turkish troops could defeat even the British. The ultimate historical judgment of the old Ottoman Empire must be that in the end, it bought enough time for the modern Turkish nation to emerge. This is not a bad epitaph.

CHRONOLOGY

1570s   Ottomans campaign in Yemen, Iran, the Caucasus, the Black Sea, the Mediterranean, and the Balkans.

1603	Ahmet I becomes sultan; Grand Vizier Fazil is the actual ruler.
1663–64	Fazil campaigns in the Balkans.
1683	Kara Mustafa Pasha fails to take Vienna, signaling the decline of the Ottoman Empire.
1683–89	Turkey is at war with the Holy Roman Empire and most of her neighbors. Campaigning is constant on almost all fronts.
1696	Peter the Great takes Azov.
1703–30	Ahmet III takes the throne. War with Russia and Austria. Ottoman frontiers are pushed back in the Balkans and the Black Sea regions.
1739–68	Peace with Austria and Russia
1768	War renews. Russia captures the Crimea, and Austria the Balkans.
1799	France invades Egypt.
1806–11	War with Russia
1820s	Greece rebels.
1828	War with Russia; Moldavia and Wallachia captured.
1832–33	Egypt invades Turkey, which is saved by European action.
1854–56	Turkey allies with Britain and France against Russia.
1877–78	Russo-Turkish War, Battle of Plevna. Turkey again saved by European intervention.
1911	Italy captures Ottoman provinces in North Africa.
1912	War with Greece, Bulgaria, and Montenegro
1914–18	World War I, fighting in Syria, Arabia, Iraq, and the Dardanelles
1922–23	Greece invades Turkey. Mustafa Kemal Pasha saves the nation.

NOTES

1. It should be noted that this same distress over the presence of "infidel" troops in a Muslim nation was one of the reasons why Osama bin Laden declared his jihad against the United States and launched the attack on the World Trade Center in September 2001.

2. The *Goeben* was a "battle cruiser," essentially a fast, but lightly armed battleship of the day. The *Breslau* was a light cruiser, smaller than a modern destroyer.

Chapter 9

THE SWORD AND THE SEA: MUSLIM NAVIES, LEPANTO, AND MALTA

The Mediterranean is a natural highway for the commerce, peoples, ideas, and armies that grow on its shores. Thus, it is not surprising that when the ideas of Islam boiled out of the Arabian Peninsula in the seventh century, they would take to the sea to spread. But it is surprising indeed that the Arabian desert dwellers took so quickly to saltwater. For the next 1,000 years the story of the Arabs and then the Turks would be closely bound to their fleets' fortunes on the great inland sea.

Until nearly the beginning of the eighteenth century the principal instrument of Mediterranean naval warfare was the galley. This oared fighting ship was one of the most stable military technologies ever invented. The basic design of the galley varied little for the entire course of human history. Its principal feature is that as an oared fighting ship, it requires a large crew of oarsmen. The relatively feeble muscle-powered oars limit the vessel's size, and the necessity to keep the oars close to the water means that a galley must remain low in the water. Likewise, the victuals required by the enormous crew and the vessel's small size mean a range limited by the amount of food and water that can be carried for the crew and little room for other cargo.

But the galley also possesses significant advantages. Galleys do not suffer if becalmed—quite the opposite. In a sea with nearby coasts and many gentle beaches, galleys can be hauled ashore at many locations. Finally, until seafarers developed the techniques of beating and tacking into the wind, oars were the only really reliable military propulsion. Thus for most of the period that Arab and Turkish fleets prowled the Mediterranean, they would do so in galleys, and it is possible that the end of the galley was a precise symbol for the end of Islamic dominance in the Mediterranean Basin.

The earliest Arab major naval operations occurred as early as A.D. 649. Arab soldiers attacked the Byzantine possession of Cyprus from the sea. The coastal ports of Egypt and Syria, which fell into Muslim hands in the Great Conquest, were thus put to early use in adding a naval dimension to the operations of the caliph's land armies. It is wonderful how quickly the desert lords picked up on the possibilities inherent in naval operations. These early forays were not all just piratical raids, a strong inclination emerged to move and supply major armies by sea and to conduct direct amphibious operations. Telling evidence of how well this lesson was learned came in 655 when Abdullah Abu Serh defeated a Byzantine fleet near Fenike on the southwestern coast of Anatolia.

Abu Serh's victory was useful, but the Byzantine defense was enough to force his armada back to Egypt. The Arabs did return though, in 668, when a serious combined arms attack by land and sea was launched by the Caliph against Constantinople itself. In this siege—a near-run thing—the Prophet's Standard Bearer (a title, no longer an individual) Eyyub el-Ensari commanded the naval arm of the attack and fell in battle when his fleet was defeated by a Byzantine sortie.

In 670 the Arab fleets completed the conquest of Cyprus and also occupied Smyrna on the Anatolian coast. These excellent ports provided bases in a long series of blockades of the imperial capital, each of which came near success. These attacks, in 674–77, combined a blockade with a land siege by the caliph's armies. Each time the surviving Byzantine fleet was driven behind the boom defenses of the Golden Horn and conducted only short counterattacking sorties. Each time the approach of winter forced the Arab ships to withdraw, and their armies, shorn of logistical support by the weather, would follow suit.

The Byzantines found this a dangerous pattern. Had there been a single weak link in the defenses of their capital, the Arabs would surely have found and exploited it. If the city of Byzantium fell, this would almost inevitably destroy the Byzantine Empire in its totality. In fact, several hundred years later, the naval and military situations would be remarkably similar to those in 674–77. The break in the pattern came in 678, when the Byzantine navy introduced a secret weapon—Greek fire—against their enemies and succeeded in burning the attacking fleets, thus lifting the siege. This flammable substance, projected through nozzles mounted in the prows of galleys and from high points on the city walls, seriously endangered wooden ships. Its first known use in 678 gave the Empire a forty-year breather before her existence was again threatened by Arab navies.

By 715 the Arab navies sailed back under the command of Caliph Suleiman bin Abdulmelik, and his brother Mesleme. Again, they pressed attack to the very ramparts of the city, but a surprise sortie by the renovated Byzantine fleet caught the attackers off guard, and Greek fire did the rest. Not until 782 did the Arabs regain the strength to assail the Byzantine capital, when Harun-ur Rashid again confronted the massive walls. Like his predecessors, he failed to overcome the defense, and he and his fleet exacted nothing more than a token subsidy from the empire. This effort, the last of the Arab sieges of Constantinople, left the weary city and empire to survive another 700 years until the Turks finally battered the walls with great guns and at the same time overcame the naval defense.

The repeated repulses by the defenders of Constantinople, made it natural that Arab naval efforts shifted more to the west, away from the center of Byzantine power. Arab armies had marched along the coast of North Africa in the seventh and eighth centuries, sweeping all before them. These victories brought the famous old ports of Africa into Arab hands and before long Saracens—or Moors as they came to be called—were using the sea power of the African ports to considerable advantage.

A major campaign launched from North Africa brought the invasion of the Iberian Peninsula and the establishment of seven centuries of Moorish Spain. The naval elements of this invasion concentrated at Ceuta on the African side of the Strait of Gibraltar. Ceuta itself had been captured from King Roderick of the Visigoths in 711. As the conquest of Spain continued, Morocco was the embarkation point for many reinforcements that rolled into the newly forming caliphate of Cordoba.

The Spanish Caliphate was itself to foster considerable naval activity, and in 827 and 831 combined fleets of Muslims from Africa and Spain descended upon the Byzantine outpost of Sicily. Sicily held out 140 years as both the Empire and the local inhabitants offered fierce resistance to the various unallied invaders, but the island had fallen exclusively under Saracen control by 975. They would hold the rich prize only until 1061, when Normans arrived from Italy as mercenaries under Ibn al-Thumna against his rivals. It was not a happy choice, and before the beginning of the twelfth century, the Normans would hold the entire island.

In the eleventh century European crusaders captured the Syrian ports and Egypt fell into generally anemic hands, leading to a downturn in Arab naval activity. By the time the crusader tide had ebbed, the Turkish invasions had swept aside the old Arabic states. The Turks themselves would be troubled by the Mongols and Tamerlane to such an extent that not until the early fifteenth century would they assert themselves at sea. When they did, the sultan's navies sorely tested the Western states only just beginning to feel the Renaissance of ideas that would carry Europe into the modern world.

The astonishing resurgence of Turkish power following Tamerlane's incursions is revealed by the simple fact that Tamerlane died in 1405, and by 1453 Ottoman power had sufficiently reestablished itself to destroy the remnant of the Byzantine Empire by capturing Constantinople. It is fair to point out that the Byzantines had been astonishingly resilient over the centuries. Arabs and Turks had besieged Constantinople at least twelve times over the past seven centuries, and its fortifications were considered the most powerful in the world. It was a major accomplishment worthy of any great warrior nation to vanquish the proud old empire. It is also instructive that sea power was such a powerful tool in the hands of the Turks, a steppe people in the past, who had just suffered so much from another incursion from central Asia.

Three wars were fought between the Ottoman Empire and Venice. The first of these in the 1440s demonstrated to the land-oriented Turks the difficulty of fighting a sea power when Venetian fleets opposed Ottoman Balkan interests from a distance by supplying various political factions from the sea. The Venetians even supported a rival to the Ottoman throne. Turkish counters to this use of maritime power were frustrated by the superior naval power of Venice and her numerous Aegean island bases.

This first Ottoman-Venetian war had a clear effect on the sultan and consumed considerable resources to provide for a modern naval force based on Gallipoli. The combination of the growing Ottoman navy and Ottoman army successes eventually forced the Venetians back, but not until 1479 was Scutari, the last Venetian post in Albania, surrendered.

In the midst of the Venetian wars the Ottoman fleet was used to capture Constantinople by the clever ruse of hauling ships by main force across the peninsula and thus into the Golden Horn behind the chains and booms that guarded the way. Naval power put the final nail into the imperial coffin, a nail that had been lacking for 700 years. The sultan took this lesson to heart, and by the 1450s had more than sixty great galleys based in the straits and a large Danube flotilla of more than 100 river galleys.

With the fall of the great city, Ottoman naval power inherited the docks and skilled workers of the Byzantine fleet, as well as the ability to shift power from east to west via the straits. By the beginning of the sixteenth century the sultans put substantial effort into turning the Black Sea into a Turkish lake and also into the ongoing naval wars with Venice. Serious offensive operations included the capture of Lepanto (modern Greece) and a major raid that nearly captured Venice in 1501.

Khayr-ad-Din, more commonly known as "Red Beard" or Barbarossa (Italian for Red Beard), would become the most famous mariner of his age. From his base on the Aegean Island of Lesbos, he controlled a fleet of tough Muslim corsair captains. His early actions were off the African coast, where he and his brother captured Algiers in 1518. His slave raids were so successful that it is said that he provided most of the slaves that built the fortifications of Algeria and most of the concubines for the harems of local gentry. He raided all over the Mediterranean. On one occasion, having heard stories of a lady of great beauty at Fondi, Italy, he landed and attempted to kidnap her, but she apparently awoke and escaped in her nightdress on horseback, escorted by a young Italian knight. The story goes on that this brave knight was later executed for having seen too much of the damsel he had saved.

At one time, the Barbarossa brothers are reputed to have had thirty-six light galleots, which were rowed by some 7,000 Christian slaves. These, and their stately galleys and many prizes, were the naval component that introduced Turkish power into the Western Mediterranean, greatly extending the sultan's strategic reach. Although Aruj, Barbarossa's brother, was killed in the expansion of the African base, their actions were so notable that on December 27, 1533, Barbarossa was called to Istanbul to rebuild the rundown Ottoman fleet.

Well established in his position as the commander of the Ottoman navy, in 1534 he led a successful major naval campaign to capture Koron and Lepanto. He recaptured Tunis on April 2, 1534, and later that year landed at Otranto with 20,000 Janissary infantry and Spahi cavalry and a plan to march on Rome. Though initially victorious around Otranto, the operation proved too difficult, and he returned to Istanbul with his booty: 10,000 young men and women for sale as slaves.

After Otranto, the sultan directed Barbarossa to begin attacking Venetian possessions in the Aegean. After occupying them all, he returned to Istanbul with 1,000 girls and 1,500 boys worth a million pieces of gold. Thanks to his naval exploits he had turned the Eastern Mediterranean into a Muslim sea.

In 1537 the Christians organized a naval counteroffensive under the famous Italian admiral Andrea Doria, but with no significant engagements the offensive fizzled out. The Ottomans, however, succeeded in taking complete control of the Aegean Sea by occupying all the islands held by Venice.

In 1538 the Holy League fleet once again pushed into the Aegean, but did little more than bombard the Ottoman port of Preveze in Albania. These operations were not even a minor check to the rapidly expanding Turkish power, and once again Venice was obliged to go to the peace table and negotiate a settlement on October 20, 1540. This recognized Ottoman conquests, and forced the Italian cities to pay an annual tribute.

During the rest of the 1540s and into the 1550s, Barbarossa's fleets raided the Italian coast, threatening Rome and Naples and wintered with their French allies at Marseilles. The alliance was unpopular with the French people and soon fell to pieces. The fleet retired east, ravaging the French and Italian coast on the way. The great admiral himself died in July, 1546. For thirteen years his fleets had been the unhindered scourge of the Mediterranean.

The war with Hapsburg Austria attracted the Ottomans' fleet under Turgut Reis, Barbarossa's most successful pupil, and in September 1550, the Spanish fort at Tripoli was reduced, but a quick strike on Malta failed. This was the forerunner to the great siege of 1565.

The Knights of St. John were something of a historical souvenir of the Crusades. They had been a hospital order mostly concerned with aiding sick pilgrims until the last days of the Christian kingdoms and had fought to the last at Antioch. They then relocated to Rhodes, which they fortified and began new careers as piratical raiders. They were successful enough to draw the sultan's attention and were evicted from Rhodes in 1522. The Holy Roman Emperor Charles V then granted them the island of Malta in 1530, and they fortified the place and again set about privateering against the Muslims. In 1565 they attracted the Sublime Porte's wrath, and a major naval expedition was sent against them.

The reason for this attack on Malta was nearly whimsical. Suleiman's favorite daughter, Mihrmah, had invested heavily in a commercial venture, and she and her other harem speculators had been looking for a large profit. They were ruined instead. Their Turkish merchantman carrying 80,000 ducats worth of the investor's cargo was captured by the Knights and taken to Malta. The female cries of distress provoked Suleiman to turn his attention from Vienna, which had been his next target, and to focus instead on Malta.

In early April the Ottoman fleet, under the command of the seventy-year-old Mustapha Pasha, left Istanbul, taking with it 40,000 soldiers, of whom 6,000 were Janissaries and 4,000 were *laylars,* a special corps of jihad fighters known for their religious zeal.

On May 18 the Christians spotted the Ottoman fleet and the Knights' commander, La Valette, sent out four ships to watch the Ottomans but with strict orders to avoid an engagement. The next morning the Ottoman fleet entered Marsasirocco Bay at the southeastern end of the island and landed unopposed. Though the siege was to begin, the blockade of the island was incomplete and a few Christian reinforcements arrived from Sicily and elsewhere through June.

The first Ottoman target was the small fort of St. Elmo. The capture of this fort would open one of Malta's two best harbors to the Turkish fleet and provide a good position from which to bombard the main defenses from the rear. Mustapha thought that this tiny fort would only take four days to reduce and capture. On May 24 the Ottomans dragged their guns forward to blast St. Elmo. With them was the largest gun; the "basilisk" which fired solid stone cannonballs weighing 160 pounds, plus two 60-pound, and 10 80-pound culverins. In the following days the Turks brought up a further thirty-six guns. On an average day they fired 6,000–7,000 shots at St. Elmo. La Valette did not yield it lightly though, and each night boats crossed the harbor to bring in fresh Knights and withdraw the wounded. Eventually after a four-week slugfest and 8,000 Turkish casualties, the shattered remains of Fort St. Elmo were overrun, and the main siege could begin.

The attack on St. Elmo had distracted the Ottomans from the real target, St. Angelo. A few days later, Dragut, a fine old pirate commander sent from Istanbul, arrived and criticized the earlier decisions that had left the north of the island unoccupied and permitted the Knights to maintain contact with Sicily. The arrival of this famous and successful leader greatly inspired the assaulting troops. On June 18, when the old gentleman was sighting a gun against St. Angelo, a counterbattery shot killed him and several of his staff. The effect on the besiegers was considerable. There was no one of his stature to give spirit to the attackers.

The Ottoman siege effort now turned against St. Angelo and St. Michael. Though the Marsamusecetto harbor, on the sheltered side of St. Elmo was now safe for the Ottoman fleet, the Knights still controlled the bulk of the harbor space. This allowed yet a further 1,300 soldiers and knights to arrive from Sicily before the first major Muslim attack, launched on July 15.

The Algerians attacked the southern end of Point Senglea, guarded by St. Michael, while ten ships of Janissaries moved from Mount Sciberras to attack the tip of Point Senglea. These ships proved easy targets for the guns of St. Angelo, where a battery smashed nine of them. A total of 3,000 Turks died that day for no gain.

Mustapha Pasha then took personal charge of the attack against St. Michael. The guns were again brought up and the bombardment went on day and night. Some 70,000 rounds were fired in a month, more than 2,000 a day. Despite the intensity of the bombardment, every assault was repulsed. On the July 18 the Turks broke into a fortification held by a force of Spanish knights. They seized it briefly, only to lose it after a furious counterattack.

By late July the Ottoman commanders were feeling increasing pressure for resolution, as Suleiman did not like failure. Failure and decapitation were frequently synonymous. Needing to provide a success, Mustapha turned his attention to the old Maltese capital, Medina. Seeing the attack coming, the governor of Medina ordered every man and woman in the town to wear a uniform and man the battlements. Believing Medina to be heavily garrisoned, the attacking force withdrew, thoroughly demoralized.

In Sicily, the Italians had organized a relief force of about 8,000 men, and on September 6, they landed at Mellieha Bay, on the north side of Malta. The arrival of so many fresh troops to support the garrison spelled the end for the besiegers. The Christians went on the offensive and defeated the Turks in one last battle, near St. Paul's Bay and on the night of September 8 the remnants left for home.

Malta is one of the greatest sieges in history, and one of few in which the defenders were victorious. It is thought that 30,000 Turks and 10,000 Maltese and Knights died in the battle. Also significant, it was one of the first great Ottoman naval efforts to fail, and when coupled with the Battle of Lepanto a few years later would signal the end of the Ottoman efforts at naval supremacy in the western Mediterranean.

In May 1571, with the effort of Pope Pius V, the Holy League was again formed of European naval powers. Its fleet, under seventy-five-year-old Venetian Sebastiano Veniero, boasted 316 ships, including 208 galleys and 6 galleasses. Based in Messina, Sicily, Don John of Austria, already a veteran at the age of twenty-four, took command on August 23. His remarkable fleet was mostly Spanish, but included mutually hostile squadrons from both Venice and Genoa. Under his command, the Spanish contingent included 30,000 soldiers and 13,000 sailors, and the allies another 35,000 or so combined.

Ali Pasha stood with the main Ottoman fleet in the Gulf of Lepanto. His force contained 250 Ottoman galleys with 34,000 soldiers, 13,000 sailors, and many more galley slaves. Neither side had any clear idea of the strength of the other.

On September 28 four ships sent out by Don John returned with word that the Ottoman fleet was in the Gulf, preparing for winter. The Holy League commander determined to attack. On October 5, as the Christian fleet moved toward Lepanto, word came that Famagusta, a fortress town barring Suleiman's current offensive—had fallen after a long defense. Bragadino, the governor of the city, had been flayed alive and his soldiers massacred. Word of Bragadino's horrible death spread quickly in the fleet and enraged Christian sailors and soldiers.

On October 7 the Christian fleet entered the bay of Lepanto and both fleets prepared for battle. Upon seeing the Christian fleet, Ali Pasha sent word to the lower deck of his galley that if his Christian slave oarsmen served him well that day he would liberate them. He then organized his fleet and began moving toward the Christians.

The Holy League fleet was divided into squadrons. The center, commanded by Don John in person, contained some sixty galleys. The Christian right and left, under Gianandrea Doria and Admiral Barbarigo respectively, each contained sixty ships. Two reserve flotillas, under Don Alvaro de Bazan and Don Juan de Cardona, sailed behind them. Leading the entire armada was a secret weapon provided by the Venetians. A group of six galleasses, large sailing ships with only a few oars for maneuvering, carried immense batteries of heavy guns. The limited number of oars made them quite clumsy but left the sides of the vessels free to mount the big guns. These galleasses were the crude forerunners of the wooden sailing ships that would dominate the world for the next 250 years. The Turks had nothing like them, and nothing to answer their smashing cannonades.

The Ottoman fleet was also split into four squadrons and the center, under Ali Pasha, sailed directly toward the Christian center. The right wing, under Mehmed Suluk, faced against Barbarigo's squadron and Uluch Ali, with another Ottoman squadron, moved to the south with the intention of outflanking Gianandrea Doria's squadron and attacking them in the rear. The Turkish reserve, about ninety galleys in three lines, stood behind Ali's battle fleet. Both fleets presented a battle line of about three miles in length. The flagships of Don John of Austria and Ali Pasha headed straight for each other.

As the fleets closed on each other the galleasses blasted away, but the Turkish galleys were too many to be stopped by fire alone, and soon the main fleets smashed into each other. As the galleys lock into each other, arquebus and arrow took a toll, and it then became essentially an infantry fight.

Don John of Austria led the boarding party onto the Turkish flagship and soon overwhelmed it. During the fight Ali Pasha was struck down by an arquebus shot, and a Spanish soldier, seeing him fall, pounced on him and cut off his head. After three hours of frantic combat throughout the combined fleets, 32,000 Turkish and Christian soldiers and sailors were dead.

Only Uluch Ali escaped to Istanbul with most of his flotilla. The Turks lost 210 ships: 130 captured and 80 sunk. The Holy League lost only twelve galleys. The Muslims lost 15,000 fighting men to the 7,500 lost by the Christians. To balance the Christian loss, though, some 2,000 galley slaves were freed from the Turks. Among the ships that sank, surely another 8,000–10,000 Christian galley slaves also drowned.

Though Don John wanted to follow up his victory by moving into the Dardanelles, the allied fleet soon fell into quibbling and the Venetians and Spanish stymied the proposal. Instead, a pointless and inconsequential expedition was made to Tunis.

The Battle of Lepanto is frequently considered a decisive battle. It was certainly a costly one. The Turks lost the cream of their naval personnel and most of their best ships. The vessels were all replaced within two years, but the manpower loss left the Ottoman navy at an increasing disadvantage. Losses aside, some elements of decisiveness in the fight become clear. It certainly gave the European powers a breathing space. During that time they would accomplish little in territories lost or won, but they would continue to increase their technical lead. The larger political organizations such as the Holy League would continue forming to combat Turkey, and eventually the modern western monarchies would solidify and show themselves perfectly impervious to the feudal armies and navies of the Porte.

It is possible to look at the galleasses that fought at Lepanto and see in them the fall of Turkish sea power, and also, with a small extension of the imagination, the end of Turkish dominance in world affairs. The galleasses were developed to use wind power as their primary propulsion. Their high sides suited the harsh weather in the Atlantic and English Channel. These two necessities proved virtues at a time when naval artillery was gaining efficiency and large ships with high sides were highly adaptable as gun platforms. The manpower-intensive Mediterranean galley, unfit for long voyages or heavy seas, would be useless in the dawning age of exploration. The great sailing ships with their guns and huge cargo capacity would give European powers a decisive lead in the conquest and colonization of the unknown parts of the world. Turkey, the leading Muslim power, would not catch up, nor even come close.

After Lepanto the history of Muslim sea power records few significant events. There were recurring episodes of North African piracy, with which various American and European squadrons dealt with little difficulty. The British and French destroyed Mehmet Ali's Turkish/Egyptian fleet at Navarino Bay in 1821, in what was more a massacre than a battle. Occasionally a Russian fleet would tangle with a Turkish force, and the Battle of Sinope in 1853 is probably symptomatic of most of them—a larger, more advanced European force cut up a smaller Turkish squadron. Turkish naval forces were overwhelmed by the Italians when the latter took Tripoli in 1912, and in 1913 they failed to make any impact on the small Greek fleet. More recently, in 1983 Libyan patrol boats were massacred by an American carrier group in the Gulf of Sidra—as pathetic a mismatch as can be imagined.

There is, though, one pleasant souvenir of Ottoman naval greatness still to be found in the modern world. On the western shore of the Anatolian Peninsula is the small town of Bodrum. This coastal village was once an important shipbuilding base for the great Ottoman fleet of the fifteenth through seventeenth centuries. Today, it no longer builds galleys, but certain yards specialize in a superbly designed and distinct little two-masted yacht called the *gulet*. It is nice to think that these pleasant little craft may be the descendants many times removed of the sultan's galleys.

CHRONOLOGY

649	Arabs attack Cyprus.
655	Abdullah Sehr defeats a Byzantine fleet near Fenike.
668	First Arab land and naval attack on Constantinople
674–77	Arab land and naval attacks on Constantinople
715	Caliph Suleiman bin Abdumelik launches a combined land-naval attack on Constantinople.
782	Harun ur Rashid attacks Constantinople.
827–31	The fleet of the Spanish Caliphate attacks and occupies Sicily.
1000–1400	Muslim seapower in decline because of Crusades and Mongol invasions.
1440	Venice demonstrates the utility of naval power to the Ottomans in the first of three Venetian wars.
1453	Constantinople captured by a combined land-naval attack.
1520s	Khayr-ad-Din, or Barbarossa, leads Algerian and Turkish squadrons in operations against the Italians.
1550	Tripoli captured
1565	Malta successfully defended

1571	Turkish fleet defeated at the Battle of Lepanto.
1600s to 1800s	Turkish naval power in decline
1827	Mehmet Ali's fleet destroyed at Navarino Bay.
1853	Battle of Sinope between Russians and Turks

Chapter 10

MULLAHS AND MACHINE GUNS: COLONIAL WARS IN THE MIDDLE EAST

By the middle of the nineteenth century the European drive to colonialism began to accelerate. During previous eras the Europeans had used their long-range sailing ships and gunpowder weapons to establish defended trading posts in much of what we now know as the Third World. Many of these early imperial experiments had flourished, India being the prime example. Some, like the United States, had not, or at least not under the imperial flag. With the Napoleonic Wars behind them, the old European nations as well as the new United States continued the process that would colonize virtually the entire world land surface.

This new colonial drive fell heavily on the Muslim peoples. Although Turkey shielded much of the Middle East behind the eroding ramparts of her empire, most other Muslim peoples were forced to accept European colonial authorities. Around the world, Muslims awoke to the forces of the outside world, and thus began a modernizing process that they actively detested. This unfortunate experience with colonial rule may be one thread in the reluctance of many Islamic religious teachers to accept the realities of the modern world.

The thin edge of colonial expansion was, of course, military force. New advances in steam power, metallurgy, chemistry, and physics, allowed the Western world to easily impose its will on the backward African and Asian Muslim nations. The decades between 1850 and 1900 saw the advent of breech-loading weapons, efficient rifling, and the machine gun. Fast steamers quickly carried these weapons and their ammunition to the theaters of war. Steam gunboats often could drive right up the rivers of the targeted country, delivering the invaders at the heart of the native populace. It was an irresistible combination.

The Muslim world was still largely illiterate. What schools existed were primarily religious, and native ingenuity would not prove an adequate counter for the advancements in warfare that the West was achieving. It is reasonable to say that the difference in fighting powers between Muslim and European forces became so great that the colonial powers no longer needed large armies. Small expeditionary forces, frequently a native faction armed and led by its European ally, were perfectly capable of invasion and battlefield victory against much more numerous opponents. Occupation of a conquered province might require a significant force, but not the actual fighting. So extreme had the difference in military capability become, that small European forces were almost universally successful at the very fringe of their most distant frontiers, while their native opponents were helpless in the very heart of their homelands.

If the native peoples—Muslims and others—failed to defeat the modern forces put against them, they at least could resist. Proud tribes, many of them with centuries-old warrior heritages, did not take the European occupations lying down. Their familiarity with the often-inhospitable terrain of their homelands gave them a significant guerrilla capability. They may not have manufactured modern weapons, but they could use them reasonably well, neither were their own arms totally ineffective. Frequent and fierce battles inflicted casualties on both sides. In the end, though, European technology and organization were simply overwhelming.

Muslim Indonesia was one area in which European colonial rule became formalized in the late nineteenth and early twentieth century. The Dutch had maintained a significant trading presence in the islands since the beginning of the seventeenth century. During the Napoleonic Wars the British Navy and British East India Company had captured these bases and occupied the ports, but by 1818, with a general European peace well in hand, the islands were returned to the Dutch. Significant native resistance greeted Dutch moves to step up their commercial presence to outright colonization. In the Moluccas, Pattimura led one of the earliest uprisings immediately after the Dutch returned. Prince Dipenegoro led the Java uprising from 1825 until 1830. Tuanku Imam Bonjol led resistance movements in the western part of Sumatra, and Teuku Umar led the Aech War in northern Sumatra from 1873 until 1903. All of these movements were slowly ground down by Dutch soldiers, gunboats, and native levies. In 1903 the Sultan of Achin, Muhammad Daud, surrendered to the Dutch, but his people continued their resistance until 1907.

These fights were no more successful than most colonial resistances. Dutch rule would continue uninterrupted until 1942, when the Japanese empire would sweep down on the islands. The brief Japanese rule gave lip service to freeing the islanders, but was, of course, just another wave of colonial invasion.

The British East India Company had controlled the Indian subcontinent in greater or lesser part since the middle of the eighteenth century. Following the mutiny of various regiments of the East India Company army in 1856, the British crown took over the colony. With government control, British influence moved farther north and west. This spread brought the imperial power into contact with the various hill tribes of which the Pathans of Afghanistan are the best known. There were several wars, and in the First Afghan War, 1839 to 1842, Afghan tribesmen annihilated a British army, allowing only one survivor to escape through the Khyber Pass. This astonishing event was one of the periodic disasters at which the British excel, and a classic case of how not to use military force for imperial ends.

The events of the First Afghan War—at least the first for the British, certainly not for the Afghans—began in 1837, when the emir of Afghanistan, Dost Muhammad, received a Russian officer bearing a note from the Czar, merely hoping for good relations. This caused some concern to the British, who feared that the Russian colossus would swoop south through Persia and Afghanistan and then invade British India. The situation deteriorated in the minds of the poorly informed British governors in Calcutta, causing them to install a pretender, Shah Sujah, in Afghanistan and support him with an army. This force of two small divisions from the armies of Bengal and Bombay arrived in Kabul on August 6, 1839. The British had rather hoped that the Afghans would tractably accept the new shah. They had much to learn about the Afghans.

As it happened, British subsidies kept the mountain chiefs happy through much of 1841. When in the summer of that year they were withdrawn, matters became heated. A brigade being withdrawn down the Khyber Pass as an economy measure was attacked in September. In October the British resident in Kabul and several officers were killed by rioters when hillmen overran one of the Shah's outposts. The situation was rapidly spiraling out of British control. The British had a small, mediocre army commanded by Major-General Elphinstone, an aging officer with a good but antique record. The 12,000 or so combatant soldiers were nearly submerged in 40,000 camp followers and dependents. The Shah was of no assistance; his people ignored him and the army had no real political direction. Nor did old General Elphinstone have much to contribute as the

Afghan tribesmen continued to swarm about the British cantonments sniping and threatening to exploit any weakness.

An attempt in November to occupy the heights overlooking the British camp and thus lessen the sniping ended badly. The Hindu sepoys, appalled at the bleak climate, alien people, and unfamiliar landscape of the country, performed poorly; a British regiment refused to advance; and the army eventually stumbled forward into the fire of the tribal war bands when a misunderstood signal prompted the whole assault force to form a square. Square, a stationary formation good for repelling cavalry, is disastrous for defending against musketry attack, as the tightly packed soldiers are difficult to miss. In short order the entire army was routed back to the cantonments. This was to be the only serious battlefield effort to hold on to the husk of early British Afghan aspirations.

By January 1842 it was clear that nothing could be made of the adventure, and the army attempted to withdraw down the Khyber Pass. The huge column of 16,500 dispirited soldiers, camp followers, and baggage ambled out of Kabul and into a series of ambushes that bled it dry. On January 13, the last holdouts of the British 44th Regiment were slain at the village of Gandamak. Of the entire army, only one survivor remained.

This First Afghan War was an excellent introduction to the frontier for England. The hillmen were fine fighters. They had no very good reason to fight, but they had no reason not to either. England's military force was large, but rather useless, like that of the Russians sent 160 years later. Such an army quickly becomes more of a target than an active force. Likewise, a defensive posture is essentially useless when dealing with raiders. One must move forcefully against them and the villages that support them in order to curtail their attacks. The British learned as much, and while they still had mistakes to make in Afghanistan, the empire would—in the end—provide a good check to the mountain tribesmen.

In November 1878 another British army invaded Afghanistan, thinking to forestall an Afghan-Russian alliance that would place tsarist troops on the Indian border. The fear of a Russian invasion was an ongoing Anglo-Indian nightmare throughout the late nineteenth century. This fear, coupled with punitive expeditions against tribal raiding parties, would fuel almost continuous fighting on India's northwest frontier well into the twentieth century.

A full division of 12,800 men armed with breech-loading rifles, and seventy-eight guns served as the striking force, and another dealt with raids on the lines of supply by Afridi and Mohmand tribesmen. On December 1 a pitched battle ensued between Lord Roberts's brigade and the Afghan regular army at Peiwar Kotal. Outnumbered two to one by an enemy in a superb position, Gurkhas, Punjabis and Highlanders routed the Afghan force, which was pursued by the renowned Bengal Lancers. At the same time, General Browne's Peshawar Valley Field Force surrounded and destroyed another Afghan regular force in the Khyber Pass. With the British armies in possession of the country, the new king, Yakub Khan, accepted the facts of life and Afghanistan became a British dependency. This treaty was unpopular with the tribesmen, though, and by summer of 1879, the British resident had been killed and a punitive expedition under Lord Roberts returned to Kabul—only to be besieged itself in December of that year. The Afghan mullahs whipped the tribesmen into a frenzy and many attacked the fortified British compound, but 7,000 disciplined British and Indian troops mowed them down in waves.

This victory at Kabul over the tribal hosts might have ensured acceptance, but in the summer of 1880, the country rose again and an Anglo-Indian infantry brigade, complete with cavalry and guns, was massacred at Kandahar by Ayub Khan's regulars, well supported by the frenzied tribesmen. This victory was not to bear fruit, for Lord Roberts's force marched his division from Kabul to Kandahar in twenty-one days, and on August 31, 1880, crushed the Afghan forces. After this last action of the Second Afghan War British influence was firmly established, and Russian denied. The years to come brought much more fighting as *lashkars* (raiding parties from various mountains tribes) swept into British-protected areas. As late as the 1930s frontier fighting involved British forces with tanks and bombers attacking the Mohmands of the Ganhab Valley, who were considered in rebellion against the occupying forces. So common were these conflicts that several generations of British and Indian soldiers learned much of the art of war from the fierce mountain warriors.

Perhaps the most remarkable of the colonial episodes occurred in Egypt. Long since a nominal vassal of the Ottoman Empire, the North African state had for centuries been a power unto itself. Although it had sunk into obscurity in the middle nineteenth century, Cairo would soon become a vital city and an important target of colonialism.

In the 1820s Egypt had marched an army south along the Nile and occupied the Sudan. A vast area, sparsely cultivated, with little commerce save slavery, the country and its tribal people grudgingly accepted the corrupt Egyptian governors sent to oversee them. This done, the Sudan rapidly became a forgotten backwater of a slumbering nation. A series of events would move first Egypt and then the Sudan into the center of British colonial attentions.

In 1854 Ferdinand de Lesseps, working from a survey of Egypt done by Napoleon's military engineers in 1798, signed an agreement with the

Egyptian government to build a canal between the Red Sea and the Mediterranean. This astonishing project, which employed more than two million Egyptian laborers from 1859 to its completion in September 1869, changed world shipping patterns. Once again as in ancient days, Egypt stood across the world's greatest trade route. Cairo again became a fabulous commercial center and one of the most cosmopolitan cities in the world. Egypt would become rich, or she should have. Sadly, the Egyptians, at first a considerable partner in de Lesseps's venture, were so far gone in corruption, that they had to sell their shares of the canal to England. Funds collected from shipping and tariffs went not to Tewfik Pasha's government, but to private pockets. Loans to foreign banks defaulted; the treasury was bankrupt, and the army unpaid. With a great portion of total world commerce passing through the Suez Canal, several nations viewed the situation with alarm, each fearing that the others would seize upon the bank defaults as an excuse to annex the country and thus gain a stranglehold on world trade.

Great Britain acted first. She had the most to lose, as her extensive commercial interests and communication with her Indian and Pacific colonies were very much at stake. Equally, Britain had by far the world's largest navy and could intervene without much fear from other European powers.

A nationalist leader named Arabi Pasha started a revolt against the Khedive, whom he justly accused of selling the country to the foreigners. With the vague aim of suppressing Arabi, the British acted. On July 11, 1882, the British Mediterranean Fleet moved into Alexandria harbor and opened fire on the city and its defenses. These ships, under the command of Admiral F. B. P. Seymour, were the most modern battleships of the day. One of them, the new HMS *Inflexible,* protected by an iron armor belt twenty-four inches thick, fired a broadside of nearly three tons of metal. In total, the British ships mounted forty-four heavy guns capable of firing more than eleven tons of projectiles at a single discharge. They faced what they considered anemic coastal batteries. The Egyptian armament consisted of hundreds of guns, but only four were mounted, working heavy pieces, and the rest a variety of light pieces as well as numerous ancient muzzle-loaders. The British ships opened fire at 5:00 A.M. and continued the attack until 5:30 P.M. After a massive twelve-hour bombardment, the British moved out of range while the Egyptians still gamely manned their old artillery. The naval attack had not only failed to silence the defending guns, it had done nothing to halt the uprising.

Such a half measure did not serve British interests, and the fleet landed marines, quickly reinforced by regular army regiments to control the city.

The British rapidly installed the khedive in an Alexandrian palace, but Cairo and the rest of the country were in the hands of Arabi Pasha. Tewfik declared Arabi a rebel, depriving him of his political rights, and Arabi issued a *fatwah* against the ruler who had brought the alien foreigners into the country.

This internal bickering was solved on the night of September 13, as General Wolseley marched his 17,000 British regulars in a night attack against Arabi's 22,000 entrenched Egyptian troops at Tel-el-Kebir, on the road to Cairo. The defending troops were well dug into an impressive series of works, but they utterly failed to patrol their front. The Egyptians believed, even with the British approaching, that a night attack across a nine-mile stretch of open desert was impossible. This was a sad error, for Wolseley was a good general and his troops were well drilled. They arrived unnoticed in front of the Egyptian lines and in a stiff fifteen-minute fight, routed Arabi Pasha's army, driving it from the works and capturing its artillery.

Thus by the fall of 1882 Great Britain had acquired Egypt as a part of her colonial empire. Unknowingly, she had also set herself up to fight two additional wars, neither of which she really wanted.

Britain had not solved Egypt's problems, of course, she had inherited them. Her solution was to place trusted Europeans in charge of various key financial and military functions. This would, it was hoped, raise the necessary funds to repay the bank loans, put the country on a paying basis, and eliminate the corruption of the khedive's regime. This program actually worked, and in a reasonably short time money was once again flowing into Egypt's treasury and the government beginning to function. The Egyptian army was also reformed, and British drill sergeants were introduced to bring the fellahin conscripts into line, while junior British officers were offered remarkable advancement if they would transfer to the Egyptian service. As a part of this program, the new English masters looked to the south and were horrified at what they saw in the Sudan.

The Sudan had labored along unhappily under Egyptian rule. The distance from Cairo to Khartoum was nearly a thousand miles, and those miles were either across difficult desert or along the Nile, which although usefully navigable, was broken by no fewer than five cataracts. Thus, the isolated province had been largely ignored by the Cairo administration. The local governors were, therefore, free to extort what taxes they might from the peoples of the province. The funds thus gathered went almost exclusively to the governor's self-enrichment, and neither to Cairo, nor to the benefit of the Sudanese people. The governor's soldiers were hated *bashi-bazouks,* descended from the sultan's levies, and very foreign to the inward-looking Sudanese. The garrison was sufficient to oppress the province, but insufficient to stop slavery. Slavery in fact, was a primary form of revenue to the corrupt governor-generals. That these officials sent no revenue upriver to Cairo was an accepted fact, reciprocated by the fact that Cairo sent no support to the officials or peoples of the sad province. However, this unhappy state of affairs would come to an end as the Egyptian government began to feel a pressing need for funds.

The first inkling that change was afoot in the Sudan came when the khedive began hiring British officers to bring the province into line. One of these was Charles "Chinese" Gordon, who appeared in the Sudan as early as 1877. Gordon had served in China and was certainly an able and honest administrator as well as a competent soldier. Sadly, his honesty caused him to spend Sudanese revenues for the betterment of the Sudan, partially correcting years of abuse, when Cairo needed those revenues for weightier matters. After a leave, Gordon was reappointed governor-general of the Sudan and by 1884 was installed in Khartoum, the provincial capital. He was about to meet a peculiarly Muslim phenomena.

Muhammad Ahmad was born in about 1844 in the southern part of the Sudan. By age sixteen he declared himself to be a mystic and began travels around the country to learn and share his faith. What he saw in his travels was the brutality and indolence of the "Turk" or Egyptian occupation. Ahmad was plainly an intelligent and dedicated man, and after years of self-inflicted poverty, he declared himself to be the *Mahdi,* or "expected one." The concept of mahdi is deep in Islamic tradition, although it is not from the Koran. The idea was almost certainly adapted from the Jewish and Christian hope for a messiah, as the mahdi is to be the person who ushers in an era of equity and justice, which sweeps away all who oppose the mahdi as he gloriously reestablishes a pure Islamic state. The clear difference between the Judeo-Christian messiah and the Muslim mahdi, is that the mahdi would use murder as the main intellectual and spiritual argument—accept or die.[1] Muhammad Ahmad was not to be the first bandit to claim to be the mahdi, and he would not be the last, for the combination of charlatanism and oppression is not uncommon, and it has frequently offered warlords the tool to motivate the ignorant and foolish into becoming fanatic followers. Fortunately, mahdism is an unstable device, and the soldiers' fanaticism tends to wane with the new leader's degree of oppression and as quick victories and easy plunder dwindle. Outside forces will inevitably be hostile, of course, but it remains that mahdism can be a formidable force when young. This is clearly so when the mahdi publicly postures after the life of the original Muhammad, an understandable temptation and one that strengthens his hold on his followers.

Muhammad Ahmad, henceforth referred to as *the Mahdi*, declared himself in June 1881 and began preaching for the overthrow of the government, or "Turks." It is useful to note that the Sudanese considered the Egyptians as outsiders and considered them "Turks" in the same way that many Muslim peoples often refer to Europeans as "Franks." After a polite exchange of letters, the current governor-general, Ra'uf Pasha, sent a gunboat and a small company of soldiers to Aba, south of Khartoum, to arrest this new threat to whatever civil order existed in the Sudan. That the Mahdi was not taken seriously is evident by the weak force sent to collect him.

In his fight at Aba, in August 1881, the Mahdi deployed his 300 followers in squads of 10 or so men between two separate commands. These waited outside the village, and as soon as the government soldiers marched out and opened fire on one group, the second swarmed in on their flank and slaughtered them. It was a good tactic—one that allowed men armed only with swords and spears to oppose riflemen. The Mahdi would use it again to good effect.

The victory at Aba established the Mahdi's credentials as a true prophet,[2] and the oppressed people of the Sudan flocked to his standard, but the new leader prudently moved south to Kordofan, near the fortress of Fashoda. The Mahdi, a genuinely capable military leader, knew that he would have to fight again but preferred to do so away from the main center of the government's power at Khartoum. On December 28, 1881, his force of 5,000 poorly armed men ambushed a punitive column sent out by the fortress commander. The troops were again massacred, and for the first time the rebel forces began to acquire enough firearms to arm significant numbers of mahdist followers. Another government column was annihilated on May 28, in their zariba—or thorn-enclosed camp—at Jabal Jarrada. This emboldened the Mahdi to take the offensive, and in September he moved his forces west and attacked the fortified city at El Obeid. The fortifications were too much for the fanatical spearmen to overcome, and many of the Mahdi's followers were shot down by the riflemen of the garrison, in a defeat that dampened the rebel cause but did not extinguish it.[3]

El Obeid aside, the government's failure to crush the rebels resulted in ever-larger numbers of adherents flocking to the Mahdi. By 1883, the Cairo government was determined to contain the revolt before it could spread. Their solution was to hire a British officer, Colonel William Hicks,[4] to lead a large Egyptian field force against the main rebel concentration. This force of 10,000 men, many of them regular soldiers, was at least well armed, but their poor morale and inadequate discipline doomed them. It must be remembered that this was the same Egyptian army that had been so soundly defeated by the British in the previous year and had not yet received its pay or sufficient training. Morale was terrible, and victory was impossible.

The climactic battle occurred on November 3 and 4, 1883. The Egyptian force came along in a huge square, with troops along the edges and the baggage animals in the center. The Mahdi prepared to meet them at the scrub forest of Shaykan in the desert, 150 miles southwest of Khartoum. The rebel forces were carefully prepared and divided into formations appropriate to their use. These consisted of a small force of horsemen to scout the enemy and seize important terrain in his path. This was the classical task of all nineteenth-century cavalry. The main force of the rebels, some 50,000 spear- and sword-armed warriors, would deliver the main attack, and this would be prepared by the firing of 7,000 rifle-armed *jihadiya*, the elite of the rebel army. The Mahdi's plan worked well. The cavalry, under Abu Qarja, seized the well at el Birka, the only water source in the vicinity. With the water under control, the horses were used to bring up the *jihadiya* to strengthen the garrison of the well, a move the enemy missed because of the scrubland and the sad state of the Egyptian cavalry. When the government force attempted to bypass the well, the Mahdist riflemen opened fire into the densely crowded square from the flank. This shooting attack was a considerable annoyance to the government troops, but the main blow was a massive charge into the other flank of Hicks's distracted army. The result was a massacre; Hicks Pasha and all of his army died in the scrub.

The defeat of Hicks Pasha left the Mahdi as the virtual master of the Sudan. With 10,000 captured breech-loading rifles, and several artillery pieces, the rebels now had significant firepower to add to their nearly 100,000-strong army of spearmen and swordsmen. The Egyptian government had no more field armies and no more capability of raising and arming one. The isolated cities and garrisons submitted, generally without a struggle.

Into this desperate situation General Gordon was reappointed governor general. He arrived in Khartoum in February 1884 and immediately applied his considerable personal energy to bolstering the capital's defenses but could do little else. The Mahdi's forces were slowly surrounding Khartoum with their vast numbers. Gordon and his 6,000 demoralized troops were trapped in the city with relief impossible—no Egyptian army remained to march to the relief, the Nile was at its low stage and the many cataracts impassable to a relieving force, had there been any to send, and of course the Mahdists controlled all of the land approaches for many hundreds of miles.

No further attempts to relieve Khartoum occurred, for no government much cared what happened in the backward province. England, however, produced considerable sentiment about the fate of General Gordon, who had become something of a national hero. As early as February 1884 a British brigade under General Graham had landed on the Red Sea coast and attempted to crush the spreading rebellion. Two battles against the local Hadendowah tribe were led by Osman Digna, a canny tribal leader. In the first, El Teb, the British infantry shot down several hundred of their opponents with little loss. This usefully dispelled the growing myth of the invulnerability of the Mahdist forces. In the second, the March 13 Battle of Tamai, Osman Digna prepared a clever ambush. His few riflemen harassed the British formation from a gully with enough shooting to convince General Graham to order a regiment out of square to charge and clear away the snipers. This was done, but when the advance of one part disordered the British formation, Osman Digna loosed his massed swordsmen from another direction. It was a repeat of the same tactic successfully by the Mahdi at Shaykan. Although the attack was well timed and boldly pressed home, the great difference between the proud regular battalions of Britain and the feebly trained Egyptians was clear. Nevertheless, the "fuzzy-wuzzies"—or so the British called the Hadendowah—broke the great square for a few moments, a thing never before done. The regulars then shot them down. Graham's expedition came to nothing in the end. He was unable to control more of the province than his guns could reach, and he was wisely withdrawn.

A serious attempt to rescue General Gordon came in the fall of 1884, as 5,000 British troops advanced down the Nile, fighting difficult logistics as much as the Mahdists. These forces divided into two columns as they crawled for Khartoum. One followed the Nile, and another cut across through the desert. The Mahdi, who by early January had Khartoum in a death grip, detached two armies to attack the invaders. Neither attack was successful, but the partial actions so strained the fragile British logistics, that they could not continue.

The stage was now set for the final act of the Sudanese Rebellion. On the morning of January 25, 1885, the Mahdi himself gave a stirring speech to his assault troops, and in a few minutes some 50,000 of them simply overwhelmed the garrison of Khartoum. Gordon was butchered and his head brought before the Mahdi.

The capture of Khartoum was the final act in the Mahdi's rebellion. He had swept away the corrupt "Turks" and their foreign helpers. The British were unwilling to send armies into the Sudan to avenge their general, but they would keep the memory of his murder for a more convenient time.

The Egyptian government, now a mere English puppet, was content to allow the Sudan to drift away. Sadly, Muhammad Ahmad did not live to enjoy his plunder. On June 28, 1885, he too passed away, and his empire fell into the hands of Abd Allahi, who came to be known as the khalifa.

The new ruler of the recently liberated Sudanese state was a Ta'aisha tribesman from the southwestern province of Darfur. He had been instrumental in the Mahdi's army as the best of the generals, and so he became khalifa, or supreme ruler. It was a difficult task. The Sudanese people had been happy to throw off the corrupt foreigners, but in general they were not amenable to the idea of a strong government—or any government at all. Many of them, particularly those from the remote tribal areas in the west, felt no loyalty outside of their own individual clans. To subdue and gain their acceptance would be a long and arduous task for the khalifa. In the end it would prove impossible. Likewise, as the administration of the country came into his hands, he learned a thing that has bedeviled conquerors since the dawn of history—it is far easier to kill and plunder than it is to govern—a problem exacerbated by an uneducated, suspicious, and jealous population, marginal industrial capability, and an isolated position in the world. Resources were adequate to feed the people in a good year, but little more. Sudan had nothing like the capability to produce modern arms, and even to replace simple parts with adequate spares was beyond Sudanese industrial ability. Perhaps the least of the khalifa's problems was that Ethiopia to the southeast was an aggressive neighbor. Much worse, fairly regular expeditions were necessary to quell his own people. In short, governing the Sudan was a difficult business, even with the spiritual blessing of the mahdi.

For better or worse, the khalifa found himself warlord of a vast domain, nearly a thousand miles from north to south, and close to that from east to west. Although he lacked the spiritual pretensions of the mahdi, he shared the dream of personal and supreme power. To inflict this dream on his countrymen, the khalifa was forced into the normal choice of dictators—for officers he could appoint capable people with no particular reason to be loyal, or hopefully loyal family members with no particular ability. Both choices generally led to civil disorder, and thus the years from 1885 to 1895 were spent in the suppression of various tribes. It is a paradox that the Sudanese people had flocked to the mahdi's standards to avoid a corrupt yet lax and distant rule, but their victory had assured a harsh and immediate government far more intrusive than the "Turk" from Cairo had ever thought to be.

Under the khalifa, the Sudanese army became a well-organized force, and much more of an army than a massed tribal array that it had earlier resembled. Permanent garrisons of regular soldiers received training, billeting, and upkeep that would seem familiar to most civilized armies. These garrisons, which varied in size, were scattered about the country with particular emphasis on the wilder areas of the tribal west and the Ethiopian frontier. They provided a defense force and kept the local people in subservience. The balance of the armed force consisted of virtually all of the male population—at least in theory. In actuality some of the manpower would volunteer for active service and some would be raised as required by the provincial administrators, generally when major field armies were to be formed. It is interesting that these levies were armed at government expense, billeted in regular barracks, and trained on a daily basis—each unit performing a daily parade in front of the Khalifa at Omdurman.

The standard fighting unit of the mahdiya, or army, was the *rub,* which might number about a thousand men. Each *rub* was divided by tactical function. The largest component was usually the spearmen, who would be further subdivided into tribal groupings, each under a banner or standard. Their mission was to close with an enemy and defeat him in melee. The second section was the *jihadiya,* or rifle-armed section. This section was broken into companies of about 100 men under a standard, and platoons of 25. These men were armed with the Remington breech-loading rifles taken from the defeated government forces. Their mission was to support the massed attack of the spearmen. The third element was cavalry, whose number varied, but at least one group was assigned to each *rub* to provide scouting and courier duties. If enough horsemen were present— they were recruited mostly from the Baqqra tribes—they could also serve as a mounted shock force. In essence, the *rub* was a combined arms formation, rather like a Western division, but on a much smaller scale. The *rub* organization was probably designed primarily for internal security duties, for which the mix of arms in such a small unit would make good sense. In larger armies, the cavalry elements would clearly be best massed together, and the rifle elements could certainly be more useful if combined together and separated from the spearmen. Separate artillery batteries— equipped with guns captured from Egyptian garrisons and field armies— usually concentrated in Omdurman and were parceled out to field armies as needed or deployed in the river forts that protected the capital. Additional units of service troops provided logistical support and maintained arsenals for the manufacture of ammunition.

When field armies were formed, the *rubs* would be placed under one of several headquarters. These were originally the Black Standard, the Red Standard and the Green Standard, each under a senior general. Each standard would include *rubs* from garrisons and volunteers and would certainly include the tribal *rubs* of the emir in command. In 1891 the Red Standard was disbanded to punish the treachery of its leader, Muhammad Sharif, who was upset at the Khalifa's preference for his own Ta'aisha tribesmen. Additional standards were formed at the end of the reign, the reserve army being formed to manage the influx of new recruits that replaced the veterans lost in the Ethiopian War, and the *mulazimin,* which was the name given to a newly raised corps of regular soldiers who were stationed in Omdurman for security purposes. The Sudanese army would have totaled more than 100,000 men. It is interesting that this army was extensively documented by the Khalifa's bureaucrats, but that many of those documents are undated, which makes them challenging for historians!

The downfall of the Sudanese state came about in 1898, as a result of a combination of circumstances, mostly beyond the Khalifa's control. The crux of the problem was that the competing imperial interests of France and Britain created a situation in which the Sudan was bound to play a major, if unwanted, role. The crisis began with the Ethiopian victory over the Italian army at the Battle of Adowa, on March 1, 1896. The Italians had been trying to expand their Red Sea coastal holdings, and Emperor Menelik II of Ethiopia had resisted. Italy had enjoyed the general benevolence of England in her colonial expansion, and the Ethiopians had accepted French weapons. Thus the English became suspicious that the French were attempting a coup that would grant the rights to a great east-west African railroad and chain of French influence. In contrast, the British hoped to build a great north-south railroad that would tie the continent together under British overlordship. The meeting place of the two contrasting dreams would have to be in the Sudanese-controlled state. Britain was therefore afraid that the Ethiopians would defeat the Mahdists and grant rights to their French allies, or that the Mahdists would defeat the Italians and thus put British aspirations even further behind schedule. These fears, coupled with the Khalifa's xenophobic policies, fear of a Mahdist attack on Egypt, and a never quite forgotten desire to avenge Gordon, all came together in 1898.

The Anglo-Sudanese War of 1898 was to be different from that of 1885. First and foremost, the whole weight of the British government was behind the enterprise, and at the end committed to the enterprise two brigades of British infantry with a powerful artillery establishment and modern gunboats. To this significant force were added four more brigades of the revitalized Egyptian army, with additional artillery, a useful cavalry arm, and yet more gunboats. The whole of the Anglo-Egyptian strike force consisted of some 25,000 men. Bringing this weight of men, animals, and machines down the Nile from Egypt relied on the superb engineers who built a double-strand railway right across the desert and on the excellent boating skills of the flotillas that kept supplies flowing and gunboats mobile, even through the Nile's five difficult cataracts between Aswan and Berber. General H. H. Kitchener, one of the ablest soldiers of the day, led the entire force.

As the Anglo-Egyptian army advanced, the weaknesses of the Khalifa's Sudan became apparent. Of the mighty army of 100,000 well-trained and disciplined soldiers, probably more than a quarter were needed to keep the provinces of the Khalifa's state in check. More had been lost in fighting against the Ethiopians at Gallabat, and the loyalty of the rest was such that the Khalifa hesitated to reinforce his northern contingents with men from the Omdurman *rubs*. With so little opposition, the Allies required no defense of the strategic cataracts, and the logistical support to continue the advance was assured.

The Emir Mahmud, with a small army, was dispatched to contest the enemy advance by threatening their flank from Atbara. Along the way, Mahmud massacred the inhabitants of Metemma, because they had refused the Khalifa's orders. The Allies saw Mahmud's 7,000 men as an isolated detachment and hardly a threat. They simply marched against the Atbara force and destroyed it on April 6, 1898. Of Mahmud's army, only the resourceful Osman Digna and his troops evaded the death trap. It was an excellent small victory for Kitchener's troops and did much to solidify the confidence that the Egyptian troops now enjoyed.

The Anglo-Egyptians continued their methodical advance down the river, scarcely pausing as their gunboats blasted the flimsy mud forts that attempted to bar their passage. By August, the end was in sight. The Khalifa still enjoyed the services of a large armed force—variously estimated as between 40,000 and 50,000. This army was concentrated near Omdurman, the capital, and as the enemy grew closer, he offered battle on September 2, 1898, near the village of Karari, just five miles north of Omdurman.

Sadly, the Khalifa ignored the sage advice of his best generals, notably Osman Digna, and chose a disastrous plan of attack. Although an attack by night would have neutralized much of the enemy firepower, he chose to advance at dawn. Likewise, the enemy army would be much more liable to attack if it was caught on the march. The Khalifa chose to attack so early that the enemy was still in its fortified night position. Thus, at first light Ibrahim al Khalil led some 5,000 well-trained riflemen forward to attack the southern wing of Kitchener's army. An hour later, Uthman

Azraq advanced his 10,000 spearmen in a wide arc against the center of the enemy front. It was hoped that the covering fire of the riflemen might allow the spearmen the chance to close the enemy without too heavy a loss. At night, this plan might well have succeeded, but by day the quick-firing artillery and maxim guns slaughtered Khalil's men so quickly that their threat evaporated before Uthman Azraq's attack was fairly begun. Worse was to follow as the Anglo-Egyptian cavalry moved to the north to scout, and to keep the front of Kitchener's force clear. In doing so they ran across the Red and Green Standards under Abu Siwar and Shaykh al-Din, with about 15,000 men, including the elite *mulazimin.* In a scrambling battle the allied cavalry engaged and pulled the two Sudanese corps after them. Thus, when the crux of the battle came, at about ten in the morning, those Sudanese forces were too far north to participate. The Khalifa's one chance to win the day came when the Anglo-Egyptian army had broken camp and was marching to the south. As their forward elements moved past the mass of the Surkab Hills, under the khalifa's personal orders the great mass of the Black Standard, with nearly 15,000 troops, lunged out at the isolated right flank of Kitchener's army. The disciplined troops quickly reformed and shot the Black Standard to pieces. Had Abu Siwar and Shaykh al-Din not left their position, they could have easily cut behind Kitchener's exposed flank and massacred his army. As it was, the Battle of Karari, or Omdurman, had taken only part of the morning and had decisively broken Mahdist power in the Sudan. The Khalifa fled with a few loyal adherents, and avoided his fate until November 1899, when he was surrounded with his tattered followers and shot down.

The destruction of the Sudan put an end to the strongest and best-organized Muslim state in Africa, and nearly the only independent nation that had not yet been absorbed by colonial powers. The real battle between Britain and the Sudan had not been decided at Omdurman. It was decided in the university cities of England that produced the knowledge to build weapons, by the arms factories that produced those weapons, and by the parliamentary system of government that kept the soldiers loyal. The Khalifa's Sudan had enjoyed none of these advantages, and like every other backward state, it had collapsed under the weight of the modern world. In the defense of the Khalifa, though, his government was at least moderately stable and for fourteen years the Sudanese people were free from foreign oppression—although not from the domestic variety. If his state was tyrannical, it should be remembered that he governed in much the same manner as virtually every nation on earth at the time, save for a dozen or so European and American states. Likewise, he prepared the

Sudanese for the idea of national rather than tribal identity, a process not yet fully completed, but one that must go forward.

Elsewhere in Africa and Asia, nations and tribes were submerged into colonial empires. With the end of World War I the Ottoman Empire was broken up and the pieces distributed among the victorious allied colonial powers—Lebanon and Syria to France, Palestine to England. Even nominally independent parts were economically and politically dominated by the colonial powers. These were the last pieces of the Muslim world to be occupied as colonies.

The colonial empires generally lasted until the immediate post–World War II years and are bitterly resented by the local peoples of most of the old colonial possessions. It is certainly understandable that people prefer to rule themselves, and it is also true that many areas were better governed by the imperial powers than by the indigenous peoples. Perhaps the saddest legacy of the colonial decades is that the reaction against them has helped to steer much of the Muslim world away from the reality of the modern world and back to the fantastical longing for an existence in which Muslim feet lie across the necks of all whom they meet. Such a world may have existed for a few years in the seventh century, but it is now long past and will not be seen again.

NOTES

1. The role of Osama bin Laden and many of the other charismatic Muslim leaders in the past fifty years can also be viewed within the context of the "Mahdi." Osama bin Laden was viewed with a near-religious fervor by the Muslim world when he proclaimed it his goal to eliminate the Americans from the Muslim world. He too used murder as his principal weapon and argument.

2. The parallels between the battles of Aba and Badr, Muhammad's first victory, are tremendous. In both instances, a small victory by a leader claiming religious leadership brought swarms of followers and launched major religious movements. In both instances, a surprising victory gave both men the aura of having God on their side in the struggle. It was then typical for the various tribes to want to be on the side of God, which, because of the military success, was the Mahdi.

3. In A.D. 625 Muhammad lost the battle at Mt. Uhud. The parallels between the Mahdi's loss at Jabal Jarrada cannot have been lost on the Sudanese and surely increased their perception that he was the "expected one."

4. It was the common practice to take the last name of Westerners and add the title "Pasha" after them when they commanded Muslim troops. This was the process used by the Ottomans for their own military commanders and was, essentially, a tradition.

Chapter 11

MULLAHS AND MISSILES: ISLAMIC WARS SINCE 1945

When the industrial world went to its two great wars in the twentieth century, much of the Islamic world was spared. Turkey was a combatant in World War I, and Muslim soldiers were raised in appreciable numbers by their French, British, or Italian colonial masters in both contests. This being said, the Islamic world was shielded from the worst of the two world cataclysms by the fact that most of those Muslim peoples did not live in independent nations. Northern Africa, the Middle East, and Asia were still much in the throes of imperial colonialism, and those fading empires had never been successful at mobilizing the full human potential of their subjugated peoples.

These colonial troops, like most other soldiers, when well led, well trained, and well supplied, could be splendid. Sadly, this was rarely the case. Most Muslim soldiers were raised for theaters of war in which their European overseers could not deploy the weight of their sophisticated mechanical equipment. Most of the best European officers were assigned to the armies of their homelands. Thus, most Muslim soldiers served as simple riflemen or labor troops in distinctly second-rate formations, though exceptions arose and many Muslim troops were employed in Europe. Indeed, much of the Free French Army that liberated France in 1944–45 was Muslim.

This military experience in the world wars, and particularly in World War II, did not provide the best possible military pool for the new Muslim states that formed in the immediate postwar decolonization of Africa, Asia and Europe. These new states had many other significant liabilities as they formed their military structures. Foremost of these was the fact that most of the Muslim world was illiterate, and thus few Muslims had any of the technical skills necessary to operate, let alone repair, maintain, or design complex machinery and weaponry. Equally, none of the new Muslim nations developed particularly successful governments. Frequently, and often for good reason, the loyalty of the officer corps and the soldiery was frequently, and often for good reason, not strong. These problems were compounded when new nations lacked the physical plant to manufacture sophisticated arms and the skills to design them. This formidable list of challenges could probably have been overcome with time, but the postwar world would place immediate political and military challenges into the paths of the Muslim states.

As early as 1947 the wartime alliance of the democratic West and the dictatorial Soviet Union was breaking apart. Western Europe, exhausted by the Nazi ordeal, shed its colonies as quickly as possible, and the new nations found themselves with bad diplomatic choices. The Soviet Union offered oppressive and atheistic dictatorship. The free states of the West were still resented for their recent colonial overlordship. While neither choice would normally appeal to the new Muslim nations, the Great Power blocs—both east and west—offered generous assistance to those that became their satellites. This assistance frequently came in the terms of weapons, which were well received by the Muslims. Tanks, ships, guns, and aircraft poured into the Middle East. Foreign troops came with them to train the local forces, and some of the newly independent nations found themselves host to military formations much more powerful than the colonial occupiers had ever imposed on them. This sad picture was made worse by the fact that the Soviet Union—the uglier by far of the foreign powers—espoused atheism and practiced the worst sorts of racial and religious intolerance. This was the price that the Muslim peoples paid to equip their armies.

The new armies of these new nations found themselves at war almost immediately. The first opponent of the Egyptian, Syrian, and Jordanian governments was to be Israel—itself a new state. The key differences between the sides would be repeatedly demonstrated, but obvious only after the fact. The Jewish soldiers were literate and familiar with machinery and weapons. They were fighting for the survival of their biblical homeland and their families. Their Muslim opponents were generally illiterate and in larger part unsure of why they were leaving their own homes to go kill people whom they did not know and who had done them no harm. Over the course of the four Arab-Israeli wars the Muslim military situation would improve, but they would never catch up to their opponents.

The Arab-Israeli wars can be traced to the Balfour Agreement, which granted the Jews a homeland in Israel in return for their support of the Allies in World War I. After World War I, Palestine became a British protectorate and the immigration of European Jews into Palestine began.

Prior to and during World War II, the mufti of Jerusalem had spoken out strongly against the Jews and had actively supported the Nazis. The British had forced him to flee to Germany during the war, but his legacy of hatred toward the Jews had taken strong root. As the Jewish population in Palestine grew, tensions increased. The Palestinians resented the increasing numbers of Jews in their midst and the pressure for a Jewish homeland. Oddly, the numbers of Arabs in Palestine grew markedly because of the improved economy that resulted from the large Jewish presence—many of the Jews being successful business people. The tensions grew into acts of terrorism as the Jews struggled to establish an independent homeland and Arabs attacked the Jews as outside invaders. The situation became too difficult for the British, who abandoned Palestine in 1947 and by their withdrawal allowed a situation where the fledgling state of Israel was faced by an invasion by the Lebanese, Syrian, Jordanian, and Egyptian armies.

It needs to be understood that the surrounding states had long histories of territorial claims on the lands granted to Israel and the deep emotional desire to control Jerusalem. The contest to conquer Israel saw the invading armies as jealous of each other's chance of success as they were eager to defeat their Jewish enemies. Their attitudes remind one more of the medieval warlordism of Zangi, Nur-al-Din, and Saladin than they do of a modern alliance.

King Abdullah of Jordan was open in his territorial claims and also sought a clear outlet to the Mediterranean Sea. Syria wanted to reestablish "Greater Syria," a process that continues to this day with its occupation of Lebanon. Egypt had similar territorial objectives, with a historical lust to claim Jerusalem that a pharaoh would have surely understood.

This competition between the Muslim states left almost no trust and cooperation between the various armies,which should have permitted the Jews to succeed in their 1948 War of Independence. However, the reasons for Jewish success went beyond just that.

The armies of the Muslim states had devolved since the years of the great conquests and the western crusades. The professional military classes that had existed and dominated Muslim military history had atrophied and finally been destroyed by the century of European colonialism and the collapse of the Ottoman Empire. The skill at arms had not only disappeared, but warfare had changed markedly. It was now necessary for generals to understand multidimensional, combined arms operations. Modern weapons could be purchased and fielded, but the Muslim armies formed after World War II were unable to employ them to their greatest efficiency because they lacked the trained officer cadre necessary to maximize the lethal effect produced by a combination of infantry, artillery, armor, and aircraft.

The one notable exception was the Arab Legion, formed and commanded by Lieutenant General Sir John Bagot Glubb during World War II. The Legion was actually a small modern army, well trained in the British military tradition and heavily officered by British mercenary officers. In a parallel process, the Turkish army in World War I had operated at a degree higher than might have otherwise been expected because supreme command of the Ottoman forces had been given to General Liman von Sanders, a professional German officer.

During the Israeli War of Independence (1948), the newborn Israeli army had the benefit of numerous Jews who had trained and served under the British in World War II. It also benefited from many Jewish officers from the American and British armies that joined the struggle of the new nation. These trained officers and NCOs fused their civilian volunteers into a well-organized, if wildly undisciplined, army. The Jewish forces were further strengthened by the knowledge that to lose the war meant the destruction of their newly formed but long-awaited homeland.

In contrast, the Muslim states, with no remaining military class in their society depended on mass armies drafted from those parts of society with no military tradition. Most were not led by officers with the necessary skill base to fully utilize their weapons systems, let alone train their soldiers in the use of the new devices. The officers were equally unknowledgeable in tactics and the motivation to win at any cost visible amongst the Jews was far less evident in the Muslim armies.

In May 1948 the Egyptians attacked the Jewish village of Kfar Darom, which was defended by only thirty Jewish settlers. This battle would clearly demonstrate the awkwardness of the new Egyptian Army. With an overwhelming combined arms force of infantry and artillery, the Egyptians should have had an easy victory—but they did not. As the Egyptian infantry attacked, the Egyptian artillery barrage fell on their own troops, shattering their attack and morale. The frightened Egyptian infantry fled, leaving seventy dead and wounded on the battlefield. The Egyptian artillery had mastered loading and firing the guns, but they had not mastered the process of aiming the guns or coordinating fire with the advancing infantry. That particular technology is complex and requires mathematical skills not readily available in an illiterate population, but even the process of firing a few spotting rounds before the main barrage, then walking the shells onto the desired target before executing the main barrage, had not been attempted. This is a clear indication that the most important aspects of the operation of artillery had yet to be mastered.

Many Muslim military operations lacked strong cadres, but this lack was most markedly demonstrated in early April when the Syrian forces, under Abd el Kader el-Husseini, attacked Kastel. The Syrian forces were using their superior numbers to gain ground when a chance bullet killed their leader. His death demoralized the entire Syrian force and their attack collapsed. Any depth of leadership would have allowed the attack to continue despite the death of their commander.

The quality of training was also apparent from the Jews' frequent success in turning the flanks of attacking Muslim forces. Once the Muslim forces found Jews on their flanks or in their rear, their attacks invariably collapsed and frequently turned into routs, abandoning much valuable equipment to the Jews, who desperately needed any heavy weapons they could capture. The fundamental tactic of posting forces at key points and on the flanks of an advance to ensure the security of the advance was unknown to the inadequately trained Muslim commanders.

In addition, the various Arab forces did not cooperate. When the Jewish forces counterattacked the Egyptians and were driving them south, the hapless Egyptian commander called to his "allies" for support. As Lieutenant General Glubb began to move the Arab Legion in to support the Egyptians, King Abdullah directly ordered him not to support his erstwhile allies. What was not lost by technical military incompetence was thrown away by internecine strife within the Muslim ranks.

Chaim Herzog, later prime minister of Israel, summed up the problem of the Muslim armies with the following observation:[1]

> On the opposing side, the Arab Legion stood out as the outstanding army, British-officered and led as it was; but even after the British left some years later, it continued to be the most effective Arab army, well led, brave and satisfactorily organized. All the Arab armies apart from Kaukji's Arab Liberation Army proved to be highly effective in the defense, and this was to characterize them over the coming years. But their failing in attack arose out of the fact that, when their set-piece attack encountered unexpected obstacles, the junior leadership in the field was incapable of adapting itself rapidly enough to the changing circumstances of the battle. Above all, the inter-Arab bickering—which over the years was to erupt sporadically in internecine strife—plagued the Arab forces. While they all fought against

the Israelis, they were inevitably looking over their shoulders at their allies in an atmosphere of mistrust. They could thus never really take full advantage of their overwhelming superiority, while the Israeli forces, operating on internal lines of communication, were able to take advantage of this situation, switching forces from front to front and developing attacks against one Arab force conscious of the fact that there would be no concerted military pressure brought to bear on them on other fronts.

The psychological importance of Jerusalem to both the Jews and the Muslims was such that the Arab Legion spent much of its military resources in an effort to capture and hold the Holy City. On May 22, 1948, the Third Regiment of the Legion—disciplined Bedouin tribesmen— pushed forward against the Old City and reached the Damascus Gate, despite heavy small-arms fire from the Jewish defenders of the city.

The Third Regiment then pushed against the principal enemy position, the old Notre Dame de France monastery complex. This large stone complex, dominated by towering stone walls, was strongly defended by a force of desperate Jews.

The spearhead attack by the Fourth Company, Arab Legion, supported by two anti-tank guns, pushed forward to the walls of the monastery, only to find itself trapped in crossfire of accurate small arms. Efforts to relieve it with an attack by armored cars were stopped when the Jews blew up a wall of the monastery and it collapsed on the vehicles. Jewish soldiers then attacked the Arab Legion's remaining armored cars with Molotov cocktails, reducing them to flaming wrecks that blocked any further motorized advance against the monastery. Despite the murderous fire, the one company held its position, losing 50 percent of its strength as killed or seriously wounded until May 24, when the attack was abandoned. During the attack the company lost all its officers and NCOs except one. As the shattered company withdrew, so too did the other Legionnaires. If all of the Muslim armies had demonstrated the discipline and staying power of this formation, the war could not have been lost. The battle had reduced the Third Regiment to a strength of 500 men.

Despite having broken the attack of the Third Regiment in Jerusalem, the Jewish situation in Jerusalem was desperate—they had little food or ammunition. They thus turned their attention to capturing the police fort at Latrun. Thus the Jews would open the road from Jerusalem to the sea and resupply and reinforce the city's Jewish defenders. The main effort in the battle to control Jerusalem now switched to the south.

Opening up the road required the Jews to attack and capture Latrun, held by the Fourth Arab Legion Regiment, another of the professional formations that General Glubb had trained. The Israeli 7th Haganah Brigade launched an attack with more than 400 troops, supported by a heavy mortar bombardment. The Arab Legion responded with a heavy and accurate artillery fire that broke the back of the Jewish assault.

On May 26 the Arab Legion counterattacked one of the principal Haganah strongholds to the north of the Jerusalem road and drove out the Etzioni garrison, capturing the Radar Hill near Biddu. Jewish forces also pushed to take positions in order to attack the Latrun-Ramallah road—the main supply route for the Arab Legion forces in Latrun. This move would then be supported by a Jewish armored battalion, an infantry battalion, and by the fire of mortars and artillery.

The Israeli armored forces pushed to the outskirts of Latrun and even pushed into the courtyard of the police post, but the Jewish infantry had been stopped by the Arab Legion's heavy small-arms fire and artillery fire. Despite the support of flamethrowers and point-blank cannon fire from armored cars, Israeli engineers failed to blow down the wall of the police station. Lacking the necessary support, the Jewish forces were stopped cold by the steady, disciplined actions of the Arab Legion. The situation had been so desperate that the Legion had even thrown its clerks and cooks into the battle. Fighting desperately the Arab Legion held until the Jewish forces were forced to withdraw. This fight at Latrun demonstrated what the Arab armies would have been capable of, had they been better led.

As the war progressed, the Arab Legion found itself stripped of its British officers as a result of United Nations political pressure against Britain as well as the Jordanian government's distrust of British officers. Lieutenant General Glubb had come under increasing criticism for his desire to support the Egyptians, since that violated the objectives of King Abdullah of Jordan, and for his willingness not to commit large forces to the defense of Jerusalem. His military perspective had not adequately taken into consideration Muslim sensitivities and jealousies. With the Arab legion neutralized by politics, no Arab or Muslim force was capable of evicting the Jews. An eight-year armed truce ensued as both sides stepped back to consider their options. During this period the Arab forces received at least rudimentary training and massive Soviet material aid. The Israeli forces received small shipments of largely obsolete weapons from the West.

The 1956 war was a preemptive strike by the Israelis into the Sinai, designed to stop incursions by Palestinian guerrillas into Israeli territory. It occurred simultaneously with the Franco-British attack against the Suez Canal after Egypt violated various financial agreements.

The Israelis, for their part, performed brilliantly. By now they had mastered the art of complex offensive operations by large-scale forces. The Egyptian forces could rarely defend themselves, but they could fight with courage.

In the battle for the Abu Ageila stronghold, fought on October 31, 1956, the Egyptians were strongly emplaced and confronted with substantial Israeli forces. Rash and ill-conceived Israeli frontal assaults proved disastrous, with the Egyptians inflicting heavy casualties on the Israelis, including their commander. However, the Egyptians were so fearful of being cut off that, despite their victory, they slipped away during the night. Abandoning this position allowed the Israelis to cut off the Egyptian and Palestinian forces in the Gaza Strip, which led to their eventual destruction. Strongly posted, the Egyptian forces could fight, but like many armies through history, they could be defeated more easily by the fear of being surrounded than by actual attack.

One major difference between the Israelis and the Egyptians in this campaign was that the Israelis lost high numbers of officers and NCOs in battle and the Egyptians lost far fewer. This contrast indicates a significantly different style of warfare, and it also indicates the Israeli leadership's commitment to the war and no parallel commitment by the Egyptian leadership. The Israeli command structure led the battle from the front lines, a military practice with a long history of success, while the Egyptian command structure did not.

If one looks back at the history of warfare in the Islamic world, Muhammad was wounded in battle. At the battle of Badr both sides sent forward champions to fight. When Muhammad sent an army off to hold a potential Byzantine attack in A.D. 633 he lost three commanders. The bulk of the sultans of the Mamluk Empire were warriors who had literally risen from the ranks. Though it would be of a stroke, the last sultan of the Mamluk Empire died on the battlefield. In the Ottoman Empire either the sultan or the grand vizier accompanied the army into the field for centuries. This tradition of leaders and officers being in the front ranks of Muslim armies appears to have vanished, and their absence in the past two centuries may be one key to explaining the almost total lack of success of Islamic military operations against non-Muslim countries.

The 1967 war was the result of Arab political pressures and persistent armed incursions into Israel. Syria had been making increasingly aggressive movements along the strategic Golan Heights and suddenly realized that it had probably provoked the Israelis into a major response. The Syrian president went to Egyptian president Nasser and formed an offensive/defensive alliance. Nasser was most eager for this as it fit in with his plans for an attack on Israel. Even the moderate King Hussein of Jordan was obliged to join rather than face charges of being pro-Israeli.

Combined, the three nations began slow preparations that eventually provoked an overwhelming Israeli preemptive strike. It is ironic that the Syrians acted aggressively but feared an Israeli response. By joining with the Egyptians, Syria guaranteed what it most feared. When war came, Syria was still far from prepared to successfully prosecute it. Again, as in both earlier wars, the Arab forces, while numerous on paper, had little fighting value.

The Israeli air force launched a series of attacks on Egyptian airfields that utterly destroyed the Egyptian air force. They then turned their attention on the Syrian and Jordanian air forces, destroying them in turn. Neither Soviet aircraft, nor Soviet antiaircraft missiles were effective in the hands of the poorly trained Arab forces. The well-trained Israeli military, using modern Western equipment demonstrated an essential truth of modern warfare—modern machines can direct and deliver massive firepower accurately, but only if their crews can master the machines.

The Israeli air staff had carefully planned these attacks on the Egyptian air force. Intelligence had determined the specific hour when the bulk of the Egyptian staff and pilots would be on the road between breakfast and their bases and designated that as the optimal time to attack. The results were devastating and gave the Israelis absolute air superiority. This excellent staff and intelligence work was possible for the well-educated Israeli forces, but not for the Arabs.

On the ground, Israeli armored forces rolled forward with equal precision. Their armored leaders had all trained at the U.S. armor school. Numerous additional officers had trained in various European military schools, including the French Ecole de Guerre. In contrast, few of the Egyptian, Syrian, or Jordanian officers had any such training. This would soon become apparent when the Israelis won every tank-versus-tank battle, employing fire, movement, support, and communication at levels that their opponents could not counter or duplicate.

In preparation for their pending attack, the Egyptians had heavily fortified the Sinai frontier, playing to their greatest strength—the defense. A frontal attack against these forts would have been a bloody affair. The Egyptians had, unfortunately, thought that areas of sand dunes would be impassable to Israeli armored columns. The Israelis knew otherwise and repeatedly turned Egyptian positions.

The Egyptian plan had failed, and once it became apparent that the situation was changed, the Egyptians showed themselves incapable of reacting spontaneously to the new situation. This and the repeated success of the Israeli turning movements caused the senior Egyptian unit commanders to fear for their lives, and they repeatedly abandoned their troops, fleeing to the western bank of the Suez. Abandoned by their officers, the lower ranks panicked and refused to face the Israelis.

The panic in the Egyptian ranks and the absence of their officers was omnipresent. At one point an Israeli force pushing toward Nakhle found the Egyptian 125th Armored Brigade, 6th Mechanized Division, abandoned with all its equipment in perfect condition and in place. The Egyptian troops had simply fled on foot.

Like the Egyptians, the Syrians had heavily fortified the Golan Heights and for a time fought hard to defend them. However, once the Israelis had broken through their defenses, the Syrians showed themselves unable to deal with a fluid military situation and so broke and fled. Only the threat of Russian intervention prevented the Israelis from taking Damascus.

In contrast to the Egyptians and Syrians, who were supplied, equipped, and trained by the Russians, the Jordanian army was equipped with American and British weapons. It was still generally regarded as the best and most professional of the Arab armies and would prove itself so when the Israelis encountered it in the June 5–7 battle for Nablus.

Israeli infantry and a supporting mechanized brigade had fought through the night of June 5 to penetrate the antitank defenses around Jenin. The next day a Jordanian counterstroke almost overwhelmed the Israelis with a powerful counterattack, though the static portions of the attack were more effective than the mobile ones. Had the mobile portion been better handled, the Jordanian Patton tanks would have had little trouble destroying the obsolete Israeli Sherman tanks. Nonetheless, the Israelis consider this attack to have been the most effective attack launched by any of the Arab armies during the war. It is not hard to see that the heritage of the Arab Legion and General Glubb remained in place. Other Jordanian forces could also fight effectively.

In another fine example of a hard fight, the 40th Jordanian Armored Brigade advanced to the Qabatiya road junction just south of Jenin and attacked the Israeli "M" brigade's rear guard. In a deliberate shoot-move attack, the Jordanian Patton tanks shot up the scattered Israeli mechanized forces that had been left behind at that road junction as the "M" Brigade had moved to attack Jenin. The Jordanian attack in the Israeli rear occurred while the bulk of the Israeli brigade's forces were engaged near Jenin.

Learning of the attack in their rear, the Israelis began to redeploy their armor to face this new attack. The Jordanians defending Jenin increased a coordinated effort to tie the Israelis in place. Israeli divisional artillery turned on the Qabatiya road junction and slowed the Jordanian assault but could not rescue the forces locked in battle with the 40th Brigade. As the Israeli tanks arrived, the Jordanians engaged and nearly defeated them. But by then the Jordanian mechanized soldiers had been fighting nonstop for nearly twenty-four hours. They were short of food, fuel, and ammunition and were utterly exhausted. At this point the Israeli air force intervened, launching a storm of bombs, rockets, and cannon fire on the hapless Jordanian force. In the subsequent slaughter, the Jordanian 40th Armored Brigade was utterly destroyed as a fighting force. Had the initial air strikes not given the Israelis absolute control of the air, the outcome of the battle would have been different.

The Jordanian front was eventually contained and crushed by the combination of Israeli ground and air attacks. The Jordanian armed forces were driven back across the Jordan River. By the time the war concluded, King Hussein had lost half his kingdom and 6,000 soldiers because he had allowed Jordan to be sucked into the war by the hysteria of the Arab world and the military agreement he had signed with Egypt ten days before the war. President Nasser of Egypt had lied to him about the status of Egyptian forces and caused him to launch his attacks prematurely. The Syrians and Iraqis had promised him support that never materialized.

The blame for the failure lay with President Nasser and his shortcomings as a military commander. General Moshe Dyan summarized the cause of Nasser's failure succinctly when he said that Nasser was blinded by the apparent strength of masses of Russian-made equipment that he had accumulated. The Egyptians and other Arab armies had learned to operate the mountains of sophisticated hardware and electronic equipment, but they had not learned to employ it in the field with any particular skill.

In addition, Nasser failed to conceptualize a rapid, hard-hitting war of maneuver in the desert. He viewed the process of war as a long-drawn-out struggle revolving around fortifications and artillery barrages, almost in the sense of the trench warfare of World War I. Nasser also failed to recognize the power of the first strike and abandoned that decisive factor to the Israelis.

The Egyptian officer corps had failed the Egyptian soldiers badly. Though there was retribution and punishment after the war, their failure to stand and fight with their soldiers had cost Egypt the Sinai and the war. As a contrast, 23 percent of the casualties suffered by the Israeli ground forces were among its officers and NCOs. They led their troops from the front and did not cower behind the safety of the Suez Canal.

If the Arab coalition was defeated, it was not discouraged. Eagerly rearmed by their Soviet allies, the Muslims prepared for a new war. This time enough Soviet advisers arrived with the mountain of Soviet equipment to make basic training a reality. The same mistakes would not be made four times.

Egyptian President Nasser had died in the course of his preparations for a renewed war with Israel, and Anwar Sadat had inherited his preparations. The Egyptian army had planned its attack with incredible care and precision. It is interesting to note that both the Egyptians and Syrians called their plan of attack Operation Badr. They had named their plan after the first major battle fought by Muhammad in A.D. 624. This was to be a jihad, and by naming it after Muhammad's most important battle, they hoped to bring upon it the blessings of their God.

When the Egyptians launched their assault across the Suez Canal it was executed with clockwork precision. They quickly formed bridgeheads across the canal as their air force engaged the Israelis. This was the major failure of the Egyptian attack. Their inability to seize air superiority from the Israelis would play a decisive role as the war developed. Instead, they defended their bridgeheads with a massive antiaircraft missile barrier that reached across the Suez from its western bank.

In the initial Israeli counterattacks the Egyptian infantry fought stubbornly and bravely. Armed with RPGs and Sagger antitank missiles they broke several Israeli armored assaults.

Facing the Egyptian attack, the Israelis rapidly mobilized their reserves and prepared for further attacks. On October 14 a massive armored battle began with 2,000 tanks on both sides locked in a battle along the entire front. The Egyptian armor advanced to attack the carefully prepared Israeli positions, moving directly into the killing ground prepared by the Israelis, where it was broken with heavy casualties. Chaim Herzog says that the Egyptian forces in this attack were "poorly led and their tactics were unimaginative." Still, they had developed a good campaign up to this point. But as the crisis developed, matters began to deteriorate badly.

On October 15 the Egyptians mounted a further major offensive, but rather than concentrating in a single powerful attack they distributed their efforts across 100 miles and in six separate thrusts. In addition, these armor-heavy attacks lacked sufficient infantry support. Some military theorists would argue that six attacks dissipated their major combat power and that one single, massive thrust would have had a greater chance of success. The nature of this attack was determined by Anwar Sadat himself, so he overruled his generals, who may or may not have understood the desirability of concentrating their armored forces into a single assault.

In one of these thrusts, the battle for the Tirtur road, a massive struggle developed. Herzog describes part of the battle as being a "scene . . . of utter confusion: along the Lexicon road raced Egyptian ambulances; units of the Egyptian infantry were rushing around in all directions, as were Egyptian tanks. The impression was that nobody knew what was happening or what to do." This behavior is typical of any army when its command structure breaks down, and the Israeli attacks demonstrated the relative ease of producing that chaos and panic in the Egyptian army.

On October 19 an Israeli force attacked an Egyptian-held outpost known as Orcha. A small infantry force, probably no larger than a battalion, garrisoned it. The Egyptians fought from their trenches and fortifications with extreme obstinacy, and though the Israelis eventually took the position, the Egyptians left 300 dead. These Egyptians were no longer the same troops who, in 1967, had fled when they saw an Israeli soldier.

The war on the Syrian front was different from that in the Sinai. The Syrians attacked two Israeli brigades with three infantry divisions and two armored divisions. They had about 1,200 tanks and 1,000 artillery pieces facing the Israeli forces with 170 tanks and 60 artillery pieces. Though the terrain was not particularly good for the offense, the Israelis had proven it could be done in 1967 and would prove it again in this war. Irrespective of how dogged the Israeli defense, a well-managed force with a nearly 10:1 superiority should have had no problem overwhelming their opponent. Yet, the Syrians were incapable of victory.

The Syrian failure had several apparent reasons. First, Syrian command and control obviously failed. It is probable that they lacked officers of sufficient authority in the leading ranks directing the battle, so the Syrian armored forces blundered forward with little coordination or direction, which allowed the Israelis to pick them off. This is the same problem the Egyptians had, but it was apparently far worse.

Second, little coordination is apparent between the various combat arms. Though Syrian artillery ranged over the battleground, the Syrian artillery spotters seemed incapable of successfully directing fire at moving targets such as tanks. The Syrian air force also failed to intervene in any meaningful manner, and once the Syrian antiaircraft missile batteries were destroyed, the Israeli air force swept the sky clear of Syrian aircraft.

As the Syrian army was pursued toward Damascus, an Iraqi armored division was moving to their support. The Israelis, seeing the Iraqi division on their flank, responded quickly and took up positions waiting for its advance. The Iraqi 3rd Armored Division advanced during the morning of October 13 directly into an Israeli killing zone and was butchered. The Iraqis were learning for the first time what it was like to face a well-trained enemy. In a like manner the reconstituted Jordanian 40th Armored

Brigade moved in to engage the Israelis. The Israelis quickly battered it into a hasty withdrawal.

In these two instances, the Iraqi 3rd and Jordanian 40th advanced without reconnaissance to probe for Israeli forces and blundered into forces ready to deal with them. They led with their chins and took a terrible pounding. In addition, the two advances were totally uncoordinated. Once again, the Arab failure to cooperate activities between the various armies cost them heavily. In subsequent actions, this failure to coordinate and communicate saw the Jordanians advancing without promised Iraqi support, or the Iraqi artillery bombarding Jordanian forces. On more than one occasion, Syrian aircraft shot down Iraqi aircraft. The Arabs suffered all the problems of coalition warfare and more.

When the cease-fire went into effect on October 22, the Syrians had lost 1,150 tanks, the Iraqis 100, and the Jordanians 50. The Israelis recovered 867 Syrian tanks from the battlefield and found many of them in good running order. The Syrians lost 370 prisoners and 3,500 killed. By contrast, the Israelis lost 250 tanks, 772 killed, 2,453 wounded, and 65 prisoners, including pilots.

On a military level, the Arab planning for the 1973 attack was sound and realistic. Detailed operational planning had been undertaken from 1970 to 1973 and supported with practical and intensive training by the Soviets and by the injection of professionalism into the Arab officer corps. Egyptian Generals Ahmed Ismail Ali, Said el Shazli, and Abdul Ghani el Gamsay, and the Syrian general staff and Generals Mustafa Tlas and Yusuf Shakur were schooled in the scientific, but rigid Soviet methods of war as well. Despite this training, or perhaps because of it, the Arab strategic plans erred on the side of caution and rigidity. The problems of professionalism had been addressed, but the Arab officer corps still lacked the innovation and spontaneity that takes a technically competent army to the next level. A few exceptions to this occurred, and the Egyptian and Syrian commando and paratroop formations displayed real daring in the missions assigned to them. Overall, the Arab troops fought competently in the face of concentrated Israeli armored attacks, while inflicting heavy casualties on the enemy.

However, the Arabs failed in two important areas. Unlike their Israeli counterparts, the Arab commanders, for the most part, failed to dominate the battlefield by their physical and moral presence in the firing line or with their forward troops. Aside from some exceptions, overall the criticism stands. In one instance the Egyptian 25th Armored Brigade advanced into prepared killing ground and was utterly destroyed. Of the ninety-six T-62 tanks that went into the battle, only ten escaped. All armored personnel carriers and the entire brigade supply train was destroyed. However, of the ten T-62 tanks that escaped, one was that of the brigade commander. With casualties like that, if the brigade commander had been leading from the front, as a good brigade commander should, the chances of his being in one of the surviving tanks is nil. He was obviously "leading" from the rear.

In contrast, the Israeli 188th Armored Brigade, which faced the overwhelming assault of the Syrians on the Golan Heights, suffered 90 percent officer casualties, including the brigade commander and his deputy. The contrast between the Israeli 188th and the Egyptian 25th Armored Brigades is striking.

The Arabs' second major failing was the inability of the Egyptian and Syrian tank divisions to conduct mobile, aggressive, and fast-moving tank warfare. The Arab infantry was solid in its defensive role, but the armor was tied to the Soviet doctrine that made them rigid, inflexible, and occasionally unimaginative. The combination of bad Soviet doctrine with only modest training was not a happy one.

The individual Arab soldiers had, during this campaign, dissipated the myth that they were unable to attack and fight in a sophisticated environment. Their performance was far and above that of their predecessors in the 1967, 1956, and 1948 campaigns, who were poorly trained and incompetently led.

The second great theater of war for a new Islamic nation was in the subcontinent. Soon the new governments of Muslim Pakistan and India would come to blows.

As India worked out its internal problems after the withdrawal of the British Raj, severe strife broke out and developed into a civil war as the forces of Azad Kashmir and India engaged in open conflict. Alarmed, the Pakistani government mobilized its army and began infiltrating forces into Kashmir to support the Kashmiri rebels. Soon a full-scale war erupted and continued with no substantial results until January 1, 1949. In the peace treaty, signed on July 27, 1949, a cease-fire line was drawn through the state of Jammu and Kashmir that split it into areas controlled, one by Pakistan and the other by India. The peace proved unstable, as Muslim Pakistan believed that Kashmir should be a state of their Islamic government, and not one of the Hindu minority.

In May 1965, the Pakistan government began sending in men to support uprisings in Kashmir. This action was known as Operation Gibraltar. These incursions provoked great tension between the Indian and Pakistani governments, and regular military forces began to clash along the cease-fire line. Many artillery skirmishes took place. In one such skirmish, forty

Pakistani soldiers were killed. An undeclared war began in the state of Jammu and Kashmir, and on September 6, 1965, India launched attacks against the Pakistani cities of Lahore and Kasur.

A full-scale war began without formal declaration. During the night of September 7 the Indian I Corps launched an attack east of Sialkot with an armored and three infantry divisions. The Pakistanis sent their armored division forward to engage the Indian armored division. The result was one of the largest armored battles to occur since World War II, known as the Battle of Assal Uttar.

The Pakistanis launched an ambitious counterattack with their armor that, had it succeeded, would have cut off all of Punjab west of the Beas. Instead, the Indians broke the poorly managed Pakistani forces.

Indian timidity and overcautiousness wasted this victory. They also failed to concentrate their forces into one solid mass and dissipated their efforts in two separate attacks, one by truck-borne infantry and the other by their armored force. The combination of Indian incompetence and Pakistani tenacity in the defense ended the battle with an inconclusive result.

The Pakistani army was holding the line, but with great efforts and heavy losses. It suffered from poor leadership from top to bottom. This deficient leadership was a major reason that the Pakistani 1st Armored Division was nearly destroyed at Assal Uttar. Indian reverses at Khem Kanar, however, so panicked the Indians that the operational commander thought about withdrawing to the Beas, only to have his decision overruled by the army commander.

After fourteen days, on September 23, 1965, the United Nations Security Council intervened, a cease-fire was declared, and the war was over. The cease-fire line of 1948 was reestablished, and the troops of both countries pulled back.

It is apparent that the motivated Muslim troops of Pakistan may not have been trained as well as possible, but they enjoyed considerable fighting ability. This distanced them somewhat from the Arab and Egyptian soldiers facing Israel and might be explained by the desire to keep their homeland safe—and it is not unlikely that some of the fine old military traditions of the British Raj had remained with both new nations.

War broke out again six years later. Clearly Indo-Pakistani relations had never been good, and they deteriorated further when civil war erupted in Pakistan. It is now frequently forgotten that Pakistan was divided into two parts, separated by the great bulk of India in between. The East Pakistanis wanted greater autonomy, and the West Pakistan army fought to deny it to them. The fighting forced 10 million refugees into India. The Pakistan army launched a terror campaign on March 25 designed to cow the Bengalis into submission.

India was not involved until Pakistan attacked Indian airfields in Kashmir on December 3, 1971. India responded by attacking both East and West Pakistan. On December 4, 1971, the Indians launched an overwhelming three-pronged attack into East Pakistan and in twelve days took 93,000 Pakistani soldiers prisoner. The Pakistani army was torn by racial problems. Many of the ethnic Bengalis in the East Pakistani Army deserted, and dissension within the ranks made that army a fragile instrument. The Indian air force quickly achieved absolute air superiority in the east and the Indian navy blockaded the East Pakistan ports, effectively isolating East Pakistan from West. Victorious in the east, India occupied East Pakistan, which declared its independence as Bangladesh, on December 6, 1971.

In the west and in Kashmir the Indians found the Pakistani army undertaking ground operations against them. A large tank battle occurred when Pakistani armor confronted the Indian 1st Armored Corps in what became known as the Battle of Chamb. The Indians underemployed their armor, sending it into battle in a piecemeal fashion. The Pakistani 23rd Division, under General Eftikhar, concentrated its armor and achieved substantial success. The combination of concentration of force and leading from the front was to bring the general much success. Unfortunately his brigade commanders did not emulate his example, which diluted the success of the attack. Sadly, the rest of the supporting Pakistani forces failed to match the 23rd Division's performance, and Eftikhar's success availed the Pakistanis little. His 23rd Division would suffer 2,216 of the 4,958 casualties suffered by the Pakistani army in the west during the entire war. Eftikhar was an aggressive, hard-charging general and might fairly be called the first of the Muslim armored warfare specialists. It is interesting that the Muslims of Pakistan were capable of mastering mobile warfare and the great complexity that goes with it.

The Battle of Hilli (November 22 to December 12) was a Pakistani defensive battle. Brigadier Tajjamal Hussain commanded the brigade posted in the Hilli sector, leading his troops from the front line. The Pakistani defense was so resolute that they held and fought after the final armistice of the war was signed. Another Pakistani brigadier had to be brought forward to surrender his brigade for him on December 18. His commander, Major General Lachhman Singh, would later write, "Brigadier Tajjamal was the only exception in my sector who showed fanatical will to fight even at the cost of his life." In sharp contrast, at Dhaka, the

Pakistanis held an impregnable position, but the officers' spirit broke and they chose to surrender.

Pakistan was defeated, but the UN intervened and forced a cease-fire in mid-December. Pakistan was thrown into tumult and political chaos and has been struggling since that time to establish a stable government.

In the three wars between India and Pakistan, some Pakistani officers demonstrated the same Middle Eastern tendency to command from the rear. The instances of leadership from the front ranks were too few to significantly change the outcome of the war, particularly as the balance of forces arrayed against them was so great. In addition, the Pakistanis failed to fully employ their forces. That is, because the artillery arm was looked down upon in the caste system within the Pakistani military, it was underutilized and the balance possible from a well-coordinated, combined arms attack was never brought to bear against the Indians.

The bitterness of the Indo-Pakistani wars has been such that in recent times both nations have felt the need to develop nuclear weapons. It is clear that the thirty years since their last great fight have seen enormous technical development in Pakistan. It is fortunate that this has been mirrored and made possible by a modernization of government and society. In fact this modernization suggests that the differences between the two governments will be resolvable only if Pakistan reaches the ability to deal with the Kashmiri question on political rather than emotional and religious lines. That both nations possess nuclear weapons is disturbing, but India, with her much larger armies, has foresworn first use of her nuclear arsenal. Pakistan is not really threatened by the large Indian army—the wars have been about Pakistani hopes for Kashmir, not an Indian invasion of the Pakistani homeland. It is difficult to imagine that either nation would have much to gain by nuclear warfare.

In the heart of the old Persian Empire, the two newly independent governments of two ancient states found Islamic theology and politics adequate for a brutal war. The roots of the Iran-Iraq war can be traced to hostilities that have existed between these two nations back before the days of the Ottoman and the Safavid (Persian) empires. The disputes revolve around boundaries and the interference in each other's internal affairs through ethnic and sectarian minorities that reach across their mutual borders. The current round of disputes began after the end of World War I and the emergence of Iraq as a quasi-independent state under the British mandate in 1921. All of these modern disagreements focus on control of the strategic waterway known as the Shatt al Arab—the mouth of the combined Tigris and Euphrates Rivers.

When the Iranian revolution occurred, Saddam Hussein, dictator of Iraq, perceived that the once powerful Iranian army would be weakened by the dissent within its ranks caused by the Ayatollah Khomeini's Islamic revolution and the elimination of American technical and material support. It was a golden opportunity for him to launch his army and not only take control of the Shatt al Arab but also grab the oil-producing territory adjacent to the Shatt and the Persian Gulf coast.

Iraqi forces flowed over the Iranian border on September 22, 1980, supported by a large-scale air attack on ten military airfields in Iran intended to destroy the Iranian air force on the ground. Though the air strikes failed in their goal, five Iraqi divisions pushed into Iranian territory. On September 28, Saddam Hussein announced that all of Iraq's territorial aims had been achieved and that he was willing to cease hostilities and negotiate a settlement, clearly demonstrating Iraq's limited strategic goals. Despite this, Iraqi forces continued pushing into Iran, besieging Khorramshahr and Abadan. Further Iraqi forces joined the initial assault, with the Iranians being totally incapable of putting up any coordinated defense.

By October 1980 the war entered a static phase as Iraq settled into defensive positions, content to hold its territorial gains. Fighting became a mere exchange of artillery barrages and air raids against both tactical and strategic targets. On January 5, 1981, a major Iranian counterattack occurred as an armored division broke out of Susangerd, crossed the Karkheh River, and pushed to the west in an attempt to break through the Iraqi lines. Air support allowed considerable initial success, and the Iranians pushed deep into Iraqi-held territory. The offensive stalled amidst heavy losses, some 100 tanks destroyed and 150 captured by the Iraqis. The Iraqis lost fifty tanks. The war once again went into a stalemate where both sides built up their forces. The Iranians mobilized large numbers of Pasdaran or religious militia and the youth brigades (Basij) were established, while the Iraqis began extensive training programs to build up the competence of its forces.

In the spring of 1981 the Iranians launched a new series of successful attacks. The army and the Pasdaran dislodged Iraqi forces from the Allah Akbar heights that controlled Susangerd and secured the approaches to the city. The Iraqi siege of Abadan was broken by a successful surprise attack. A multidivision Iranian assault recaptured Bostan and forced the Iraqis to withdraw. Both sides suffered heavy casualties and substantial equipment loss during these engagements.

When the winter rains came, the war again subsided until March when the Iranians began two large offensives that practically drove the Iraqis out of Khuzistan. Operation Undeniable Victory was launched on March

22 in the Sush-Dezful area and lasted a week. Iran deployed 40,000–
50,000 troops and 30,000 Revolutionary Guards. The Iraqis faced this
assault with 40,000 men. The combined-arms operations of both sides
made effective use of infantry, artillery, armor, and close air support. The
Iranians inflicted a humiliating defeat on the Iraqis in this operation and
are reported to have taken between 15,000 and 20,000 Iraqi soldiers
prisoner.

The Iranians then launched Operation Jerusalem on April 24 to clear
Khuzistan completely. As in the previous offensive, the Iranians used a
mixture of classical military maneuvers and guerrilla tactics. After two
weeks of bitter fighting the Iranians drove the Iraqis out of the Ahvaz-
Susangerd area and pushed a bridgehead to the west bank of the Karun
River near Taheria and Haloub. This threatened to cut off the Iraqi forces
besieging Khorramshahr and was followed by an Iranian assault on Khorramshahr with 70,000 troops. The Iraqis, faced with the prospect of losing
the 30,000–40,000 men besieging Khorramshahr, withdrew them before
they could be surrounded and captured. Despite this timely retreat, Iraq
lost 12,000 prisoners and large quantities of military equipment.

Faced with defeat, the Iraqi dictator, Saddam Hussein, decided to withdraw from Iranian territory. He used the Israeli invasion of Lebanon to
cover his decision, announcing that his troops were withdrawing on June
20, 1982. The Iranians were not to be placated and prepared yet another
offensive. Once launched, it encountered a solid, well-entrenched Iraqi
defense and broke. Between July 13 and August 2, Iran sent out 100,000
men (four regular divisions and 50,000 Pasdaran and Basij) in five con-
secutive attacks. Though they did penetrate five to ten miles into Iraqi
territory, they did not break the Iraqi lines. Iraq responded with nonlethal
tear gas, reported to have stopped the attack of one Iranian division. To
support Iraq in its war, both Egypt and Jordan provided many volunteer
soldiers to serve with the Iraqi army. These were supported by a steady
flow of arms and equipment from both the United States and the Soviet
Union, but the Soviets had also provided, by 1982, 1,500 military advisers.
Though the Iraqis were more sophisticated than the Iranians when it came
to operating military equipment, they still required substantial technical
support and other military support.

Iran continued to launch numerous offensives during the summer and
autumn of 1982, but none were successful. The Pasdaran and Basij became
the backbone of the Iranian attacks, and the regular army reduced its
participation to a minimal level. By this time, the Iranian regular army,
deprived of resupply for its American and British equipment, and suffering
from the revolutionary purge of its officer corps, became almost combat

ineffective. The Pasdaran and Basij, being little more than untrained militia, were generally slaughtered in front of the prepared Iraqi positions.
Huge numbers of casualties resulted.

In 1983 Iran mounted five large-scale offensives, all of which failed
and were repulsed with heavy losses. Iraq intensified air and naval attacks
against Iranian strategic targets, including ports, industrial facilities, tank-
ers, and merchant shipping in general. Targets included the oil wells in
the Nowruz field and the oil terminal at Kharg Island. The Iranian air force
was also rapidly disappearing as the lack of American spare parts began
to bite into its operational capabilities.

In 1984 the war resumed its intensity with the Iraqis standing on the
defensive and launching bombardment attacks on Iranian cities. On February 15 the largest Iranian offensive to date was launched with 500,000
men involved on both sides and repulsed with 20,000 casualties. Again
the regular Iranian army played little part in this offensive—a mere quarter
of the 250,000 Iranians involved. Stalemate resumed from 1984 to February 1986. In February 1984 the Iraqis first used poison gas on a large
scale. They are reported to have killed 40,000 Iranians on Majnoon Island
in this attack.

The Iranian offensives continued to be mostly Pasdaran and Basij
troops. On January 28, 1985, the Iraqis launched their first offensive since
1980. Convinced of their equipment superiority and witnessing the inability of the Iranians to launch a successful offensive, the Iraqis thought
the opportunity ripe. The attack was only a marginal success and failed
in its goal of deterring or frustrating Iranian preparations for their next
offensive, which was launched on March 11, 1985.

This new Iranian assault abandoned frontal human-wave assaults and
returned to conventional military operations. The Iranian government had
successfully worked to turn the Pasdaran into a military force capable of
conventional military operations. The offensive launched in February inflicted about 10,000–12,000 casualties on the Iraqis for a loss of 15,000
Iranian casualties. However, it failed to dislodge the enemy from their
positions. The war once again became static, marked by intermittent artillery barrages and local operations. The focus of operations returned to
a strategic level, with both sides attacking civilian shipping and strategic
targets.

On February 9, 1986, the Iranians launched Operation Dawn VIII and
finally cleared the Iraqis from Iranian territory. The Iranians captured the
Faw Peninsula at the southeastern tip of Iraq and retained it despite repeated counter-attacks. Unable to recapture Faw, the Iraqis launched an

attack that took Mehran, in Iran, which the Iraqis then offered in exchange for Faw, but Iran refused.

Throughout the remainder of the war neither side accomplished much militarily. In 1987 stalemate ended when continuing attacks on merchant shipping and the presence of the American and other navies in the gulf to protect tanker traffic provoked the United Nations to end the war. In July 1988 the UN forced Iran to accept a cease-fire. Estimates are that the war produced 1.5 million casualties and failed to resolve the issue of access to the Shatt al Arab.

The situation Iraq faced when the war broke out was certainly one that a well-coordinated and managed army could have successfully exploited. However, instead of large-scale, coordinated operations, the Iraqi invasion was characterized by engagements between small, brigade-sized units. Indeed, the initial invasion force was only five divisions. It was far from an all-out assault. The 1991 Gulf War made it clear Iraq had little ability to manage large-scale operations, shown by its policy of falling back onto prepared defensive positions and surrendering the initiative to the Iranians. A defense is much easier to manage than an offensive, and the Iraqis proved themselves capable of holding an enemy whose tactical skills were limited to human-wave attacks. Iraqi tactics on the battlefield placed heavy reliance on minefields, heavy artillery barrages, and poison gas. The Iraqi efforts at strategic operations, that is, air strikes and Scud missiles launched against Iranian cities, were ineffectual.

The Iranians, on the other hand, proved themselves even less capable of modern warfare than the Iraqis. They used brute force and willingly sacrificed thousands of lives in uncoordinated, futile, and unsophisticated frontal assaults that charged directly into the Iraqi killing zones. Stories have emerged of children roped together and sent forward to clear minefields. As the war progressed the regular army was little used in favor of the more politically reliable Pasdaran and Basij.

The reduced use of the regular army and its trained officer cadre probably shared two influences. First, the army was the Shah's creature and was, as a result, probably not well trusted by the new government. The lack of trust induced a purging of senior officers, the very men capable of implementing large-scale, combined-arms operations. The second problem was that Iran's army had been outfitted with American equipment. With the seizure of the American embassy during the Iranian revolution, the flow of spare parts and ammunition from the United States ended abruptly. It is impossible to prosecute a modern war without spare parts and munitions. In addition to the lack of spare parts, the multitude of American advisers and contractors who had trained the Iranians in the use of modern weaponry and even performed much of the equipment maintenance, were gone. The Shah had mostly bought those services, rather than training Iranians to perform them. This may well be because the Shah had realized that his subjects, on the whole, had not yet achieved a level of literacy sufficient to provide him with the number of trained technicians he needed to maintain his armed forces. As a result Iran's arsenal was filled with equipment it could not maintain and could only barely operate.

Iraq—a dreadful secular dictatorship—did declare a jihad but did not carry it to an extreme. In contrast, Iran not only declared a jihad but made extensive use of volunteer martyrs who were inspired by their Shia Islamic faith to join the war against Iraq. The Iranians Shias viewed death in this war as martyrdom in the path of God that granted immediate entry into paradise. This was supported by the following Koranic verse:

And call not those who are slain in the way of Allah "dead." Nay, they are living, only ye perceive not. And surely We shall try you. (Surah II, 154)

The Martyrs' Foundation was established to provide for the families of these martyrs, once they had been killed in the holy war against Iraq. Funds came from the Iranian government, religious trusts, and income from exiled Iranians. This foundation looked after the families of those slain, assuring widows or parents a monthly income of $280 per month, plus child allowances of $56 per month. In addition, the family survivors were given preference in the allocation of scarce consumer goods such as cars, motorcycles, refrigerators, housing, and admission to universities. In the case of military personnel, an outright grant of $24,000 was made. The government combined these material incentives with an appeal to Islamic zeal to build and motivate its forces.

As deadly as the actions of Saddam Hussein had been, the Muslim world was about to meet the genuine "Great Satan" of the globe, the atheistic militarism of the Soviet Union.

The Russian invasion of Afghanistan occurred in December 1979. Some suggest the invasion was a continuation of the historic Russian endeavor to continue its push for warm-water ports. Those people have obviously never considered the problems of road transport through the mountains of Afghanistan, nor the fact that Iran or Pakistan would have to be tackled next. Some suggest that it was an effort to continue the spread of international communism. Others would suggest that Russian paranoia drove the Soviet Union to surround itself with a line of puppet states that would absorb any assault from the west. Some might also suggest concern for a militant Muslim state forming on its southern border that would stir up the Muslim population in those portions of the Soviet Union that bordered on Afghanistan.

Whatever the reason, the Russians sent thousands of men into Afghanistan over ten years, during which 15,000 Russians and an estimated 1,000,000 Afghans would die. It was a guerrilla war that had no major battles. It featured large-scale military operations, but no set-piece battles between modern armies.

The Afghanistan government had been taken over by a radical branch of the Afghan communist party in the late 1970s. After purging those communists inadequately submissive to the Soviets, these radicals had begun an immediate "sovietization" of Afghanistan. They persecuted and murdered mullahs, seized and redistributed land, prohibited arranged marriages, and generally attacked the roots of Afghan culture in order to bring Afghanistan into the world of socialism.

The attacks on the mullahs were a particular mistake, which the Afghani communists should have understood, but apparently did not. Outside of the few major cities, Afghanistan was organized in tribes. Illiteracy was almost universal, and the mullahs in each community were not only the spiritual leaders, they frequently served their villages as teacher, scribe, and sage. Mullahs were highly respected by their communities; they played a critical role in the fabric of the village and tribe.

The redistribution of land was equally destructive of Afghan culture. The mullah, the elected *malik,* who was generally the wealthiest landowner of the community, and possibly one or two other individuals formed the principal part of village administration. The redistribution of land attacked this second leg of the civil government and further exacerbated the political disarray. Afghan communist party attacks against them provoked a rebellion, and central governmental officials were either driven out of the villages or murdered. When the Soviets invaded, Afghanistan was already in a civil war.

A further aspect of Afghan society made the eventual Soviet invasion a disaster. Afghan society revolved around three essentials, the family, the *Pashtunwali* (an unchanging set of rules learned from childhood that provided guidelines for behavior, including the blood feud or *badal*), and the Islamic religion.

The last two caused the principal problem for the Soviets. First, when indiscriminate Soviet attacks against villages killed women and children, every surviving male was obliged by *Pashtunwali* blood feud rules to avenge the dead members of their family.

This blended with the Islamic concept of the jihad. The devout Islamic Afghans believed that by fighting a foreign invader they became *gazi,* or

Islamic warriors. If they died fighting an infidel, which definitely included the atheistic Soviets, they would become *shakhid* and go to paradise.

Thus, the combination of blood feud against an infidel and jihad turned the male population of Afghanistan into most tenacious guerrillas. The feud imperative obliged revenge and the jihad guaranteed the reward of paradise if they were killed.

As a result, the war was marked by extreme savagery on both sides. A discussion with E. Vovsi, a veteran of the Soviet army and of the Afghan war who served in Afghanistan from October to November 1982, reveals that the Soviet soldiers had no idea what awaited them when they went into Afghanistan. Early in the war battalions were rotated in and out after a few months' service, so disconcerting was the fighting.

Mujahedin war was something the Afghans understood quite well as heirs to a rich martial history and continuing experience of banditry and tribal conflict. The Soviet invasion, however, was an assault by infidels, by "crusaders" seeking to destroy Islam. It mattered little that the Soviets were officially atheists; they were no different to the hill men than the Catholic crusaders that had marched into Palestine 800 years earlier.

To the mujahedin, the war was a holy war. They had little concern for their personal safety in combat and could stand and fight to the death rather than run away from the superior Soviet firepower. Vovsi says that when he encountered Afghan prisoners he saw nothing but hatred in their eyes. He doubted that they had any concept of the struggle in Kabul to establish a puppet Afghan regime, subservient to the Soviets. They were simply filled with anger at the Soviet infidels who had intruded into their country.

Most of the Afghan attacks were hit-and-run in nature. For obvious reasons they avoided open confrontations with the militarily superior Soviet forces. Instead, they would throw grenades in marketplaces, poison wells, and snipe at Soviet supply convoys. The Afghans had no vehicles and operated entirely on foot, or on horseback. They were more fit, as a result, and their greater endurance, coupled with their knowledge of the countryside, gave them tremendous advantages over the Soviets.

In contrast, the Soviets were frequently overly wedded to their vehicles and maneuvered on roads or by air. The Afghans were well informed of Soviet movements and frequently caught these convoys as they moved about. They also caught and savaged airborne detachments while landing, before the Soviets could bring up supporting arms.

When cornered, however, they were ready to fight to the death. The Soviets often remarked that the Afghans did not know the meaning of the word "retreat." They had no concern if they died, or if their women and children died, if a Soviet soldier could be killed. Vovsi perceived that the Afghans saw it as an obligation imposed on them by a higher authority, be it Allah or their mullahs, to kill every Soviet possible. Soviet prisoners were savagely tortured. If a Soviet woman was taken, Vovsi reported that she was brutalized such that she "would never bear another Christian child."

The anti-Soviet military struggle was the defense of a Muslim state against an infidel invader. The Afghan warriors frequently carried Korans into battle, wore religious necklaces or even had verses from the Koran tattooed on their bodies. In the early days of the war the mujahedin often wore the white robes of the martyr. Their military leaders were their religious leaders. It was a holy war, pure and simple. As such, it drew volunteers from all across the Muslim world, including the notorious Osama bin Laden. These men saw a struggle between Dar ul Islam and Dar ul Harib, the World of Islam and the World of War. The "Harib" (residents of the Dar ul Harib) were infidels, be they Soviet atheists or twelfth-century Frankish Crusaders. The ancient Arabic saying, "My enemy's enemy is my friend," in an incredible twist of irony, allowed them to accept American military support with a glad hand. Thirteen years later, in an act of cold calculation, they would bite that same American hand simply because it was an infidel hand.

As Vovsi noted, Afghans knew nothing of the world outside of their villages and what their religious leaders told them. The mullah is the voice of Allah on earth and the hand of Allah that guides them on this earth. Their entire existence, their demeanor in war, and their death were inseparable from their religion.

The Soviets attempted to fight as much of the war as they could with a theoretically loyal Afghan army formed from draftees. The young and capable generally escaped the press gangs, leaving the old and less alert to be swept up and armed. Those conscripts who were physically fit generally stayed only to be equipped and armed by the Soviets before they defected to the mujahedin. This conscript army failed miserably for many reasons; a major consideration was their total lack of commitment to the communist cause.

A second cause can be illustrated by an interesting quotation dating from 1882. A Victorian military writer, in speaking of the individualism of the Afghan warrior said, "once he [the Afghan soldier] is asked to sink his identity and become merely a unit in a battalion he loses all self-confidence and is likely to think more of getting away than of stubbornly holding his ground as he would have done with his own friends led by his own chief." This comment clearly indicates that the tribal associations were still a critical element in the mind of the Afghan warrior one hundred years later.

The situation in Afghanistan was little more than a festering sore for the Soviets, and their prestige began to suffer badly. In April 1984 they decided to launch a major offensive against the mujahedin along the Russian border. On April 20, 1984, the Panjshir offensive began with saturation bombing raids by more than 200 Tu16 medium bombers. On April 21 they began a rolling artillery barrage followed up by infantry, armor, and leapfrogging special forces, airborne units supported by ground attack aircraft, and helicopter gunships. The Afghan leader, Shah Massoud, and most of his forces escaped relatively unscathed, yet inflicted major blows against the Soviets. The Panjshir Valley was, despite the Soviet losses, cleared of mujahedin by September, but as soon as the Soviets withdrew, the Afghans began to return. By winter they had completely reoccupied the valley. The offensive had resolved nothing.

Accomplishing nothing in the war, and with their own political structure crumbling, the Soviets withdrew from Afghanistan. After a futile attempt at turning the war over to the Afghan communist government, they pulled out completely in 1988. The Afghan communist regime, left to defend itself, was quickly destroyed and Afghanistan fell into a civil war that continued until the U.S.-Afghan war of 2001.

Just as the Soviets were leaving Afghanistan, and indeed the pages of history, Saddam Hussein again committed Iraq to a foreign adventure. This one would be shorter and less costly than the Iranian War, but would have much more lasting consequences.

On August 2, 1990, a massive Iraqi attack descended on the tiny neighboring principality of Kuwait. The Kuwaiti national guard force, a brigade-sized unit, either died under the weight of the oncoming armor or disengaged to the south into neighboring Saudi Arabia. Saddam Hussein, frustrated at his defeat against Iran, had come for the Kuwaiti oil. His soldiers in Kuwait City looted and raped like those of any other medieval despot.

Although the Iraqi attack had overwhelmed Kuwait, a real fear was that his troops would keep moving and occupy Saudi Arabia, the rich but weak center of the Arabian world. The Saudis were terrified, and the United States was justly alarmed. Had Iraq taken Saudi Arabia, a despotic madman would have controlled approximately 40 percent of the world's oil, a picture with chilling ramifications. The world acted.

On August 6, 1990, Saudi officials asked for United States military protection. Two days later, American air force planes began arriving in the country and were joined by the beginnings of an enormous naval presence in the Indian Ocean. Marines landed next and were slowly reinforced by regular army divisions. While American air and military power grew, the two sides' diplomats growled at each other. Hussein may have misjudged Western resolve because of the weakness with which Jimmy Carter had acted—or failed to act—when Iran had kidnapped American embassy staff in Tehran. President Bush was cut from sterner stuff and built a decisive military and political coalition to defeat the Iraqi invasion. By January hosts of modern fighter planes faced Iraq's aging Mirages, and a large U.S.-led army had shouldered up to the Kuwaiti-Iraqi border. The only question was the ability of the American armored forces, who hadn't seen serious action in fifty years. If Saddam's troops could sufficiently bloody the Americans, he must have hoped that the pacifist and isolationist elements of the American Congress would win his battle for him. He ordered his army into action.

A few hours after darkness fell on January 29, 1991, U.S. Marine Corps outposts along the border reported the advance of a major Iraqi armored attack. Realizing that they were terribly outnumbered, the marines loaded into their vehicles and fled Khafji five minutes before the T-62s of the Iraqi 3rd Armored Division rolled over their now empty post.

The Iraqis were advancing in three distinct spearheads, two moving at positions to the west and one striking down the coastal highway. The 1st Mechanized Division was assigned the task of guarding the western flank of the attacking forces. The 3rd Armored Division was to cross the Saudi-Kuwaiti border south of Wafra and then strike against the Saudi port of Mis'hab. Simultaneously, the 5th Mechanized Division was to strike straight down the coast, clear out the Saudi forces posted on the border, then push south to link up with the 3rd Armored Division near Mis'hab. This was the spearhead of the only Iraqi advance into Saudi Arabia, and it was intended to be their major assault on the Saudis. If successful it would break the political back of the coalition.

The westernmost column consisted of a T-62 tank battalion and armored personnel carriers drawn from the 1st Mechanized Division. The central column was formed by elements of the 3rd Armored Division and contained about fifty tanks and thirty armored personnel carriers. The eastern column contained forty or more tanks and armored personnel carriers and moved directly down the coastal road. Once spotted, all three columns were brought under continuous air attack.

The 5th Mechanized Division's line of advance led it through the city of Ra's al Khafji, an oil and resort city on the Persian Gulf coast, about eight miles from the Kuwaiti border. Because of its proximity to Kuwait, when the war erupted, the Saudis had evacuated its 15,000 inhabitants.

The city was garrisoned by a battalion of the Saudi National Guard and a Qatari tank battalion, and supported by a U.S. liaison team intended to provide artillery support from the U.S. ships or aircraft as appropriate.

The Iraqi 5th Mechanized Division attacked southward, capturing Al Khafji, chasing from it the Saudi National Guard and Qatari forces that had garrisoned the city.

A counterattack was quickly mounted by Saudi National Guard and the Qatari armored forces, accompanied by a few U.S. marines and supported by massive American air attacks. The counterattack had little finesse, and the Saudis rolled through the streets of southern Khafji firing wildly. The Iraqis fired back with as little discipline, resulting in an utterly chaotic battle with little or no direction from above. The counterattack was repulsed. When the morning of January 30 arrived, the Iraqis still held Khafji.

The next morning the 2nd Saudi National Guard again advanced into Khafji supported by two companies of Qatari tanks that positioned themselves to block Iraqi reinforcements that might move against the city. The Saudis again drove into the city, Saudi officers screaming into bullhorns demands that the Iraqis surrender. Iraqi defensive fire slowed the Saudi thrust, bringing some pause to the battle. The Saudis, however, were not to be denied and resumed their attack. Eventually they cleared the city and recaptured it, claiming 30 Iraqis killed, 37 wounded, and 429 prisoners. Their attack had cost them 19 dead and 36 wounded. During the attack the allied air strikes claimed to have inflicted 2,000 casualties on the Iraqis and to have destroyed 300 vehicles. The Iraqi 5th Mechanized Division was virtually destroyed. Ground engagements cost it 40 tanks and many armored personnel carriers. The Allied command reported destroying 544 tanks, 314 armored personnel carriers, and 425 artillery pieces between January 29 and February 3 in all parts of the war zone. Most of these were from the corps that had attacked Khafji.

The Battle of Khafji was the only offensive by the fourth-strongest army in the world. Instead of attacking, the Iraqis built massive sand fortifications of the type that had served so well against Iran. These fortified dunes, and their dictator's bluster, were to be equally ineffective against the Allied bombing, or the armored assault that followed.

On February 24 Saddam's house of cards collapsed as the Allies attacked in a huge armored advance led by two American corps and incorporating elements from most other nations of the world. With superior reconnaissance, maneuvering, firepower, and leadership, the Allied storm was neither stopped nor delayed by the Iraqi defenses. In a few hours the Allies had reentered Kuwait city and enveloped most of the Iraqi army.

In a mad rush to escape, thousands of enemy soldiers were massacred by concentrated air attacks on the "Highway of Death" leading to Iraq from Kuwait. Thousands more surrendered to anything remotely resembling an American presence—including the media.

Despite the crushing defeat there were instances of skillful Iraqi operations and generalships. The technological gap in war-fighting capabilities was, however, too great for any Iraqi general to overcome. The conventional war ended after 100 hours in a negotiated settlement. Sadly, the peace that followed has gradually eroded into a meaningless farce as Saddam Hussein thumbed his nose at an irresolute West. When the fighting stopped, the American doves reasserted themselves, and Iraqi failure to comply with peace terms has been met with pointless sanctions and random bombing attacks. In 2003 this would lead to a new and more devastating confrontation with the United States.

The Gulf War was at least comprehensible to Western minds, in that it was a conflict in which nations were contestants for understandable national goals. The next major United States military involvement into the Muslim world would pit the freedom of the modern world against the dark medievalism of fundamentalist hatred.

The destruction of the World Trade Center is still fresh in the mind of the world, as is President Bush's demand to the Taliban that it surrender Osama bin Laden for prosecution by the U.S. government. When the Taliban refused, President Bush ordered military action that began with air strikes first aimed at the elimination of Afghanistan's primitive air defense system and then focused on tactical bombing of the Taliban's field army facing the Northern Alliance.

The war itself was militarily interesting, in that it included no great maneuvers and battles of the old style. However, it provides some lessons. Afghanistan, as mentioned earlier, functions on a tribal basis. Alliances between weak tribes are the basis on which all Afghan governments are built. Just as with the Arab tribes that Muhammad organized into a single, nominally unified mass, these alliances produce something resembling a sense of national unity for Afghanistan, but one infinitely more fragile than the Western sense of nationalism provides.

As discussed in Chapter 1, Muslims view victory as an indication of Allah's support of the victor and defeat as a sign of Allah's disfavor. When Muhammad won at Badr he was perceived as having Allah on his side, and the tribes, wishing to be on the winning side, flocked to his banner. When, in 2001, the American bombing had broken the Taliban forces' ability to resist the Northern Alliance and organized Taliban resistance collapsed, the various alliances it had with the numerous tribal groups also collapsed. Allah was no longer on the side of the Taliban, because the laurels of victory had passed to the Northern Alliance. Each Northern Alliance step toward Kabul as it swept south was seen as a further sign of Allah's favor and even more tribes and commanders joined the Alliance forces. In a more basic sense, the process of shifting alliances might be summarized as, "It is better to pick the corpse than to be the corpse, even if its previous occupant is now in paradise." This is a clear demonstration of how fragile any system of alliances has been in Afghanistan and how fragile they likely will continue to be until the people of Afghanistan evolve away from their tribal roots.

If one steps back and examines the U.S. campaign plan, it was an incredibly subtle exploitation of the Islamic perception of God being on the side of the victor when the victor is a Muslim. Had the United States landed troops and launched a ground attack on the Taliban, they would have simply melted into the mountains, declared a jihad, and by definition had God on their side. Attacked by infidels, they would not lose face or the support of their allied tribes, because God cannot be, by definition, on the side of an infidel.

On the other hand, the Taliban could not withdraw in the face of the Muslims of the Northern Alliance, even under the pressure of U.S. bombing. To do so would be political suicide. If the Taliban moved away in order to escape the air attacks they would appear beaten by the Northern Alliance, which actually happened.

Knowing this, the Taliban troops remained in their positions, locked in place not by the military prowess of the Northern Alliance, but by their own cultural imperatives—to back away is to surrender God to your enemy. As a result, the Taliban stood as U.S. air power bombed them into oblivion.

Stationary Taliban military forces were ground down and blasted into nothing. When the morale of the survivors was so shaken by the hand of God, in the form of cluster bombs, Daisy Cutters, and carpet-bombing, the Taliban was incapable of resisting the military pressure of the Northern Alliance. Some Taliban defected to the Northern Alliance soldiers to escape the terrible weight of explosives showered on them by naval bombers and B-52s. Others melted into the mountains and desert. When the Taliban army vanished, the Northern Alliance, with God now on its side, drove forward. With every step south it took, tribe after tribe came to offer fealty to God's designated victors. Like a train rolling downhill, the Alliance gained irresistible momentum.

Another factor is the average Afghani's hatred of the Taliban. The Taliban was supported by large numbers of non-Afghans: Arabs and Pakistanis. The Arabs were simply foreign devils, as any other non-Afghan would be perceived, but the Pakistanis occupy a place of particular hatred in the Afghan heart. Aside from the border issues—the Pakistan border cuts off many ethnic Pushtuns from their Afghan brothers and prevents the formation of an ethnically cohesive Pushtunistan; a longstanding rivalry exists between these two states. Both have meddled in the other's internal affairs. In addition, the Afghans have long viewed the Pakistanis as objects of prey. When Pakistani volunteers came into Afghanistan to join the Taliban, they were already despised foreigners, but even more they were now perceived as supporting the oppressive central government. It is not at all surprising that many Arab and Pakistani Taliban fighters were slaughtered if caught.

In March 2003 the most recent Muslim experience in war occurred. Saddam Hussein's continued violations of the First Gulf War's armistice and continued weapons programs provoked an alliance of western nations to remove him once and for all. From the Muslim perspective the onslaught that exploded over Baghdad was stunning in its precision and magnitude. Technological progress and the science of applied military force had undergone a massive evolution since the 1991 Gulf War that was beyond the comprehension, not only of the Iraqi military, but of the world that watched it nightly on their televisions. Precision munitions absolutely eviscerated the Iraqi command and control system, leaving their combat troops directionless and easy victims to the rapidly moving American columns. The only Iraqi successes were, strangely enough, achieved by the para-military militias that had hidden from and were bypassed by the American armored columns. The tanks past, they suddenly found themselves confronted by the noncombatants of the American logistical system, which did not have the combat training or weapons systems of their big brothers. These limited successes, the destruction and capture of elements of a single ordnance company or the random sniping of stray Western soldiers, stand in poor comparison to the overrunning of their country in three weeks. However, they can easily be seen as yet a further example of the historical Middle Eastern flair for small actions of a hit-and-run nature. This is a form of guerilla or nonconventional warfare, but the geographical environment of Iraq and most of the Persian Gulf region is not as conducive to that style of warfare in an age of pilotless drones, reconnaissance satellites, and laser guided bombs as it was 1,000 years earlier. The very best it can hope to accomplish is to produce a politically difficult situation for the Western powers that occupy Iraq until a new Iraqi government is established and they withdraw. This, however, becomes a political and diplomatic issue and not a military one.

The backwardness of the Taliban and, to a lesser degree, Iraq, are only the most recent evidence of a long trend in Islamic military circles—a backwardness mirrored by their societies. In the Balkan War of 1912–13, the Bulgarians, who were about as backward a European nation as one could imagine at that time, proved themselves militarily superior to the Turkish army, despite the long Turkish military tradition. During the course of World War I the Turks proved themselves generally incapable of anything but a stubborn defense against the western armies. The few bright moments were mostly brought about because of the presence of German officers.

After World War II, the only Muslim successes in 1948 were, again, when their troops were led by the British officers of the Arab Legion. Through the 1956, 1967, and 1973 Arab-Israeli wars the Arabs proved themselves vastly inferior to the Israelis, despite their huge numerical and equipment superiority. They moved about clumsily when attempting an offensive. Once their initial plan was completed or went awry, they were bewildered by the changed circumstances and appeared to have little concept of what to do next. This was most notable in 1973 after the Egyptians had breached the Israeli Suez Canal defenses.

Some Muslim armies did have a flare for the defense and could be formidable on those occasions, but once their leadership was killed or its morale broken, they generally decamped in great haste. They could operate in a static war of attrition. In the Iran-Iraq war the Iraqis clearly recognized their inability to maintain an offensive against the vastly superior Iranian forces arrayed before them, fell back on the defense, and proceeded to slaughter thousands of Iranian soldiers. The Iranians—once their small Western-trained, professional army was bled white—had no skill at the offense, but they certainly demonstrated a willingness to accept huge and needless casualties.

The Russian invasion of Afghanistan faced a guerrilla war. Here, the Islamic warriors avoided pitched battle and fell back on the techniques of ambush and mountain warfare where the prowess of the individual and small groups were familiar keys. They did not attempt to conscript large numbers of civilians into their war bands, nor to mold them into soldiers as the Egyptians, Syrians, Iranians, and Iraqis had done in their wars in the latter half of the twentieth century. Instead, they relied on the natural Afghan proclivity for war based on tribal military tradition. They were also reinforced by both their hatred of foreign invaders and the religious imperative to defend their homeland from infidels. Their success can be ascribed to many issues: the lack of real dedication on the part of the Russians to pursue the war, financial support from the rest of the Muslim world, and the introduction of superior technical weaponry from the United States in the form of Stinger missiles that checked Russian close air support. However, the overwhelming reason for their success was their reliance on guerrilla tactics and a military tradition ideally suited for guerrilla warfare.

When the United States attacked Iraq in 1991, during the Gulf War, the Iraqis abandoned the initiative to the United States when their limited incursion into Saudi Arabia was brutally crushed. They fell back on their strength in defensive warfare and hoped to repeat the same tactics they had used against the Iranians. Their mistake was to play the warfare game with a superpower that excels in conventional warfare.

In the subsequent ground battle, the Iraqis proved totally incapable of dealing with the U.S. air-ground battle system. Their officers fled the front and abandoned the troops to their fate. There were instances in the 1991 Gulf War where the Iraqis had shown a fair level of aggressiveness and military capability in the Republican Guard. However, by 2003 the technological gap had greatly widened and the moral decay of the Iraqi army was such that in barely three weeks Iraq was completely overrun. The poor performance of the Iraqi army was as much of a shock to the entire Arab world as was the massive superiority of the American army. This overwhelming and crushing victory will temper the behavior of Muslim states, but may well force them to shift to unconventional warfare.

When the War on Terrorism began in 2001 and the United States attacked Afghanistan, the United States wisely chose not to introduce large numbers of "infidel" troops into Afghanistan. The Americans carefully exploited the cultural and internal political situation to their advantage, kept the war in a conventional mode, and avoided a guerrilla war. The United States played to its strength and the Taliban weakness.

Overall, the Muslim world has shown little talent for the complexities of modern warfare. In 1948 they had every reason to expect to crush the nascent Israeli army, but their lack of a trained officer and NCO cadre, in addition to intra-Muslim political problems, led to a decisive failure.

In the subsequent Arab-Israeli wars they again showed themselves incapable of modern warfare against a capable foe, no matter how small. When facing other Muslim states they were evenly matched, but again showed no capability for controlling large military forces in a mobile warfare environment. The Iranians reverted to mass infantry attacks, the height of wasteful military incompetence.

Modern warfare develops its power from the combination of movement and firepower. This style of warfare requires educated, trained, and sophisticated soldiers capable of operating and maintaining complex mechanical and electronic equipment. It also depends on highly trained and educated command and control systems—officers. The Muslim world is decisively deficient in these commodities. The military tradition that once produced such ferocious warriors as the Janissaries and the Mamluks has long vanished. Even if the Muslim military societies still existed, the social environment on which Western military techniques, and the technology upon which it rests and depends, will not exist in the Muslim world until there are major cultural changes.

The officers produced by Middle Eastern cultures come from elements of society different from those that provide the common soldiers. Though this is true throughout the world, the difference is far greater in the Middle East. This prevents the bonding and trust that provides the staying power of Western armies. Education in the Middle Eastern states is so poor that the technical skills necessary to maintain tanks, aircraft, and electronics simply do not exist in sufficient depth to support a modern military force.

It is impossible to say if Osama bin Laden recognized these failures of his world, but he did come to a correct conclusion: the Muslim world can not engage in conventional warfare with the West. He has chosen terrorism as an alternative. Terrorism is such an anemic form of warfare that it hardly qualifies as such. It is difficult to imagine that his terrorism will avail much. For several generations it hasn't helped the Palestinians and seems unlikely to help Bin Laden. Still, it may be the only type of warfare that backward nations can employ against the forces of the modern world. If so, some Muslim forces will still be in the mold of practicing futile and unsuccessful military arts, a bleak prospect indeed.

CHRONOLOGY

1947	India and Pakistan become independent. War breaks out.
1948	First Arab-Israeli war
1948	Cease-fire between India and Pakistan
1956	Second Arab-Israeli war (Suez War)
1965	First India-Pakistan war
1967	Third Arab-Israeli war (Six Days' War)
1971	India attacks Pakistan, creating Bangladesh from East Pakistan.
1973	Fourth Arab-Israeli war
1979	Soviet Russian invasion of Afghanistan. Fighting continues into 1989.

1980	Iraq attacks Iran. Fighting continues into 1988.
1991	Gulf War: United Nations forces remove Iraqi forces from Kuwait.
2001	Taliban regime in Afghanistan defeated by United States and rebel forces.
2003	Second Gulf War

NOTE

1. Herzog, C. *The Arab-Israeli Wars, War and Peace in the Middle East from the War of Independence through Lebanon,* New York: Vintage Books, 1984, 107–108.

Chapter 12

ISLAM AND JIHAD: FOR IT IS ORDAINED UNTO YOU

Now when ye meet in battle those who disbelieve, then it is smiting of necks until, when ye have routed them, then making fast of bonds; and afterward either grace or ransom until the war lay down its burdens. That is the ordinance. And if Allah willed He could have punished them (without you) but (thus it is ordained) that He may try some of you by means of others. And those who are slain in the way of Allah, He rendereth not their actions vain.

Koran, Surah XLVII, 4

The word *jihad* originates in the Arabic word *jahada,* which is translated by Lane in his Arabic-English lexicon, as "He strove, labored, or toiled; exerted himself or his power or efforts or endeavors or ability." Jihad, however, as a historical tradition and a general practice has come to mean a "military action with the expansion of Islam and, if needs be, the defense of Islam."

Prior to the Islamic period, the Arabs were nomadic shepherds. Historically they had been warriors who supplemented their livings by pillage and the exploitation of settled populations. Injected into this Arabic culture, Islam would become a war machine, which once started could not be stopped. Before Islam, the Arabs did not even search for a motive to conduct their wars; their social organization needed war, and without victories it would have collapsed. To them war was a natural part of life.

However, without Islam it is unlikely that the conquests of Syria and Iraq would have occurred. Without Islam and the charismatic personality of Muhammad it is unlikely that they would have overcome the fractious nature of their clan society and the incessant feuds. Islam unified them, suppressed the clans and gave them the unity that permitted conquest. Many details of Arab expansion and conquest can be explained by the words of Muhammad, but its force is found elsewhere. In the Arab culture, Muhammad would not have succeeded had he preached humility and submission. For the Arab warriors, "true" meant successful, and "false" meant unsuccessful. The primary cause of the Arab conquests was this attitude that God's will is expressed by success and failure of the individual. In a society that supplements itself by robbery and pillage, a successful military foray that is rewarded with substantial spoils was seen as God's approval of that action. It is ironic that many of the early heroes of Islam were, in fact, little interested in religion. Khalid, who successfully fought against the Byzantines has been described as someone who "cared for nothing but war and did not want to learn anything else." The same goes for Amr, the conqueror of Egypt, and Othman, who amassed a fortune from these conquests.

The failure of the Meccans at the Battle of the Trench, the siege of Medina in A.D. 627, branded them as "false" and gave credence to the "truth" of Muhammad. It is little wonder, in this light, that key individuals such as Khalid, Othman, and Amr went over to Islam even before the capture of Mecca. In light of the Arab culture at that time, the story of their conversion merits little credence. The defeat before Medina had shown them where the "truth" lay. This is exactly the concept found in the medieval European concept of "trial by combat" where God—or Allah—granted victory to the truthful combatant.

Within the Arabic culture of the time, the young men needed to prove themselves to the older men, while the older men felt obliged to lead and reaffirm their virility in war. Much of this related to the idea of the vendetta or feud. Arab culture included a necessity to avenge the death of a family member, and this led to an almost endless cycle of revenge killings. As a result, some Arabic tribes lived for generations in a state of conflict with other tribes. The original cause of the conflict could be long forgotten or become totally meaningless, but neither tribe would willingly end the struggle. Battles were even arranged on an annual basis, such as those fought by the Kuraish and the Hawazin tribes. At the appointed time the warriors would appear and fight until they felt that enough men had been killed and maimed to satisfy the feuders.

This was the clay from which Muhammad would mold his army, and it was the culture into which Allah revealed his word. As language reflects the culture in which it exists, it is not surprising that Allah revealed his will to Muhammad using words and concepts that Muhammad knew and understood and that he imparted unto Muhammad an understanding of the concepts he was revealing. The problem, then, comes when Muhammad had to communicate those revelations in words and concepts that the Arabs around him would understand, so any divinely granted comprehension was not passed on to the next generations and the transmission of Allah's will left to the vernacular. The result was a huge introduction of Arabic culture into Allah's words as they were inscribed in the Koran. This included the Arabs' predisposition to war.

The history of Islamic military operations dates from March A.D. 622 when Muhammad met with the seventy-three men of Yathrib (Medina) and they decided to join Islam. This was a time when such acts entailed great personal danger. In doing so, these men came to Muhammad along different trails and in groups of two or three, to avoid detection. They swore loyalty to Muhammad and Muhammad is reputed to have cried out, "I am of you and you are of me! I will war against those that war against you and I will be at peace with those who are at peace with you!" The pledge these men made to Muhammad is known as the "Second Aqaba." Not only did it establish Islam, it also established one of the five principals of Islam—the Jihad.

After the Hegira, or flight to Medina, Muhammad was visited again by the Angel Gabriel, who brought Allah's order to "Fight the idol-worshipers." This was an order to war by Allah. Initially, this declaration of war was aimed at the Meccans, who were idolaters and who had cast Muhammad out of their midst. Muhammad began his war against the idolaters by attacking their wealth, the caravans that were the lifeblood of their economic interests. This not only trained his followers in the ways of war, but brought in much needed loot.

In January A.D. 624 Muhammad sent out Abd Allah Hajash and twelve men on a secret mission. Their mission was secret because of its inflammatory nature. The sealed orders were opened up two days out into the desert. They were ordered to Nakhla, between Mecca and Taif, and once there to attack a Meccan caravan. The raid was a success, but the attack occurred during a sacred period of peace observed by the Arabs and would arouse much anger.

When the anger burst, Muhammad initially denied responsibility, but after the return his raiding force and the arrival of the loot, a revelation came, Surah II, 217:

> They question thee (O Muhammad) with regard to warfare in the sacred month. Say: Warfare therein is a great (transgression), but to turn (men)

from the way of Allah, and to disbelieve in Him and in the Inviolable Place of Worship, and to expel his people thence, is a greater with Allah; for persecution is worse than killing. And they will not cease from fighting against you until they have made you renegades from your religion, if they can. And whoso becometh a renegade and dieth in his disbelief: such are they whose works have fallen both in the world and the Hearafter. Such are rightful owners of Fire: they will abide therein.

Subsequent Islamic scholars have stated that if the people of Mecca obstructed the new faith, old traditions were not to stand in the way of Allah. It should also be recognized that no movement that seeks to establish itself can succeed without breaking from old traditions.

The battle at Badr followed shortly upon the heels of the attack on this caravan. Before going to battle Muhammad prayed in a small tent, and it is reputed in some sources that he emerged reciting a new revelation, "Soon shall the hosts be routed, and they shall turn their backs." This revelation, surprisingly, is not found in the Koran. This revelation inspired his forces and convinced them that their cause was Allah's cause.

In a later passage in the Koran Muhammad spoke directly to the issue of Allah's support of their action at the battle of Badr. Two such passages are found:

Surah III, 123. Allah had already given you the victory at Badr, when ye were contemptible. So observe your duty to Allah in order that ye may be thankful.

Surah III, 13. There was a token for you in two hosts which met: one army fighting in the way of Allah, and another disbelieving, whom they saw as twice their number, clearly, with their very eyes. Thus Allah strengtheneth with His succor who He will. Lo! Herein verily is a lesson for those who have eyes.

This Koranic reinforcement of Allah's presence with them as they fought under Muhammad was the "lesson for those who have eyes," and it applied to all. This contributed to the problem of taking up arms against kinsmen, which was strictly forbidden by existing Arab tradition. Muhammad's approach worked. In one instance, Abd Allah Ubayy asked Muhammad's permission to kill his own father for "treachery" that his father had committed against Muhammad. Had someone else punished his father, existing tradition would require that the son kill his father's murderer after the fashion of the vendetta.

The battle of Badr began with stylized duels between the champions of both sides. Each side sent forward three champions. Two of the Muslim champions won their duels, but the third was wounded and bled to death. With the prelude over, the overture began with a bloody engagement. Muhammad, distraught over the forces arrayed against his tiny band, cried his prayers aloud, calling on Allah to intervene. As the battle proceeded he called out, "All who die today will go to Paradise!" This promise was formalized in Surah IV, 74:

> Let those fight in the way of Allah who sell the life of this world for the other. Whoso fighteth in the way of Allah, be he slain or be he victorious, on him We shall bestow a vast reward.

A young man standing by Muhammad, upon hearing the promise of paradise asked, "What, is it only necessary to be killed by these people to enter Paradise!" Being told yes, he then charged into a group of enemy warriors, cutting several down before being wounded himself. The rest of his band, inspired by the same promise, fought with such furor that the Meccans were driven back, leaving fifty dead and as many prisoners behind them.

At first, some of the Muslims wanted to slaughter their prisoners. In what would become a common occurrence—though usually after many had been slaughtered—they realized that the prisoners had ransom value and should be preserved.

The battle of Badr became a fundamental pillar in the formation and foundation of Islam. Had it gone differently, Islam would have ended on its bloody field. From this battle, a holy battle, Islam was founded and its continuance assured. In the light and impact of Badr, one can argue that "war" was a sacrament of the Islamic religion. Indeed, an argument for this can be found in the Koran as well. Surah III, 123, says that the victory at Badr came from Allah. The subsequent passages follow:

> Surah III, 124. And when thou didst say unto the believers: Is it not sufficient for you that your Lord should support you with three thousand angels sent down (to your help)?
>
> 125. Nay, but if ye persevere, and keep from evil, and (the enemy) attack you suddenly, *your Lord will help you with five thousand angels sweeping on.* [Italics added for emphasis.]
>
> 126. Allah ordained this only as a message of good cheer for you, and that thereby your hearts might be at rest—Victory cometh only from Allah, the Mighty, the Wise—

127. That He may cut off a part of those who disbelieve, or overwhelm them so that they retire, frustrated.

128. It is no concern at all of thee (Muhammad) whether He relent toward them or punish them; for they are evil-doers.

Allah sending angels to support the Muslims when they are in battle is surely an indication that their battle is a matter of Allah's interest, thereby making it a holy undertaking. Surah III, 126, says that "Victory (at Badr) cometh only from Allah," which states clearly that the fight at Badr was Allah's fight and the implication, when looked at in conjunction with Surah IV, 74, which promises eternity in paradise to those who fall in combat for Islam, is clearly that war for Islam is a holy act.

As history marched on, Islam, weaned on the field at Badr, would spread across the Middle East, North Africa, and the Indian subcontinent in the same manner. Jihad came to mean "holy war," and its main goal would evolve into the method by which infidels would be converted to Islam. Scholars agree that jihad is a collective, not a personal, obligation. According to the majority of scholars, the compulsory nature of the jihad is founded on Surah II, 216, "Prescribed for you is fighting, though it be hateful to you." Islamic scholars also agree that all polytheists should be fought. This is founded on Surah VIII, 39, "Fight them until there is no persecution and the religion is God's entirely." God, of course, refers to Muhammad's God.

The militarily aggressive nature of Islam is nowhere more apparent than in the concept of jihad, the holy war. The ultimate aim of this holy warfare is to conquer the entire world and force it to submit to Islam or the sword. Islam alone has been granted the truth and salvation is impossible outside it. It is the sacred duty of all Muslims to bring it to all humanity. Jihad is a divine institution, birthed at Badr and specifically decreed for the purpose of advancing Islam. Numerous scriptures in the Koran make it clear that Muslims must strive, fight, and kill in the name of Allah:

Surah IX, 5. Then, when the sacred months have passed, slay the idolaters wherever ye find them, and take them (captive), besiege them, and prepare for them each ambush.

Surah IV, 76. Those who believe fight in the cause of Allah . . .

Surah VIII, 12. I will instill terror into the hearts of the Infidels, strike off their heads then, and strike off from them every fingertip.

Surah VIII, 39–42. Say to the Infidels: If they desist from their unbelief, what is now past shall be forgiven them; but if they return to it, they have already before them the doom of the ancients! Fight then against them till strife be at an end, and the religion be all of it Allah's.

Surah II, 256. But they who believe, and who fly their country, and fight in the cause of Allah may hope for Allah's mercy: and Allah is Gracious, Merciful.

Surah V, 33. The only reward of those who make war upon Allah and His messenger (Muhammad) and strive after corruption in the land will be that they will be killed or crucified, or have their hands and feet on alternate sides cut off, or will be expelled out of the land. Such will be their degradation in the world, and in the Hereafter theirs will be an awful doom."

Aside from those scriptures, other scriptures declare it a mortal sin for a Muslim to shirk the battle against the unbelievers, "those who do will roast in hell":

Surah VIII, 15, 16. Believers, when you meet the unbelievers preparing for battle do not turn your backs to them. [Anyone who does] shall incur the wrath of Allah and hell shall be his home: an evil dwelling indeed.

Surah IX, 39. If you do not fight, He will punish you severely, and put others in your place.

Surah IV, 74. Let those fight in the cause of Allah who barter the life of this world for that which is to come; for whoever fights on Allah's path, whether he is killed or triumphs, We will give him a handsome reward.

It is abundantly clear from the preceding verses that the Koran is not talking of metaphorical battles or of moral crusades; it speaks of the battlefield in all its horrors as mandated to all the faithful Muslims. These passages establish the rules and concepts of the jihad and set them in the concrete of holy, divinely revealed scripture.

Various Islamic schools of thought differ on the application of the jihad. These are found within the four main schools of Islamic law. However, these differences are and must be on superficial issues only, because of the Koranic roots of the jihad.

The Koran divides mankind into two groups—Muslims and non-Muslims. The Muslims are members of the Islamic community, the *umma,* who possess territories in the Dar ul-Islam, the Land of Islam. In these lands the edicts of Islam are fully promulgated. The non-Muslims are the

Harbi, people of the Dar ul-Harb, the Land of Warfare, any country belonging to the infidels and not subdued by Islam. These lands are destined to pass into Islamic jurisdiction either by conversion or by war (Harb). All acts of war are permitted in the Dar ul-Harb.

Once the Dar ul-Harb has been subjugated, the Harbi, the surviving residents of the Dar ul-Harb, become prisoners of war. The imam has full license to do what he might with them. Those men taken prisoner are immediately faced with two choices: conversion to Islam or death. The option has not always been made clear. If it had been, many more would have accepted Islam. In the past, women and children had a worse fate awaiting them—slavery.

When Constantinople fell in 1453 the conquering army was allowed three days of pillage and rapine. The blood ran in rivers down the streets until the lust for slaughter was assuaged. The soldiers then realized that captives would bring them greater profits when sold as slaves. This was the same furor and blood lust that had first appeared at Badr when some of the victors had sought to slaughter the Meccan captives.

Other conquered peoples faced exile. Christians, Jews, or Zoroastrians, who had also received the Scriptures from Allah, might become *dhimmis,* tolerated second-class subjects forced to pay a regular tribute known as the "*jizya.*" Islamic scholars have interpreted Surah IX, 29

> Fight against such of those who have been given the Scripture as believe not in Allah nor the Last Day, and forbid not that which Allah hath forbidden by His Messenger, and follow not the religion of truth, until they pay the tribute readily, being brought low.

to mean, "the *jizya* shall be taken from them with belittlement and humiliation. [The *dhimmi*] shall come in person, walking not riding. When he pays, he shall stand, while the tax collector sits. The collector shall seize him by the scruff of the neck, shake him, and say: 'Pay the *jizya!*' and when he pays it he shall be slapped on the nape of his neck."

A critical issue is that the Dar ul-Harb are lands destined to submit to Islam. Some Islamic scholars contend that the wars that spread Islam are now long over and have completed the promise of the Koran. They claim that no more holy wars remain. They also contend that Islam, the true world religion, was complete from the moment of its revelation to Muhammad and did not have to evolve or develop, as Christianity evolved through the period of the writing of the Bible. As a result, they claim that Islam is stronger than Christianity, Judaism, Hinduism, Buddhism, and all other "misconceived" religions.

The idea of the jihad, born at Badr, fed on Islamic confidence and a sense of righteousness of Islam's cause. Inspired by their sense of right and the promises of paradise if they fall in their cause, jihadic warriors can be fanatically courageous and ferociously single-minded. They should never be underestimated because of this.

Islam added a new motive to the natural proclivity of the Arabic people to war. Despite this, in the early years of Islam the jihad was not limited to open war. Other forms of combat, aggression, and conflict could be justified as holy. What the Koran states—or is interpreted to have stated—is so absolute, however, that justification is meaningless and irrelevant. As a result, murder and assassination have been part of holy wars throughout the history of Islam.

Tradition and Koranic instructions about the jihad take the requirement to participate in it to an individual level. This is clearly stated in Surah III, 167–68:

167. *And that He might know the hypocrites, unto whom it was said: Come, fight in the way of Allah* [italics added], or defend yourselves. *They answered: If we knew aught of fighting we would follow you.* [i.e., refusing to engage in the jihad.] *On that day they were nearer disbelief than faith.* They utter with their mouths a thing that is not in their hearts. Allah is best aware of what they hide.

168. Those who, while they sat at home, said of their brethren (who were fighting for the cause of Allah): If they had been guided by us they would not have been slain. Say (unto them, O Muhammad): Then avert death from yourselves if ye are truthful.

The Surah III goes on to say that those who were "slain" have gone to Paradise. As far as these verses go, however, it is clear that those who were called to war and did not go were "hypocrites." In later verses, the Koran is clear as to the fate of hypocrites. By this verse, in the context of others, the believing Muslim finds himself called to war or to face the fate of hypocrites. That fate is laid out in several verses.

Surah LVII, 13. On the day when the hypocritical men and the hypocritical women will say unto those who believe: Look on us that we may borrow from you your light! It will be said: Go back and seek for light! Then there will separate from them a wall wherein is a gate, the inner side whereof containeth mercy, while the outerside thereof is toward the doom.

Surah XXXIII, 24. That *Allah may reward the true men for their truth and will punish the hypocrites* [italics added] if He will, or relent toward them (if He will). Lo! Allah is forgiving, Merciful.

Surah IV, 14. Lo! *The hypocrites (will be) in the lowest deep of the fire*
[italics added], and thou wilt find no helper for them.

Under tradition, the jihad became a *fard ala`l–kifaya,* or duty, imposed
on all free, adult, male Muslims who were sane and had the means to
reach the Muslim army as it assembled for war. The qualifications about
sanity and ability had no meaning because not joining was considered, of
itself, a form of insanity. In addition, the lengths and privations expected
of any male to attempt to join the army were such that there was no
escaping it. The jihad eventually became what might be considered the
sixth *rukn,* or fundamental duty of the Muslims. This is the tradition of
the Kharidjis, members of the earliest of the religious sects of Islam. These
sects are not comparable to the various Christian monks or holy orders,
but more akin to such groups as Protestants, Catholics, and Orthodox
Christians, where substantial theological differences separate them.

Islam is not just a religion, but a way of life that entails both the secular
and religious life of the fundamental Islamic state, that is, Islam is essentially a theocracy. When implemented as interpreted by modern fundamentalists such as the Taliban in Afghanistan and the ayatollahs in Iran,
the concept of sovereignty becomes inseparable from the concept of Allah.
Indeed, passages in the Koran specifically address this issue and give all
sovereignty to Allah:

Surah III, 26. Say: *O Allah! Owner of Sovereignty* [italics added]! Thou
givest sovereignty unto whom Thou wilt, and Thou withdrawest sovereignty from whom Thou wilt. Thou exaltest whom Thou wilt and Thou
abasest whom Thou wilt. In Thy hand is good. Lo! Thou art Able to do all
things.

Surah III, 189. Unto *Allah belongeth the Sovereignty* [italics added] of the
heavens and the earth. Allah is Able to do all things.

Under these circumstances, to the true believer, rebellion against the
state becomes rebellion against Allah. This evolves, especially in light of
the second-class nature of the *dhimmis* (non-Islamic followers of Allah
allowed to live within the Islamic state). The Koran says that all men
should subscribe to the will of Allah, and those who do not are obviously
the enemies of Allah and to be subjugated or eliminated. Submission to
rule by an Islamic government is insufficient. It must be submission to
Allah and his one true prophet.

Some interpret the jihad as having ended because the modern Muslim
world exists and its expansion has stopped—that is, the Dar ul-Harb (land

of war) as defined in the Koran has been brought to Islam. Other scholars see the "duty to fight" until the whole world is ruled by Islam and is controlled or headed by a Muslim imam or leader.

Until recently it was considered, in theory, that the Shia Muslims could not launch into a jihad until their "invisible" imam reappeared. This invisible or missing imam was, in 1979, considered to be the Ayatollah Khomeini—at least by many in Iran.

Wars against nonbelievers were always right in the religious sense, in that they are supported by many verses in the Koran. However, from a legal sense they were also right. The Shari'a, or Islamic Law, required that a Muslim head of state organize annual raids into enemy territory as a legal ritual to remind everybody, including the faithful, of their Islamic obligations. Even in times of peace they were expected to undergo military training as well as prepare their weapons for the jihad to come.

As time passed, later Islamic legal experts determined that a ruler could fulfill his obligations by simply making the annual preparations for the jihad, even if he did not then go to war. Historically, however, even these preparations produced a momentum that made conflict almost inevitable. The organization of an army in times past brought with it anticipation of loot, women, and slaves. When a medieval Muslim ruler brought together such a force without giving it the opportunity to vent its desire to gather the anticipated booty, he ran the risk of mutiny.

When a holy war was declared and combat engaged, those about to be attacked or those just defeated were given the opportunity, by Koranic edict, to embrace Islam. The period for reflection, as mentioned earlier, could be short. On occasion, select groups, that is, the "children of the book" (Christians, Jews and Zoroastrians) were given the opportunity to reconsider and accept status as *dhimmis* and to pay the *jizya* (tribute) and *kharadj* (a tax paid on land). This was regarded as a generous concession. Those who accepted Islam to escape this and reverted to their previous religion faced death.

Surah III, 85–91. *How shall Allah guide a people who disbelieved after their belief and (after) they bore witness that the messenger is true and after clear proofs (of Allah's sovereignty) had come unto them* [italics added]. And Allah guideth not wrongdoing folk.

87. *As for such, their guerdon* [reward] *is that on them rests the curse of Allah and of angels and of men combined* [italics added].

88. They will abide therein. Their doom will not be lightened, Neither will they be reprieved.

89. Save those who afterward repent and do right. Lo! Allah is Forgiving, Merciful.

90. Lo! *Those who disbelieve after their (profession of) belief, and afterward grow violent in disbelief: their repentance will not be accepted* [italics added]. And such are those who are astray.

91. Lo! Those who disbelieve, and die in disbelief, the (whole) earth full of gold would not be accepted from such an one if it were offered as a ransom (for his soul). Theirs will be a painful doom and they will have no helpers.

Surah III, 105. *And be ye not as those who separated and disputed after the clear proofs [that Islam was the true faith] had come unto them. For such there is an awful doom* [italics added].

106. On the day when (some) faces will be whitened and (some) faces will be blackened; and as for those whose faces have been blackened, it will be said unto them: Disbelieved ye after your (profession of) belief? Then taste the punishment for that ye disbelieved.

Though the surah does indicate a chance for redemption for the individual who accepted Islam and later returned to his disbelieving ways, recidivists were seldom given an opportunity to exploit this opportunity. Historically, they tended to meet their "doom" quickly when discovered.

Islam contains an interesting problem within the context of the jihad. Any war can become a holy war, even when Muslims fight Muslims. Both sides can and do invoke the name of Allah. In 1980 both Iraq and Iran, then engaged in a bitter war, proclaimed a jihad against the other. This cleaved along the rift between the Sunni and the Shia sects, both of which have a strong antipathy for the other. Iraq used poison gas against the Iranians and both bombed each other's cities. Where this becomes interesting is in Surah IV, 93–94:

93. *Whoso slayeth a believer of set purpose, his reward is Hell for ever* [italics added]. Allah is wroth against him and He hath cursed him and prepared for him an awful doom.

94. O ye who believe! *When ye go forth (to fight) in the way of Allah* [the jihad], *be careful to discriminate* [italics added], and say not unto one who offereth you peace: "Thou are not a believer," seeking the chance profits of this life (so that ye may despoil him). With Allah are plenteous spoils. Even thus (as he now is) you. Therefore take care to discriminate. Allah is ever Informed of what ye do.

One must accept, by these two surah, that one true believer killing another true believer sentences the murderer to hell for eternity. If the war between Iraq and Iran was seen by both as a legitimate holy war, then each must have rationalized the other as being an infidel. This would also indicate that they are subject to the fate of those who accept and then abandon Islam, that is, death. Clearly this indicates that the Muslim world today is not a monolithic organism.

In the case of Iran, one can legitimately say that they surely have the right to self-defense, and verses can be found in the Koran to support that right. However, the later Iraqi invasion of Kuwait for the sole purpose of despoiling it of its riches, plus the murder and rapine practiced by the Iraqi soldiers against men, women, and children, violates Surah III, 94.

However, under normal circumstances the fundamental target of the jihad is conflict with idolaters and non-Muslims of every kind, including what Muhammad describes as "people of the Scripture"—Christians, Jews, and Zoroastrians. The Koran includes frequent references to the Jews as having broken their covenant with Allah. Frequent references that damn the Jews also generally appear in the Koran after Muhammad had some problems with various Jewish communities. Much of this comes from the Hebrew tribes who shifted their alliances away from Muhammad after his defeat at Mt. Uhud. In a second major incident the Hebrews turned on Muhammad during the siege of Medina and openly sent forces to join those fighting against him.

The question now comes to how these non-Muslims are treated within the context of the jihad. The answer is that terror and brutality are appropriate. The Koran makes numerous references to this issue:

Surah III, 151. *We shall cast terror into of those who disbelieve* [italics added] because they ascribe unto Allah partners, for which no warrant hast been revealed. Their habitation is the fire, and hapless the abode of the wrong-doers.

Surah XXI, 98. Lo! *Ye (Idolaters) and that which ye worship besides Allah are fuel of hell. Thereunto ye will come* [italics added].

99. If these had been Allah's they would not have come thither, but all will abide therein.

100. *Therein wailing is their [the nonbelievers] portion* [italics added], and therein they hear not.

101. Lo! Those unto whom kindness hath gone forth before from Us, they will be far removed from thence.

102. They will not hear the slightest sound thereof, while they abide in that which their souls desire.

103. *The Supreme Horror [Terror] will not grieve them* [italics added], and the angels will welcome them, (saying): This is your Day which ye were promised;

104. The Day when We shall roll up the heavens as a recorder rolleth up a written scroll. As We began the first creation, We shall repeat it. (It is) a promise (binding) upon Us. Lo! We are to perform it.

105. And verily We have written in the Scripture, after the Reminder: My righteous slaves will inherit the earth:

Surah XXVII, 88. And thou seest the hill thou deemest solid flying with the flight of clouds: the doing of Allah Who perfecteth all things. Lo! He is Informed of what ye do.

89. Whoso bringeth a good deed will have better than its worth; and such are safe from fear [terror] that Day.

90. *And whoso bringeth an ill deed, such will be flung down on their faces in the Fire* [italics added]. Are ye rewarded aught save what ye did?

91. (Say): I (Muhammad) am commanded only to serve the Lord of this land which He had hallowed, and unto Whom all things belong. And I am commanded to be of those who surrender (unto Him).

Surah VIII, 65. O Prophet! Exhort the believer to fight. If there be of you twenty steadfast they shall overcome two hundred, and if there be of you a hundred steadfast they shall overcome a thousand of those who disbelieve, because they (the disbeliveers) are a folk without intelligence.

66. Now hath Allah lightened your burden, for He knoweth that there is weakness in you. So if there be of you a steadfast hundred, they shall overcome two hundred, and if there be a thousand (steadfast) they shall overcome two thousand by permission of Allah. Allah is with the steadfast.

67. *It is not for any Prophet to have captives until he hath made slaughter in the land* [italics added]. Ye desire the lure of this world and Allah desireth (for you) the Hereafter, and Allah is Mighty, Wise.

Surah XLVII, 5. And when you meet in regular battle those who disbelieve, smite their necks; and, *when you have overcome them, by causing great slaughter among them* [italics added], bind fast the fetters—then afterwards either release them as a favor or by taking ransom—until the war lays down its burdens. That is the ordinance. And if Allah had so pleased, He could have punished them Himself, but He has willed that He may try some of you by others. And those who are killed in the way of Allah—He will never render their works vain.

To summarize these surah, idolaters and infidels of every kind are condemned to hell. Horror and terror are their lot in the afterlife. Surah VIII, 67, "*It is not for any Prophet to have captives until he hath made slaughter in the land. . . .*" could not be clearer in its commandment that there must a great slaughter of nonbelievers BEFORE the war is ended, that is, when captives are taken. A question arises from this. Consider the following: (1) Horror and terror are to come to the nonbelievers in the afterlife; (2) it is the role of Islam to cause a great slaughter among nonbelievers, which sends nonbelievers to their hellacious afterlife; and (3) this being so, then what does it matter by what means they are sent to the afterlife? Does it matter if the suffering of nonbelievers and the horror and terror that is their doom begin in the process of their leaving this life for the next, especially when those sending them to the afterlife are the instrument of Allah?

Answers to this question can be found in the historical record. And this historical record of conquest must be examined in light of the era and its military practices. Massacres were not uncommon. It was the inevitable result of any siege that the soldiers were turned loose on the inhabitants of the city for a time to loot and rape. However, the inhabitants of the captured cities and provinces were valuable commodities to the conquerors. Not only were they potential slaves, but by continuing in their lives and occupations, they added their economic potential to the economic structure of the conquering nation, thereby giving its king more subjects to rule over and more subjects to tax. When you're king, taxes are good, and the more subjects the greater the king. Therefore, a conquering king does not just whimsically slaughter the economic resources of the newly conquered province.

One must examine the record of Arab conquests in light of the conquered people's economic value. As will be chronicled, many massacres occurred after areas were conquered. To a degree this is typical, and the following list is a far from complete list of such massacres that occurred at the hands of the conquering Arabs. In many instances they could have been solely for the purpose of cowing the conquered people and impressing on them who was now their ruler. On the other hand, in a few instances religion was certainly the reason for the massacre. Both prospects are discussed so as to provide the reader a perspective on the events that followed the Arab conquests of the Middle East and beyond.

After the death of Muhammad, Caliph Abu Bakr organized the invasion of Syria. During the campaign of A.D. 634, the entire region between Gaza and Caesarea was devastated. During the military operations in that region 4,000 peasants, Christians, Jews, and Samaritans who were simply defending their land, were massacred. During the campaigns in Mesopotamia, between A.D. 635 and 642, monasteries were sacked, the monks were killed, and Monophysite Arabs were executed or forced to convert. In Elam the entire population was put to the sword, and at Suza all the dignitaries suffered the same fate.

John, the Bishop of Nikiu, chronicled the events of the invasion of
Egypt between A.D. 693 and 700. He described the Muslim yoke as
"heavier than the yoke that had been laid on Israel by Pharaoh."

During the Muslin advance into Egypt, Amr captured the town of Beh-
nesa, near Fayum, and exterminated the inhabitants. John recorded, "whoever gave himself up to them [the Muslims] was massacred, they spared
neither the old, nor the women or children." The towns of Fayum and
Aboit suffered the same fate. At Nikiu, the entire population was put to
the sword. Only at Cilicia did the conquering Arabs take the population
into captivity.

In A.D. 642, the citizenry of Dvin was put to the sword or forced to
convert. In A.D. 643, the Arabs returned to the region bringing "extermination, ruin, and slavery." The conqueror of Cyprus, Mu'awiya established
his domination by a "great massacre" that accompanied the pillaging of
the island.

The same process was repeated in North Africa when Tripoli was pillaged in A.D. 643; Carthage was razed to the ground and most of its
inhabitants killed. The invasions and conquests of Mesopotamia, Syria,
Iraq, and Iran were simply more of the same. It is impossible to determine
if these massacres were based on a religious imperative or on the need of
the conqueror to establish his dominance over the now conquered territories, however, some clear examples of purely religious massacres do
exist.

The conquest of India came after the fall of Iran. Hajjaj, the governor
of Iraq, masterminded the conquest of the Sind and then dispatched his
military commander, Qasim, to implement the plan in A.D. 712. Qasim
was ordered to "bring destruction on the unbelievers . . . [and] to invite
and induce the infidels to accept the true creed, and belief in the unity of
Allah . . . and whoever does not submit to Islam, treat him harshly and
cause injury to him until he submits." These instructions are quite within
the scope of the mandate given in the Koran.

When the Indian port city of Debal was captured, the Muslim army
took three days to slaughter the inhabitants. When the slaughter was finished, Qasim allowed the survivors to continue their professions and even
to practice their religion. He had obviously decided that the economic
value of their labor was worth preserving.

When Hajjaj read of this in Qasim's report, he wrote back: "My dear
cousin, I have received your life-augmenting letter. On its receipt my
gladness and joy knew no bounds. It increased my pride and glory to the
highest degree. It appears from your letter that all the rules made by you
for the comfort and convenience of your men are strictly in accordance

with religious law. But the way of granting pardon prescribed by the law is different from the one adopted by you, for you go on giving pardon to everybody, high or low, without any discretion between a friend and a foe. The great Allah says in the Koran [Surah XLVII, 4]: 'O True believers, when you encounter the unbelievers, strike off their heads.' The above command of the Great Allah is a great command and must be respected and followed. You should not be so fond of showing mercy, as to nullify the virtue of the act. Henceforth grant pardon to no one of the enemy and spare none of them, or else all will consider you a weak-minded man. Concluded with compliments. Written by Nafia in the year ninety three [A.D. 715]."

In a later letter Hajjaj writes: "My distinct orders are that all those who are fighting men should be *assassinated,* and their sons and daughters imprisoned and retained as hostages." Serious note needs to be taken of the word *assassinated.* This clearly shows that Hajjaj understood the nature of the act he was ordering. The operation had ceased to be purely military and had become religiously supported murder.

His orders in hand, Qasim arrived at the town of Brahminabad and ordered all the men of the military classes beheaded. It is said that about 6,000 fighting men were massacred on this occasion, some say 16,000. The survivors were then forced to submit to the will of Hajjaj, through his lieutenant Qasim.

Qasim's invasion was but the prelude of Islamic incursions into India. The true conquest began in the eleventh century when Mahmud of Ghazni, head of the Turko-Afghan dynasty, passed through India like a whirlwind destroying, pillaging, and massacring, all of which he justified by constant references to the Koranic injunctions to kill idolaters, whom he had vowed to chastise every year of his life. Mahmud was a most zealous Muslim and of the ferocious type prevalent at that time. He believed it a duty as well as pleasure to slay idolaters.

Surah IX, 5. And when the forbidden months have passed, *slay the idolaters wherever you find them* [italics for emphasis] and take them captive, and beleaguer them, and lie in wait for them at every place of ambush. But if they repent and observe Prayer and pay the Zakát, then leave their way free. Surely, Allah is Most Forgiving, Merciful.

With that Koranic verse in hand, effectively a *carte blanche* to slaughter idolaters, it mattered little that Mahmud was also greedy for treasure and took good care to derive a handsome profit from his holy wars. Besides, the Koran is explicit about spoils. Surah VIII is entitled "Spoils of War." Other relevant passage are

> Surah XLVIII, 19. Surely, Allah was well pleased with the believers when they were swearing allegiance to thee under the Tree, and *He knew what was in their hearts, and He sent down tranquility on them, and He rewarded them with a victory at hand,*
> 20. *And great spoils that they will take* [italics added]. Allah is Mighty, Wise.
> 21. Allah has promised you great spoils that you will take and He has given you this in advance, and has restrained the hands of men from you, that it may be a Sign for the believers, and that He may guide you on a right path;
> 22. And He has promised you another victory, which you have not been able to achieve yet, but Allah has, surely, compassed it. And Allah has power over all things.

As it says, *"He* [Allah] *knew what was in their hearts, and He sent down tranquility on them, and He rewarded them with a victory at hand, and great spoils that they will take."* Allah knows what is in the heart of man and gives him the victory and the subsequent spoils. Therefore Mahmud was perfectly justified in gathering in the spoils of the victory that Allah had given him.

In the course of seventeen invasions of India, Mahmud utterly ruined the country and scattered the vanquished Hindus. The desolation that he wrought was the seed of the reaction of Hindus to Muslims when India and Pakistan formed. Now that both Pakistan and India have nuclear weapons, this historic hatred becomes much more relevant, even to those of us in the West.

Mahmud invaded Multan in 1004. When he occupied the district of Ghur, he forcibly converted the inhabitants to Islam. The rich Hindu temples were particularly desirable targets for Mahmud, as the smashing of idols was mandated in the Koran by Muhammad's destruction of the idols of Mecca when he conquered and occupied it. Mathura, the holy city of Krishna, was Mahmud's next victim. Its temple was incredibly rich. After it was pillaged of its five golden idols and priceless jewels, the Sultan gave orders that all the temples should be burnt with naphtha and fire and leveled to the ground. In that fire perished works of art that must have been among the noblest monuments of ancient India. At the battle of Somnath, the site of another celebrated Hindu temple, 50,000 were reputed to have been killed as Mahmud's warriors assuaged their lust for blood and booty.

Mahmud was equally ferocious with those whom he considered heretics such as Dawud, the ruler of Multan. In 1010, Mahmud invaded Dawud's kingdom and slaughtered many of his heretical subjects. This may be the first example of Muslim-on-Muslim holy war and indicates the attitude of the various sects toward one another.

In A.D. 1351 Firuz Shah ascended the throne and became ruler of Northern India. Though in many ways an enlightened man, when it came to religion he was a strict fundamentalist. Based on Koranic interpretation, he indulged in wholesale slave raiding and is said to have had 180,000 slaves in his city, all of whom became Muslims.

A zealot, Firuz Shah was particularly dangerous when his religious zeal was roused. In one instance he seized Shias, some of whom he executed, others he lectured, and then he burnt their books. He caused the *ulama* to kill a man who claimed to be the Mahdi [false prophet], "and for this good action," he wrote, "I hope to receive future reward."

When Firuz Shah encountered a Hindu religious festival and ordered the leaders of that "abomination" put to death, he then inflicted severe penalties on the population in general. He destroyed their temples and had mosques raised on the sites.

Old sins are not easily forgiven: Recently, enraged Hindus destroyed an ancient mosque in India claiming it was on the site of an even earlier Hindu temple. In March 1995 the Charar-e-Sharief mosque was destroyed, and the Babri Masjid, specifically claimed to have been built on the site of an ancient Hindu temple destroyed by the Muslims, was itself destroyed in 1992.

Overall, Firuz Shah, who also had a Brahman who had practiced his rites in public burnt alive, was simply carrying on the tradition of the early Muslim invaders. He sincerely believed that he served Allah by treating the public practice of their religion by the vast majority of his subjects [i.e., Hindus] as a capital crime.

Firuz Shah also used the *jizya* or poll tax to push many Hindus into converting to Islam. He exempted converts from the tax, which was otherwise rigorously enforced. The Muslims of the fourteenth century, seven centuries after the death of Muhammad, were still dominated by ideas current in the early days of Islam. They were convinced that the tolerance of idolatry was a sin.

Aurangzeb (1618–1707) was a Muslim puritan who wished to turn his Indian empire into a land of orthodox Sunni Islam and ruled in accordance with the principles laid down by the early caliphs. He began this process by destroying Hindu temples. During the campaigns of 1679–80, he destroyed 123 temples at Udaipur, 63 at Chitor, and 66 at Jaipur. He reduced all non-Muslims to the status of *dhimmis*, that is second-class citizens in their own country.

Aurangzeb reimposed on the newly ordained *dhimmis* the hated *jizya* that his predecessor Akbar the Great (1542–1605) had wisely abolished early in his reign. The ruler's aim was to curb the infidels and demonstrate the distinction between the Dar ul-Islam (the Land of Islam) and the Dar ul-Harb (the Land of Warfare and of the infidels). With that decision he brought warfare to the Dar ul-Harb to make the distinction clear for all to behold.

Concurrent with the war on Hinduism, the Muslim invaders of India waged war against the Buddhists. Between A.D. 1000 and 1200 Buddhism disappeared from India through the combined effects of its own weaknesses, a revived Hinduism, and Muslim persecution. Buddhism was eradicated from the homeland of its peace-loving and inspirational founder by Muslim persecution in A.D. 1200.

The merciless and fanatical Qutb ud din Aibak sent his general, Muhammad Khilji, to the northern Indian state of Bihar to continue the Muslim conquests that had started in the late twelfth century. Buddhism was the main religion of Bihar. In A.D. 1193, the Muslim general, who knew nothing of Buddhism and considered it mere idolatry, put most of the Buddhist monks in Bihar to the sword and destroyed a great library. His troops went on a rampage of destruction, destroying the Buddhist sanctuaries at Sarnath near Benares. Many noble monuments of the ancient civilization of India were irretrievably wrecked by the iconoclastic Muslim invaders. Those invasions were fatal to the existence of Buddhism as an organized religion in northern India. The monks who escaped massacre were scattered over Nepal, Tibet, and the south.

The Muslim conquests of Central Asia focused on the destruction of Buddhist art that continues today with Afghanistani Taliban destruction of the ancient Buddhas of Bamiyan in February 2001. The iconoclasm of Islam is nothing new, for as early as the eighth century the monasteries of Kizil were destroyed by the Muslim ruler of Kashgar and the Sphinx at Giza, Egypt, was defaced.

We have mentioned already that the Christians, Jews, and Zoroastrians who came under the control of Islamic conquerors had, in theory, a fate different from those to whom the holy Scriptures had not been revealed. Muhammad had some strong feelings about these peoples and inscribed them upon the pages of the Koran:

Surah V, 57. O ye how believe! *Chose not for friends such of those who received the Scripture before you* [italics added], and of the disbelievers, and make a jest and sport of your religion. But keep your duty to Allah if ye are true believers.

Surah V, 80. *Thou seest many of them making friends with those who disbelieve. Surely ill for them is that which they themselves send on before them: that Allah will be wroth with them and in the doom they will abide* [italics added].

Surah V, 82. *Thou wilt find the most vehement of mankind in hostility to those who believe (to be) the Jews and the idolaters* [italics added]. And thou wilt find the nearest of them in affection to those who believe (to be) those who say: Lo! We are Christians. That is because there are among them priests and monks, and because they are not proud.

Surah IV, 144. *O ye who believe! Chose not disbelievers for (your) friends in the place of believers. Would ye give Allah a clear warrant against you* [italics added]?

Surah III, 118. O ye who believe! *Take not for intimates others than your own folk* [italics added], who would spare no pains to ruin you; they love to hamper you. Hatred is revealed by (the utterance) of their mouths, but that which their breasts hide is greater. We have made plain for you the revelations if ye will understand.

Surah III, 28. *Let not the believers take disbelievers for their friends in preference to believers. Whoso doeth that hath no connection with Allah unless (it be) that he but guard yourselves against them, taking (as it were) security. Allah biddeth you beware (only) of Himself* [italics added]. Unto Allah is the journeying.

Surah V, 57, in speaking of "those who received the Scripture before you" is specifically pointing at Christians and Jews. Surah V, 80, essentially states that if you make friends with a nonbeliever, which includes the Christians and Jews, you will abide in "doom." Surah V, 82, reflects what may have been a great stress between the Hebrew tribes and the early Muslims and lumps the Jews with the idolaters as the greatest enemies of Islam.

When Islam began its expansion the first groups that it encountered in any numbers were the Jews, Christians, and Zoroastrians. The invasion of the Middle East by the Muslim Arabs was not an uplifting experience for the victims. It came with death and destruction—not evangelism. The inhabitants of any town captured, be they Christian or Jew or other, were either killed or lead off into slavery. Those that remained were reduced to the status of *dhimmi* and burdened with *jizya* and *kharaj* taxes that often were a crushing burden that forced non-Muslim peasantry to live at a subsistence level. The purpose of these taxes was twofold. First, economic pressure presumably would eventually pressure the less spiritually strong to convert to Islam. Second, taxation would so oppress those who stood defiant in their resolution and commitment to their religion that they could never become a threat to Islam's domination in the land. These non-Muslim communities within the Muslim world did, however, obtain a certain amount of autonomy in that they governed their own affairs within their own communities. However, if at any time they had dealings with a Muslim, the Islamic courts ruled and second-class citizenship proved a crushing burden that left the non-Muslim totally at the mercy of the Muslims with which he conducted business. If they chose to rob him it was perfectly legal, and not only would the Islamic courts support the robber, but his religion reaffirmed the behavior that we would see as immoral, because it was done to a non-Muslim.

It should be noted that the degree of repression and the quality of life of the *dhimmis* did vary considerably depending on the period and the Islamic state in question. Certain Islamic rulers were noted for their enlightened rule and tolerance of other religions. However, many others closely followed the Koranic teachings and imposed the full rigor of Islamic law.

Because of this, Jewish communities within the Islamic cultures would frequently live precariously in times of famine, civil strife, or other catastrophes. The Jews were a small, defenseless community of infidels and humble tribute bearers who could be abused without response, particularly in light of the Koranic verses relating to them.

With Koranic support, anti-Semitism was not unknown in the Islamic world. Even in the best of times, Jewish *dhimmis* in all walks of life and at every level of society could suddenly and rudely be reminded of their true status.

Another form of discrimination against the *dhimmis* was forced mass conversion. Under the Almohad caliphs Al Mumin (d. 1165), Abu Yaqub (d. 1184) and Al Mansur (d. 1199), there were forced conversions. If one assumes only one conversion per reign, this identifies three forced conversions. In Yemen the Jews, who were already part of the Islamic world and declared as *dhimmis,* were forced to choose between death and conversion to Islam in 1165 and again in 1678. Apparently some had either escaped the first forced conversion or had reverted to their old ways. The same happened in Aden in 1198. The Jews of Tabriz were obliged to convert in 1291 and 1318, and those of Baghdad in 1333 and 1344.

Throughout Persia, forced conversions from the sixteenth century to the beginning of the twentieth century decimated the Christian and, even more, the Jewish communities.

The forced conversion of Jews was only part of the story. Forced conversions of Christians, Hindus, Zoroastrians and others occurred on a more massive scale.

With the institution of the *dhimmis,* discrimination was institutionalized within Islamic law and practice. It was a permanent and necessary part of the system by which the Islamic conquerors of the Middle East controlled those conquered races that were under their heel.

How then were the *dhimmis* to be controlled? The first phase of controlling them was in the conquest where thousands were ruthlessly slaughtered. The terror inflicted on them by their Muslim conquerors began with the ruthless butchering of thousands of surrendered male captives.

There is a phrase from English history that describes this well. An English admiral named Byng failed to defeat the French fleet of Mallorca in 1756. He was not defeated, he just failed to win. He was court-martialed and shot for his failure, *"pour encouragez les autres"* (to encourage the others). In the same sense, the slaughter of thousands of captives would impress on the group psyche of a conquered people that their conquerors were absolutely ruthless and had no qualms about butchering anyone who opposed them. It was intended to "encourage the others" to remain docile and obedient. This imposition of terror, as we have already said, was their lot in the afterlife, and why did it matter if the Islamic overlords imposed it on them prior to their death? In addition, terror has historically been the principal method used by conquering nations to suppress their victims.

The process of control by terrorizing the *dhimmis* continued under Islamic institutions because any Muslim could perpetrate any act he might wish against a *dhimmis* without fear of any retribution. The *dhimmis* had no recourse under Islamic law.

In all litigation between a Muslim and a *dhimmi,* the validity of the oath or testimony of the *dhimmi* was not recognized. In other words, because a *dhimmi* was not allowed to give evidence against a Muslim, his Muslim opponent always got off. The *dhimmi* was forced to bribe his way out of the accusations.

Accusations of blasphemy against *dhimmis* were quite frequent, and the penalty was capital punishment. With his testimony not accepted in court, the *dhimmi* was forced to convert to save his life.

A *dhimmi* would often be sentenced to death if he dared raise his hand against a Muslim, even in legitimate self-defense. The accidental killing of a Muslim could condemn the whole non-Muslim community to death or exile. Could this situation be considered anything other than a life spent in constant terror where at any instant death could be whimsically applied?

In 1033 more than 6,000 Jews were massacred at Fez, Morocco; hundreds more were killed between 1010 and 1013 near Cordoba, Spain; the entire Jewish community, some 4,000 in Granada were slaughtered during the Muslim riots of 1066.

In Kairouan, Tunisia, the Jews were persecuted and forced to leave in 1016, returning later only to be expelled again. In Tunis in 1145 they were forced to convert or to leave, and during the following decade fierce anti-Jewish persecutions occurred throughout the region. In Morocco a similar pattern of events followed the massacre of Jews in Marrakesh in 1232.

In all fairness, at this time the treatment of Jews in Western Europe was no kinder. Western Jewry was destroyed in the Middle Ages. The Spanish Inquisition was an instrument of forced conversion or death to the Spanish Jewish community. Pogroms against the Jews occurred in Russia until the twentieth century, and no one can ever forget the horrors of Auschwitz. Then again, no one is attempting to imply that any enlightenment has altered European treatment of Jews, nor is there an effort to claim that terror was not a tool frequently used by western society against Jewish minorities. This is in stark contrast to the current trend of the media and of many scholars vis-à-vis the history of the treatment of minorities under Islamic rule.

Under no circumstances should this be seen as an attempt to ignore such acts of terror and repression that have occurred in Christian lands or at Christian hands. The principal difference between Islamic and Christian oppression is that when committed by Christians, that is, the Crusades, it was done in spite of the teachings of Christianity. This contrasts sharply with Islam, where acts of oppression and terror were in accordance with Koranic scripture.

A similar history exists for the Islamic persecution and destruction of the Zoroastrian communities of the Middle East. By about A.D. 944 Islam had been imposed on the reluctant Zoroastrian inhabitants of Bukhara. The Bukharans reverted to their original beliefs no less than four times, and three times the Muslims returned and reinstated Islam. On the fourth reversion the Koranic commandment of death was instituted. The Muslim leader, Qutayba, came with fire in hand, waged war, seized the city, and reestablished Islam after considerable bloodshed. In response, the Zoroastrians took their religion underground.

Many Zoroastrians were induced to convert by bribes, or by the economical pressure and eventual financial ruin of the *jizya* tax. Many of these "economic converts" were later executed for having adopted Islam to avoid paying the *jizya* and land taxes. Coexistence between Muslims and Zoroastrians was rarely peaceful, and conflict remained the prime form of contact between these two groups from the initial Arab conquest of Transoxiana until the late thirteenth century. A similar situation existed in Khurasan, where violent military conflicts produced lasting enmity between Muslims and Zoroastrians. The early conquests of Zoroastrian Iran were punctuated with the usual massacres. At Sarakh, only a hundred men were granted amnesty, the women were enslaved, and the children taken into captivity were brought up as Muslims. At Sus a hundred men were pardoned, the rest killed. At Manadhir, all the men were put to the sword and the women and children enslaved. At Istakhr, more than 40,000 Iranians were slaughtered. The litany of Muslim terrorism and atrocities is quite long.

Forced conversions were frequent, and the pressures for conversion often led to conflict and riots as in Shiraz in A.D. 979. To escape persecution and forced conversion, many Zoroastrians emigrated to India where to this day they form a much respected minority and are known as Parsis. Conditions for the Zoroastrians in Iran became even worse from the seventeenth century onwards. In the eighteenth century, their numbers declined disastrously due to the combined effects of massacre, forced conversion and emigration. By the nineteenth century their existence was one of total insecurity and poverty. Houses were frequently looted, and the Zoroastrians had to wear distinctive clothing and were forbidden to build new houses or repair old ones.

Little can be gained from a recitation of each of the long litany of massacres, but one more needs to be discussed. Surely the greatest and most recent such act of mass Muslim terrorism was perpetrated by the Turks against the Armenians. This was not simply a single outburst of xenophobia or political concern that erupted in World War I about a discontented minority behind the lines that might become a fifth column supporting the Russian invaders of Turkey. The history of Muslim persecution of the Armenians stretches back to the initial conquest of the Transcaucasus by the Turks. In Armenia, during the seventh century, the entire population of Euchaita was wiped out. Armenian chronicles recount how the Arabs repeated the process in Assyria, decimating that population and forcing many to convert to Islam. They then moved into the region southwest of Lake Van and in the district known as Daron repeated the process.

However, the massacres of 1894, 1895, and 1896 are of particular note. It is true that the Armenians looked to Russia for protection at this time and the Russians were unable or unwilling to intervene in the massacre of 250,000 Armenians in Sasun, Trapezunt, Edessa, Biredjik, Kharput, Niksar, and Wan. Further massacres followed in 1904 and in 1909 when 30,000 Armenians lost their lives at Adana. These massacres have been described as a deliberately planned and implemented extermination of the Armenians.

The pressures of the Russian armies in the Transcaucasus theater in 1915 against the Turkish armies provoked great concern for the internal security of the Turkish state. The Turkish government began to worry what might be going on behind their lines. They had already, by either their ineptness or because of a calculated plan, begun stirring the pot of Armenian discontent in the 1890s. Having created the mess, they reverted to old methods that had worked in previous crises—slaughter the problem—and this led to the infamous mass murders of 1915, described as the first case of genocide in the twentieth century and discussed at length in Chapter 8.

If one looks at the Armenians' situation in 1915 within the context of the jihad, the logic flows as follows: The Armenian *dhimmis* were non-believers. They were co-religionists of the attacking Russian army, and they had, in the past, made appeals to the Russians to aid them. As a result, they were a threat to the Islamic state of Turkey. The jihad is a holy war to either expand or defend Islam. The Armenian *dhimmis* were a threat to the state as it defends itself against the assault by the infidel Russians and, therefore, they became a legitimate target for military operations. Surah XLVII, 5, says, *"And when you meet in regular battle those who disbelieve, smite their necks* [cut off their heads]; *and, when you have overcome them, by causing great slaughter among them, bind fast the fetters."* Clearly this is an injunction to kill and enslave those that threaten the state. In the Turkish mind in 1915 the Armenians fell under the prescription established in this surah. Sadly, these genocides seem to have deeply impressed Hitler, and he may well have seen the lack of world reaction to them as a model for his later genocidal attacks on the Jews.

This genocide of the Armenians was the first genocide of the twentieth century and was but the natural culmination of a divinely sanctioned policy toward non-Muslims. It was nothing less than a jihad, implemented by Muslims, who alone benefited from the booty. Historically the possessions and the land of the victims went to the murderers, while the women and children were reduced to slavery. Armenia in 1915 was not an isolated incident, but a deliberate policy to eliminate any possible escape of Armenian *dhimmis* from Muslim domination and to keep the conquered territory under Islamic jurisdiction. The inner logic of the jihad could not tolerate religious emancipation or equality before the law by non-Muslims. The Islamic concept of permanent war in the Dar ul-Harb (Land of War) and the inferiority of the conquered *harbis* constituted the three interdependent and inseparable principles underlying the expansion and political domination of Islam.

In summary, the Islamic perspective divides the world into two classes—Muslims and others. Only Islam is valued. In some enlightened Muslim societies this was not the rule, but those were exceptions. The general statement is true. The Koran established the jihad to defend and expand Islam. Muhammad divided the world and its people into two parts, Dar ul-Islam, the Land of Islam, where the edicts of Islam are fully promulgated and the Dar ul-Harb, the Land of War, where Islam is yet to take power. The Koran established the jihad as the duty of every Muslim male and identifies eternal damnation for those that fail to participate. The jihad is targeted specifically at non-Muslims. The Koran repeatedly states that the afterlife of nonbelievers is a horror in the flames of hell and mandates that Muslim warriors convert nonbelievers or send them to their horrible fate. This process has historically seen the deliberate murder of prisoners to establish a reign of terror that will ensure the docility of the survivors.

Islam does not exempt from this terror those who have submitted to Muslim rule but not accepted Islam. Those people, the *dhimmis,* accept a tenuous existence. The history of the Islamic world is filled with *dhimmis* who suddenly found themselves subject to slaughter and reduction to slavery, a fate that they absolutely would have escaped if they had been Muslim.

In order to fully understand the concept of the jihad it is necessary to draw together some of the cultural threads discussed in Chapter 1. In that chapter we discussed briefly the Arab cultural predisposition toward the vendetta or blood feud. We spoke of how, in some instances, it had become ritualized as a regularly scheduled combat, even though the initial reason for this feud had long since vanished.

Earlier in this chapter we also spoke about Surah IV, 93–94, which forbade Muslims to deliberately kill other Muslims. Muhammad attempted to use this Surah to control the natural tendency of the Arab people to the vendetta.

In contrast, Muhammad sought not only to redirect the jihad away from an internally destructive process in order to preserve Islam, but to harness it as a tool for the expansion of Islam. By providing divine sanction for warfare under specific circumstances, Muhammad provided an acceptable outlet for the naturally combative nature of the Arab people. He allowed the urge to vent in a manner nondestructive to Islam.

The concept of jihad served the early Islamic states well, but only for a time. In a few short years after the death of Muhammad, politics and greed—the normal corrupters of man—were as much at work in Islamic countries as they have always been elsewhere. In the modern world, religious imperialism is as dead as national imperialism. Simply put, the world is no longer available for armed conquest. However, much of the world is still certainly available to teaching and conversion, and Muslims have not been backward in these endeavors. It is sad that the fundamentalist Muslim world is trying to wage armed jihad against the free states of the Western world, when it is in just those states—those that practice freedom of religion—that the peaceful jihad of conversion might be most successfully waged.

Chapter 13

DYING FOR GOD: THE ASSASSINS—PAST AND PRESENT

By the eleventh century, a new and unusual state arose in the Arab Empire. This state was formed by one Hasan-as-Sabah, a Shia Syrian mullah and convert to the Ismaili sect of Islam. Hasan's accomplishment, one that has entered both our history and our language, was the foundation of the order of Hashishyun—or Assassins.

With the support of the Egyptian Fatimids, Hasan built his base in Khorassan, or northeastern Iran. From this fortified base—known as the Eagle's Nest—he began a career of political murder against his foes, the Seljuq Turks and Abbasid caliphs of Baghdad. The Assassins were his chief weapon.

In fact, the Assassins, with their unmatched fervor, were his only real offensive weapon. Like all other rulers in what was an essentially medieval state, Hasan had soldiers as well, but they were deployed only to protect his holdings. Thus, whenever possible Hasan employed what must be considered the most efficient type of warfare possible. By striking with carefully trained murderers he could keep his enemies off guard and at bay. A particular plus to this style of warfare is that it spends few fighting men and little treasure. Conventional forces normally require thousands of men and great economic effort to upset an opposing government. Hasan learned to do the same thing with a handful.

In A.D. 1092 the Assassins implemented their political assassination with the murder of Nizam. Nizam was one of the main supporters of the

Seljuqs in Iran. After learning who had perpetrated this attack, the Seljuqs attempted to reduce the Eagle's Nest but failed.

This particular assassination went into legend, and its horror was enhanced by the declaration that Nizam and Hasan had studied together, along with the poet Omar Khayyam, under the learned Muwaffaq of Nishapur. The legend goes that these two had sworn an oath to aid each other throughout life, which in the eyes of Islam made the assassination all the more terrible.

So successful was Hasan that he expanded his influence into Syria. Here he established several "lodges" eventually centered near the Syrian coastal fortress of Banyas.

By the time of the Crusades the Assassins found ready allies in the Franks. The Assassins were quite willing to work with the crusaders, whom they considered no more odious than their Sunni Muslim foes. The crusaders of Antioch profited from the murder of the Emir of Apamea, so their alliance with the Assassins may well have begun as early as A.D. 1106. The Assassins were on friendly terms with Tancred, the great Norman warlord who became Prince of Antioch.

It is certainly true that the Assassins made miserable allies. It is difficult to reproduce the mindset of a ruler who would accept as friend those who make political murder a practice. Buzurg-Ummed, one of the earliest Assassin grand masters, was welcomed by Emir Toghtekin, the ruler of Damascus. In that city, the cult became prominent but also aroused the antipathy of the local populace—they were Sunni Muslims, and the Assassins were Shia. Buzurg appealed to the Emir, who, in 1126 granted him the fortress of Banyas.

This clever move on Toghtekin's part gave his ally a base secure from the sophisticated and hostile Damascenes, but it also put Buzurg square in the path of a likely advance by the Christian Crusader states. In this way Emir Toghtekin would have solved two problems at once—he would honor his word and at the same time secure a dangerous frontier. Assassin leader Buzurg had other ideas. After renewing his fortifications, he immediately began terrorizing the local population and made plans to murder his benefactor.

In the event, Toghtekin died without Buzurg's assistance, and Buzurg himself alienated one local tribesman too many. He was killed in a border skirmish with a tribe whose leader he had ordered killed. But the hostilities and animosity did not die with the principals. As was so often the case with medieval societies, the struggle became hereditary.

Buzurg's grandson Hasan eventually took power and declared himself the *Ismail*—or promised Imam and Caliph of God. He took the name Ismail, and went about the normal business of the assassins.

Buzurg was succeeded by his son Muhammad I in whose reign the Masyad fortress became the chief seat of the Syrian branch of the Assassins. Muhammad I's son Hasan declared himself the promised Imam, the caliph of God and lineal descendant of Ismail, taking the name Ismail. But Toghtekin's heir, his son Taj al-Mulk Buri had other ideas. He instigated a mass rising against the cult and had their followers slaughtered wherever they could be found.

Frightened by these events, Ismail opened up negotiations with the Frankish crusaders. King Baldwin agreed to take the Assassins under his protection. Ismail and his sect were settled within the Frankish territories. Ismail soon fell ill of dysentery and died a few months later, dealing conclusively with his claim to divine selection. His followers dispersed. With Ismail dead and much of his forces in disarray, the Assassins were at a low ebb. Baldwin moved to protect Banyas in early November, and in A.D. 1149 the Assassins fought alongside the Crusaders.

The new Kurdish leader of the Assassins' Syrian sect, ibn Wafa, hated the Muslim military leader, Sultan Nur al-Din, more than he hated the Christians. In A.D. 1148 ibn Wafa surprised Nur al-Din as he moved through the Aswad plain. Nur al-Din's army was forced into a hasty and ignominious retreat. The next year, at the battle of Murad, a combined force of Crusaders and Assassins moved to defend the fortress of Inab. Nur al-Din, misinformed of the size of this force, again retreated.

On June 28, 1149, Nur al-Din surrounded the combined force of Christians and Assassins. In the subsequent attack the Christians and Assassins were defeated and the leader of the Assassins killed.

In A.D. 1152 Raymond II of Tripoli had the honor of being the first Christian victim of the Assassins. No motive for his murder was ever discovered.

After Raymond's death a decade of quiet began. The sect had approximately ten fortresses in Syria, and their numbers were estimated at 60,000, including both fighting men and the population they controlled. They consolidated their power in the Nosairi Mountains and maintained their enmity with Nur al-Din. One night during this period he received a warning that he was going too far. He awoke to find a dagger on his pillow. One can only wonder at this story—warnings were not the main stock-in-trade of the sect.

In 1169 the Assassins at Alamut, Persia, sent a new governor to the Nosairi province. The Persian branch was the senior half of the Assassin sect, and the Syrians the junior. This new leader was Rashid ed-Din Sinan of Basra. He was a formidable man and would be known by the Crusaders as the "Old Man of the Mountains." With his arrival, the Syrian Assassins roused from their slumbers and quickly made themselves separate from the main branch of the order. In A.D. 1173 Rashid sent to the Christian warlord Amalric a note suggesting that they form a close alliance aimed against both Saladin and Nur al-Din. He subtly suggested that he and his flock were considering conversion to Christianity. He also sought to have cancelled the tribute paid by various Assassin villages to the Templars at Tortosa.

The Templars, however, unwilling to accept this loss of income, acted. Walter of Mesnil, acting on the orders of his grand master, ambushed the envoys and murdered them near Tripoli. King Amalric was horrified and sent troops to deal with the situation. He had Walter kidnapped and thrown into prison in Tyre. The Assassins were assured that justice would be done and accepted the apology. Relations between the Assassins and the Christian crusaders stabilized.

The following year both Amalric and Nur al-Din died and the Assassins concentrated their focus on the elimination of Saladin. They made several unsuccessful attempts. During the first attempt all the Assassins were killed—one of them actually succeeded in penetrating Saladin's tent. In the second attempt, only a small mail cap saved Saladin's life from an Assassin's dagger. Three *fedais* involved in the plot had succeeded in enrolling in his personal bodyguard.

Saladin became convinced that action was required, and in A.D. 1176 he marched into the Nosairi Mountains and attacked the Assassin's interests in that region, laying waste to the territory and besieging their main fortress at Masyaf. The new Assassin grand master, Sheikh Sinan, was away when the attack began. He hurried home and some "mysterious power" prevented Saladin's men from capturing him. Saladin began having terrible dreams. One morning he awoke to find on his bed some hot cakes of the type that only the Assassins baked. With them was a poison dagger and a piece of paper with a threatening verse. Saladin believed that the Old Man of the Mountains had personally been in the tent. Saladin's nerves failed and he sent a messenger to Sinan requesting forgiveness for his sins and promising, in return for a safe-conduct, to leave the Assassins undisturbed. Sinan accepted the proposal and a treaty was made between them. It is interesting that the Assassins had such good intelligence that they could not only penetrate Saladin's defenses, but that they also knew that he was of more use to them alive. This story, by the way, sounds unlike Saladin.

For a period the Assassins were certainly neutral, if not tacitly on the Muslim side of the Crusades. In A.D. 1192 Conrad of Montferrat was murdered by the Assassins at the orders of Sinan, just before he was to become king of Jerusalem.

Sinan died in A.D. 1194 and his successor sought out the Crusaders for a new alliance. This was signed with Henry of Champagne, and by 1213 the Assassins were paying regular tribute to the Hospitallers. This was probably because the Hospitaller fortress of Krak des Chevaliers dominated their territories.[1]

Few assassinations occurred during the reign of Hasan III (1210–20), and he actually developed a high reputation among the other princes in the region. However, his alliance with the Christians was not particularly solid, and in A.D. 1213 the Assassins killed Raymond, son of the Prince of Antioch. The Templars attempted to avenge this assassination, but they failed in their siege of the Assassin fortresses. Hasan III was poisoned— dying in character, one might say. His son, Ala ad-Din Muhammad III abandoned the mild principles of his father and launched a new era of assassination. In A.D. 1255 he too was murdered, this time with the contrivance of his son, Rukn ad-Din, last ruler of the Assassins. The senior branch in Persia was also about to expire.

In A.D. 1256 the Mongols invaded Persia. After a siege of Alamut and many other Assassin castles, Rukn ad-Din was captured. Initially Hulagu, brother of the Tartar Mangu Kahn, treated him kindly. Rukn ad-Din was sent to Mangu, who ordered him put to death and sent a messenger back to Hulagu that commanded him to slay all his captives. The businesslike Mongols had little patience with fanatics. About 12,000 of the Assassins were massacred, and their power was permanently crushed.

Though the Persian branch was destroyed, the Syrian branch continued and cooperated actively with the Mamluks of Egypt. In A.D. 1270 they assassinated Philip of Montfort at the request of the Mamluk sultan Baibars. The Assassins removed Montfort out of gratitude for Baibar's conquests, which had freed them from the necessity of paying tribute to the Hospitallers. They also strongly resented the crusaders negotiating with the Mongols, because the Mongols had destroyed their Persian branch. In 1272 Baibars requested the assassination of Prince Edward of England and the Prince was wounded in the attempt. In this instance the Assassin, disguised as a native Christian, had used a poisoned dagger. Prince Edward was seriously ill for several months.

Eventually, Baibars, not unlike the Mongols, found the Assassins more trouble than they were worth and crushed them. The few survivors of the sect continued in the mountains of Syria for many years, and some are thought to exist there still.

To understand the Assassins, King Louis XI of France sent one of his knights, Yves le Breton, to Masayaf in order to gain insight into these people. After many interviews with them, Yves le Breton wrote to his king, reporting these words of the Old Man of the Mountains:

> Know that one of the rules of the law of Ali [Ali is more revered by the Shia sect than Muhammad] is that when a man is killed in the service of his lord, his soul enters a more pleasant body than it had before; and therefore the Assassins do not hesitate to get themselves killed when their lord commands because they believe they will be in more pleasant circumstances after they are dead.
>
> And there is another rule: they believe that no one dies except on the day appointed for him; and no one should hold this belief for God can prolong or shorten our lives. But the Bedouins support this rule of the law of Ali, and thus they refuse to put on armor when they go into battle, for otherwise they believe they would be acting against the commandment of their law. And when they curse their children, they tell them: "May you be cursed like the Franks, who put on armor for fear of death."

It is reported, in legend, that the Assassins had a particular method by which they recruited their members. Of course, they were all Muslims, so the seeds of the recruiting methodology were already planted in the potential recruits.

> Legend claims that it was at Alamut that the leader of the sect [Assassins] had a private garden of infinite beauty, with the sparkling fountains so precious to the desert dweller and a selection of the most beautiful and most sexually accomplished young women in the land. A young member of the sect would be given hashish to numb his mind to the point of unconsciousness. When he awoke, he found himself in the fabled garden, where the beautiful young ladies fed him morsels of the most delicious foods. They treated him to every sexual delight he had ever heard of, and to some he had never even imagined. As the day progressed, more and more hashish would be pressed upon him until he passed out again.
>
> When he awoke the next morning to his usual surroundings he was encouraged to recount his drug-induced adventure. After he had spelled out the unbelievable delights, he was told that he had been favored by Allah by being given a tiny glimpse of the highest level of heaven reserved for those martyrs who "*die for their faith*" [italics added]. For such loyalty and devotion to God, the delights he had experienced so briefly were available for all eternity. Now he longed for nothing more in this world than the chance to die in the service of Allah.
>
> In answer to his plea, he was given intense training to kill an enemy of God, who would be identified for him by the leader of the sect, called by chroniclers the grand master. Thus would he earn eternal bliss in paradise,

because his would be a suicide mission. His mind and heart must be set on a successful kill and not at all on his own escape. He learned techniques of the dagger: where and how deep to strike, and how to circumvent armor. He was taught the use of poisons. He was instructed in the use of disguises and, if necessary, instructed in other religions, including Christianity, in order to be able to pass himself off convincingly as a member of the victim's own faith.

With a corps of such young men ready to kill and die, the grand master had a weapon that was often as powerful as an entire army. It inspired such fear that even the greatest rulers would think twice before going against the wishes of the grand master. (Robinson, 66–67)

The Garden of Paradise legend may or may not be apocryphal. In view of the Koran's promise, there has never been a shortage of young Muslims ready to die for their faith.

Surah IV, 74. Let those fight in the way of Allah who sell the life of this world for the other. Whoso fighteth in the way of Allah, be he slain or be he victorious, on him We shall bestow a vast reward.

Numerous other passages promise Paradise for the faithful. This particular surah, spawned on the battlefield at Badr, specifically says that when you die fighting "in the way of Allah" you receive the "vast reward," which has come to mean immediate entry into Paradise and the services of seventy-two virgins. To understand how this influenced these young men, one must step back into the twelfth century, imagine young men with no understanding of drugs who were given a taste of heaven for a day and then dumped back into their primitive squalor. Is it surprising that such young men would, upon the command of their imam, die without thought?

Today, it is easy to say that the Assassins lived 800 years ago and are irrelevant to the modern world. But they existed, and their philosophy was and still is a real force in the Middle East.

The ideology that brought the Assassins into the world and the surah in the Koran that made the promises of eternal life in paradise are alive and well. In May 1982, during the Iran-Iraq war, it is reported that young Iranian boys were "volunteered" by their parents to sacrifice themselves in the front line. The method, so it is reported, was for the boys to be roped together and advanced through minefields, detonating the explosives and clearing the way for the better-trained soldiers with their tanks. They are said to have had black cloths tied around their heads, with the inscription *"One who will love martyrdom."* These were the *Bassij,* or young martyrs. Their parents had willingly given them up for Khomeini's holy war.

If this story is true, and there is no particular reason that it should be, the black cloth about each head was the key to paradise, the same paradise that the Assassins expected to enter when they followed the orders of their imams. The parents of these tiny victims had the blessing of knowing their sons had gone to paradise and also received and proudly displayed martyrs' certificates from the government. The parents of these children actually enjoyed higher social status than others.

In addition, the Martyr's Fund was established and became a massive economic enterprise supported directly by the Iranian national treasury as well as by nationalized industries and private donations. Monies were dispensed from this fund to the families of the martyrs. The families were also given access to food and consumer goods that were, otherwise, heavily controlled and rationed.

Today, families of Palestinian suicide bombers receive much the same treatment. Their sons' pictures hang not only in their homes, but also along the streets where their martyrdom is extolled. Palestinian society confers the same elevation in social status, and a fund doles out money to the families. The process of martyrdom and suicide are well accepted and even admired in Palestinian society. When a young man has "martyred" himself, neighbors and friends visit his family and congratulate them on the accomplishment. Heroic pictures of their son quickly appear throughout the community. At the young man's funeral, be the body present or not, members of the Palestinian police forces present arms in salute as the martyr's coffin is paraded past. Crowds gather and the funerals become a major national event. All of this pressures the family to accept and support their son's death.

However, the use of suicide bombing or otherwise suicidal attacks does not end there. A Muslim assassin killed Mahatma Gandhi on January 30, 1948. Suicide bomb attacks have occurred in Chechnya, Kashmir, and Istanbul, Turkey. The attack on the USS *Cole* in Yemen on October 12, 2000, was launched by suicide bombers as were the 1983 attacks on the U.S. Marine barracks in Lebanon, and on Khobar Towers in Saudi Arabia during 1996.

Modern reports and studies indicate that these suicide attackers are not psychotic. The only abnormality found in the psychological profiles of bombers who have been evaluated is the lack of fear at the time of the attack.

A Palestinian suicide bomber who failed in his attack and was taken prisoner related that his own brother recruited him for a suicide bombing to be launched in a market in Haifa. He said that when his brother gave him the bomb, his brother "was giving me a ticket to heaven. I took his hand and kissed it because he wanted to give me something precious. . . . Because he loves me he wants me to become a martyr. . . . The most exalted thing in our religion."

This suicide bomber sees himself as someone already dead. There is no abandonment of this course, once it is set upon, without a loss of self-respect. The bomber sees nothing actually suicidal about the act, because the Koran prohibits suicide. This is a nice piece of logic and little appeals to the average Westerner. The bomber perceives his pending death as merely a momentary inconvenience in his propulsion into heaven. Any pain that he might suffer is merely a temporary annoyance on the road to immortality. Once in paradise he will live forever with seventy-two virgins and a river of honey. In addition, he is assured that he wins entry into paradise for seventy of his relatives.

The suicide bomber's attitude is exactly the same as that young man standing next to Muhammad during the battle of Badr (A.D. 624), who when hearing Muhammad's exclamation that death in battle granted immediate entry into heaven, charged into the midst of his enemies, heedless of his personal danger. So too do these suicide bombers charge into the midst of their enemies. In the same sense, the modern Muslim fanatic sees himself as a holy warrior, on a jihad to defend or promote Islam with extreme action. These men see the jihad as a pillar of Islam, an obligation that they must undertake.

Some would suggest that the profile of suicide bombers would show that the bombers are the young and unattached males who are religiously devout, extremely poor, dismally educated, and not particularly intelligent. Overall, it is true that such individuals may be more likely recruited into the ranks of suicide bombers, but they are not alone. A surprising number of female suicide bombers have been seen. These have surfaced in the attacks against Israel and in the Chechnyan attack of June 8, 2000, where two women drove a truckload of explosives into a Russian headquarters. There are also university-educated young men and married men with young families. The members of this unusual group defy Western understanding.

The only single, clearly identifiable thread is a devout attachment to Islam and the firm belief in the paradise to follow their death.

The Middle East has been the focus of considerable conflict in the past fifty years, and the term "jihad" has frequently been heard on the tongues of political and religious leaders directed at Israel, the United States, Britain, and even other Muslim states. Indeed, *jihad* has been institutionalized in the names of many of these groups. Fatah, one of the major Palestinian organizations is itself such a term. In Arabic, "Fatah" is a reverse acronym of Harekat at-Tahrir al-Wataniyyeh al-Falastiniyyeh, which means "conquest by means of jihad."

These jihads are frequently "low intensity" wars, as no armies actually face one another on battlefields. Instead, these are frequently fought in the streets of cities, marketplaces, discotheques, and so forth, and their attacks are aimed at civilians. The operative word is terrorism; the groups and states supporting jihad are far too weak in political, economic, and military terms to support successful armies. In the broadest sense, these jihads are bent on the violent overthrow of corrupt, or anti-Islamic governments and their replacement with Islamic governments.

Islamic fundamentalist groups have arisen from the revivalist works of select Muslim scholars. From these educated individuals have arisen such groups as the Muslim Brotherhood and Jamaat-I-Islami. These groups have steadily become more militant. Their beliefs focus on Islam as an all-encompassing ideology—a foundation of life and law that interprets the Koran literally and without exception or discussion. Their members are from all groups of Islamic society. They are students, workers, merchants, and young professionals.

A great many such terrorist groups exist, but Hamas is one of the more interesting. It was organized in late 1987 in the Gaza Strip when the "Intifada" or Palestinian uprising against Israeli rule began in the occupied territories. Its name is an acronym of Harakat al-Muqaqana al-Islamilya and translates as the Islamic Resistance Movement.

Hamas was founded on the idea of Islamic nationalism. Its goal is the establishment of an Islamic Palestinian state that will encompass all of historical Palestine, including modern Israel. As its action has attracted attention, Hamas has expanded its membership by drawing in those with little to lose and who might be influenced to hate—the disgruntled young males of the slums and lower-class neighborhoods.

Hamas has an armed militant wing known as Iz el-Deen, which carries out continued bombings and suicide bombings, assassinations, and kidnapping of those opposed to its existence. Like many terrorist organizations, they have a strong appetite for suicide bombings. Their primary targets are Jewish settlers in the West Bank.

Hamas draws its strength from the Palestinian community. They have established a network of schools, clinics, mosques, and charity funds. It makes active use of these establishments to provide social services to the community that increases its influence as well as providing those social services to the families of deceased suicide bombers.

The goals of Hamas are laid out in their Covenant of the Islamic Resistance Movement, issued August 18, 1988. Article 15 of this covenant is highly informative: "The day that enemies usurp part of Muslim land, *Jihad becomes the individual duty of every Muslim* [italics added]." It goes on: "It is necessary to instill in the minds of the Muslim generations *that the Palestinian problem is a religious problem* [italics added], and should be dealt with on this basis."

It ends with, "I swear by the holder of Muhammad's soul [Allah] *that I would like to invade and be killed for the sake of Allah, then invade and be killed, and then invade again and be killed* [italics added]."

Article 22 of the Hamas covenant is interesting in that it specifically identifies the Free Masons, Rotary Clubs, Lions Clubs, B'nai B'rith, and the like as their enemies. It is probable that this is because these organizations have loyalties to groups outside of Islam and might, as a result, bring pressure against a Muslim to choose other than their Islamic community.

Dr. Abdel Aziz al-Rantisi, a leading figure in Hamas and its spokesman in Gaza, was interviewed by the *Kul al-Arab* newspaper on January 9, 2001. A self-proclaimed fundamentalist member of the Muslim Brotherhood, in that interview he said, "You call them 'suicide operations,' and I call them 'martyr operations.' They are not terrorism. They are a response to Israeli terrorism, individual and governmental, against Palestinian civilians. We should remember that these martyr operations began after the massacre committed by the terrorist Baruch Goldstein [in the Hebron mosque in 1994] and intensified after the assassination of Yahya Ayash." Dr. al-Rantisi's linking of martyrdom with terrorism is a clear indication of how modern fundamentalists view the legitimacy of any methods of killing those perceived as enemies of Islam.

If one uses the Assassin sect as a template for Hamas, several points seem to coincide. The emphasis on murder for political or religious reasons is one. The inherent weakness of the sponsoring group is another. If the Assassins or Hamas had a culture strong enough to attract sufficient followers, they would have been able to field the military forces that could ensure their goals. But murder and suicide are not strong lures to large numbers of people. Thus the Assassins caused their own destruction, and it is difficult to imagine Hamas doing much better.

Apparently the largest Islamic murder organization is Al-Qaeda. Al-Qaeda was established by Osama bin Laden in the late 1980s to fight the Soviet invaders of Afghanistan. This initial purpose has, however, changed since the expulsion of the Russians, and its current goal is twofold: (1) to remove Western influences from the Middle East and particularly Saudi Arabia where Osama bin Laden believes the presence of American troops is a violation of Koranic proscriptions, and (2) to establish a pan-Islamic caliphate throughout the world by working with allied Islamic extremist groups to overthrow regimes it deems non-Islamic.

To restate the second point, it is Al-Qaeda's goal is to "unite all Muslims and to establish a government that follows the rule of the Caliphs." He has stated that the only way to establish the caliphate is by force, a thread clearly supported by the Koran. Al-Qaeda's goal, therefore, is to overthrow all Muslim governments viewed as corrupt, to drive Western influence from those countries, and eventually to abolish state boundaries, essentially reestablishing the Islamic state that had existed under the early caliphs.

According to Osama bin Laden's "Declaration of War against the Americans," occupation of the land of the two "Holy Places" (Mecca and Medina), is the greatest aggression suffered by the Muslims since the death of the Prophet. He considers it even worse than the Crusades.

Beyond that, it sees the United States as the chief obstacle to reform in Muslim societies. To support its ends, Al-Qaeda also supports Muslim fighters in Afghanistan, Algeria, Bosnia, Chechnya, Eritrea, Kosovo, Pakistan, Somalia, Tajikistan, and Yemen. It also trains members of terrorist organizations from such diverse countries as the Philippines, Algeria, and Eritrea. These diverse connections clearly indicate that Al-Qaeda and its leader Osama bin Laden have world-level plans and are not simply focused on the Middle East. They seek to bring death and destruction to Dar ul-Harib (the Land of War), as defined by Muhammad, in their movement toward the establishment of Islam as the single world religion.

Bin Laden has said, in reference to some of his terrorists, "What I know is that those who risked their lives to earn the pleasure of God, Praise and Glory be to him, are the real men, the true personification of the word men [i.e., true Muslims], They managed to rid the Islamic nation of disgrace." His response clearly demonstrates his total commitment to the concept of a religious jihad against the United States and belief that those involved were implementing the will of Allah.

Al-Qaeda is not a numerically large organization and until recently was believed to consist of about 3,000 members, including an estimated few hundred each of Egyptians, Jordanians, Yemenis, and Iraqis, and a few dozen each of Syrians, Algerians, Sudanese, Tunisians, Moroccans, and Palestinians. Other estimates place the number of members much higher.

Many Al-Qaeda members are veteran mujahedin of the Afghan war against the Soviets. These militants fight not only for their cause, but also because it is the only life they know. The mujahedin connection is an important one. When the old Soviet Empire invaded Afghanistan, the Muslim response was a legitimate call to jihad—although it was answered on a personal level, not a national one. When Afghanistan was in fact defended against the Red Army, it was partly the result of a great international and individual crusade—or jihad. It seems that bin Laden believes he can harness the same forces against the West and its influence.

The mujahedin in Afghanistan were surprisingly successful. After ten years of savage fighting they drove the Soviet Union from their land. What had begun as a fragmented army of tribal warriors ended up a well-organized and equipped army capable of defending the country against invasion. The departure of Soviet troops left behind in Afghanistan thousands of seasoned Islamic warriors from a variety of countries, who were heavily armed and highly motivated.

Using these veterans as his base, bin Laden began extending his campaign to purge Western influences from the Middle East to all corners of the globe. In 1988 bin Laden founded "Al-Qaeda" (the military "base"). Though maintaining a position within his family's Jeddah-based construction business, he continued his organization to support opposition movements in Saudi Arabia and Yemen.

Through this period bin Laden ran the Jihad Committee, an organization that included the Egyptian Islamic Group and the Jihad Organization in Yemen, the Pakistani al-Hadith group, the Lebanese Partisans League, the Libyan Islamic Group, Bayt al-Imam Group in Jordan, and the Islamic Group in Algeria. This committee also runs the Islamic Information Observatory center in London, which concentrates on the organization of media-related activities for the other organizations. There is also an advisory and reformation body.

After his return to Saudi Arabia, bin Laden continued his political activities. However, the Saudis were ill disposed toward his calls for insurrection and acted against him. In April 1994 he was stripped of his Saudi citizenship for irresponsible behavior and expelled from the country. He, his family, and a large band of followers moved to Khartoum, Sudan. There he set up factories and farms, some of which were established solely for the purpose of providing jobs to unemployed mujahedin. He built roads and infrastructure for the Sudanese government and established training camps for the Afghan veterans.

Bin Laden's construction company, el-Hijrah for Construction and Development, Ltd., was in partnership with the National Islamic Front and the Sudanese military when it built the new airport at Port Sudan and a 1,200-kilometer-long highway linking Khartoum to Port Sudan.

Osama bin Laden's numerous Sudanese commercial interests included a factory to process goat skins, a construction company, a sunflower plantation, an import-export operation (Wadi al-Aqiq Company), and the el-Shamal Islamic Bank in Khartoum. In view of his fundamentalism, operating a bank where interest is charged is an interesting activity. Osama bin Laden is said to be close to Sudanese leader Omar Albashir and to Hassan Turabi, head of the National Islamic Front (NIF) in Sudan. This seems a reasonable supposition, as his residence in Khartoum was guarded by the local security forces.

Because of Saudi pressure and the threat of UN sanctions, bin Laden was expelled from the Sudan in May 1996, despite Sudanese involvement with many terrorist organizations. The principal refuge that remained open to Osama bin Laden was Afghanistan, where he still had a large network of supporters.

Upon his return he was welcomed in Kabul. Shortly after his arrival in Afghanistan the Taliban seized power in Jalalabad and Kabul. Because of their similar ideologies, bin Laden found the Taliban ready allies. Despite that support, his situation was precarious, and two assassination attempts against him failed in early 1997. After those attacks he moved to Kandahar, the stronghold of the Students of the Shari'ah, and the central residence of the Commander of the Faithful al-Mulla Muhammad Omar.

Bin Laden has issued three *fatwahs,* or religious rulings calling upon Muslims to take up arms against the United States. On August 23, 1996, his first *fatwah* identified the United States as an enemy and urged Muslims to kill American military personnel abroad. A second *fatwah* was issued on February 23, 1998, by Al-Qaeda under the newly organized "World Islamic Front for Jihad Against the Jews and Crusaders." It was signed by the founders of the World Islamic Front: Osama bin Laden, Ayman al-Zawahiri, emir of the Jihad Group in Egypt; Abu-Yasir Rifa'i Ahmad Taha, Egyptian Islamic Group; Shaykh Mir Hamzah, secretary of the Jamiat-ul-Ulema-e-Pakistan; and Fazlur Rahman, emir of the Jihad Movement in Bangladesh.

The *fatwah* begins with a reference to Surah IX, 5, then quotes Muhammad: "I have been sent with the sword between my hands to ensure that no one but God is worshipped, God who put my livelihood under the shadow of my spear and who inflicts humiliation and scorn on those who disobey my orders."

Then, after describing the "crusader armies"[2] as spreading across Saudi Arabia like locusts, it proceeds to enumerate what it describes as the crimes of the United States. The first is the occupation of "the lands of Islam in the holiest of places, the Arabian Peninsula, plundering its riches [probably a reference to oil], dictating to its rulers, humiliating its people, terrorizing its neighbors, and turning its bases in the Peninsula into a spearhead through which to fight the neighboring Muslim peoples [Iraq]."

It then goes on to complain of "horrific massacres" in Iraq committed by the Americans by their blockade of Saddam Hussein's regime, claiming it is aimed at the "annihilation of what is left of [the Iraqi] people."

This is an incredibly self-serving statement. First, Osama bin Laden forgets the tenets of Surah IV, 93–94, which prohibits the plundering of a fellow Muslim, that is, what Saddam Hussein did when his army invaded Kuwait. In addition, if he believes the Kuwaiti government was totally corrupted by the West and deserved annihilation, he is arguably aligning himself with a horribly secular dictatorship that has perpetrated innumerable atrocities against its own and other Islamic peoples, including the use of poison gas against the Shiites both inside Iraq and in Iran in violation of other Koranic scriptures.

The third crime ascribed to the United States is supporting the Israeli occupation of Jerusalem and its purported murder of Muslims.

It continues by saying, "All these crimes and sins committed by the Americans are a clear declaration of war on God, his messenger, and Muslims. Ulema (religious leaders) have, throughout Islamic history, unanimously agreed that the jihad is an individual duty if the enemy destroys the Muslim countries. . . . As for the fighting to repulse [an enemy], it is aimed at defending sanctity and religion, and it is a duty as agreed [by the ulema]. Nothing is more sacred than belief except repulsing an enemy who is attacking religion and life."

In response to American "crimes," this statement declares it the duty of all Muslims to kill any and all U.S. citizens, civilian or military, and those of U.S. allies, wherever they may be encountered.

In May 1998, it was reported that clerics in Afghanistan had issued a *fatwah* stipulating the necessity to remove U.S. forces from the Gulf region. In addressing the Muslims of the world, the Afghan ulema said, "The enemies of Islam are not limited to a certain group or party; all atheists are enemies of Islam, and they take one another as friends."

This Afghan ulema declared jihad within the scope of the Shari'a, against the United States and its allies. They urged Islamic governments to perform the duty of armed jihad against the enemies of Islam, claiming that the US intended to occupy the mosques in Medina and Mecca, as they had occupied the al-Aqsa Mosque, in Jerusalem.[3] Going on, they said, "This *fatwah,* with the evidence and the rulings issued by early and current ulema, on which it is based, is not merely a *fatwah* issued by the ulema of a Muslim country, but rather a religious *fatwah* that every Muslim should adopt and work under."

Osama bin Laden immediately circulated this *fatwah* and convinced people to begin their training in Afghanistan. It was estimated that 4,000 Muslims went to Afghanistan as a result of his call. The Saudi government was not happy with his activities and limited his movement to Jeddah only. His relationship with the Saudi government grew extremely tense, with the regime raiding his farm in the suburb of Jeddah. Bin Laden was not there during the raid and was angry when told it had occurred. He wrote a letter of protest to Prince Abdullah. Abdullah apologized and claimed he was not aware and promised to punish whoever was responsible.

Bin Laden justifies the formation of the anti-American and anti-Israeli fronts with arguments contending that Muslims everywhere in the world are suffering at the hands of the United States and Israel. He said the Muslims must wage holy war against their real enemies not only to rid themselves of unpopular regimes backed by the Americans and Israelis, but also to protect their faith, which he claims is under assault.

The threat posed by this new front is that it combines all the organizational levels by establishing a consultative council. This council is led apparently by Osama bin Laden, which increases the front's effectiveness.

If bin Laden's *fatwahs* and claims are absurd—and they show nothing like coherence—his activities are dangerous.

Reports have existed that claim Osama bin Laden has attempted to acquire nuclear material as well as ready-made warheads from freelance individuals in Russia, unspecified chemical weapons from Iraq and Sudan, and biological agents such as botulinum toxin, plague, and anthrax from individuals in the Czech Republic, Kazakhstan, and Indonesia. Recent events in the United States support the probability that anthrax was obtained, but no evidence to supports the other claims, particularly those reports regarding possession of nuclear weapons.

The acquisition of nuclear weapons has been of significant interest to Osama bin Laden. In September 25, 1998, his aide Mamdouh Mahmud Salim was arrested in Munich, Germany, and charged with acting on behalf of bin Laden to obtain nuclear materials. In particular, Salim reportedly attempted to obtain highly enriched uranium in the mid-1990s.

Jamal Ahmad al-Fadl, a Sudanese national and the star witness in the embassy bombing trial gives this rumored purchase of uranium credibility. He described his role in the preliminary phase of a $1.5 million purchase of an unknown quantity of uranium in Khartoum, Sudan. He said he did not know if the deal was ever concluded.

In August 1998 Israeli military intelligence sources reported that bin Laden had paid over £2 million to a middleman in Kazakhstan. The purported deal involved the promised delivery of a suitcase nuclear weapon to him within two years. This threat was credible enough that the Israelis sent a cabinet minister to Kazakhstan to stop this exchange.

On October 6, 1998, a London-based Arabic newspaper, declared that bin Laden had obtained nuclear weapons. It was later reported that he was engaged in a comprehensive plan to acquire nuclear weapons. The report is supposed to have come from information provided the Russian intelligence agency, the Federal Security Service (FSB). The report stated that bin Laden had established contacts with organized crime members in the former Soviet republics in Central Asia and the Caucasus.

Later, Osama bin Laden reportedly gave his contacts in Chechnya $30 million in cash and two tons of opium in exchange for approximately twenty nuclear warheads. Sources stated that bin Laden planned to have the warheads dismantled by his own team of scientists, who would then transform the weapons into instant nukes or suitcase nukes.

This claim was, of course, absurd, as Osama bin Laden is unlikely to have access to the technology necessary to construct a suitcase-sized nuclear weapon. In addition, the systems necessary to make a small weapon that can achieve critical mass could not be stripped from a larger strategic weapon.

Al-Watan Al-Arabi also reported that bin Laden's original strategy had been to develop his own in-house nuclear manufacturing complex in which small, tactical nuclear weapons would be manufactured from scratch. As early as 1993, Osama bin Laden had instructed some of his aides to obtain weapons-grade uranium that could be used to develop nuclear weapons. However, the $300 million that he is reputed to have would not be sufficient to establish the facilities necessary to do this work.

But if bin Laden lacks nuclear weapons, his comments on them are not comforting. "Acquiring weapons for the defense of Muslims is a religious duty. If I have indeed acquired these weapons, then I thank God for enabling me to do so. And . . . if I seek to acquire such weapons, this is a religious duty. How we use them is up to us."

Even without atomic weapons, bin Laden has been responsible for considerable murder around the world. Attaching responsibility to him for specific terrorist acts has been difficult, but he has been connected with the attacks in Riyadh (November 1995) and Dhahran (June 1996). Because of the structure of the Islamic World Front it is probable that he had no direct involvement in them. He has also been implicated in the attacks on a Yemenite hotel (December 1992), the assassination attempt on Egyptian president Mubarak in Ethiopia (June 1995), and the first World Trade Center bombing, February 1993. His culpability in the September 11, 2001, attacks on the United States seems assured.

The U.S. State Department fact sheet assigns blame to Osama bin Laden for the conspiracy to kill U.S. servicemen in Yemen as they were en route to the humanitarian mission "Operation Restore Hope" in Somalia in 1992 as well as plotting in the deaths of American and other peacekeepers in Somalia. The State Department contends his network assisted in a car bombing against the Egyptian embassy in Pakistan in 1995. Bin Laden is also accused of plotting to blow up U.S. airliners in the Pacific and of conspiring to kill the pope. Several of bin Laden's followers were convicted of the suicide bombing attacks on the American embassies in Nairobi and Dar-es-Salaam. The connection with bin Laden was established on August 15, 1998, when Muhammad Sadiq Odeh was arrested at Karachi International Airport in Pakistan. Odeh's description of bin Laden's international network and his role in the bombing of the American embassies gave conclusive evidence of the extent of bin Laden's activities.

The U.S. government also claims having classified information that clearly demonstrates his responsibility for the destruction of the World Trade Towers and the attack on the Pentagon on September 11, 2001. This evidence has been reviewed and found conclusive by numerous other governments.

After the destruction of the World Trade Center, Osama bin Laden issued a statement. He directed his comments to the entire Islamic world. In that statement he said, "The nation must know that 'terror' and the terror of the United States is only a ploy. Is it possible that America and its allies would kill and that would not be called terrorism? And when the victim comes out to take revenge, it is called terrorism. This must not be acceptable." This statement is, essentially, an admission of his involvement and a justification for the murder of the 5,000 who lost their lives in New York, Washington, D.C., and Pennsylvania.

After declaring the jihad as a duty of all Muslims and citing the Koran, he went on to say, "those youths who did what they did and destroyed [the World Trade Center] America with their airplanes did a good deed. They have moved the battle [that he has demanded in his *fatwah*] into the heart of America. America must know that the battle will not leave its land, God willing, until America leaves our land, until it stops supporting Israel, until it stops the blockade against Iraq."

Bin Laden went on to say, "The Americans must know that the storm of airplanes will not stop, God willing, and there are thousands of young people who are as keen about death as Americans are about life."

One consistent thread in all these groups, Fatah, Hamas, and Al-Qaeda, is that they have cast their operations in completely religious terms. The word "jihad" rings as a constant refrain that links all three together philosophically. They quote the Koran to support their positions and actions. Their foot soldiers, the suicide bombers, are convinced that they are destined for an eternity in paradise because of their actions.

Osama bin Laden, and to a lesser degree, the leaders of Fatah and Hamas are doing exactly what the grand masters of the *Hashishyun,* the Assassins, did nine centuries earlier. They murder to achieve their political aims because, militarily, they are too weak to deal with the military powers with which they are in contention. Like all terrorists, they justify their actions by the goal they seek to achieve. They hide behind the masses of innocent people in which they operate, clearly stating that they are unconcerned for the deaths of their fellow Muslims because greater good is achieved by their attacks than the ill caused by the deaths of those innocents. They are simply continuing in the footsteps of Hasan as-Sabah, and Osama bin Laden is certainly the successor to Rukn ad-Din, the last grand master of the Assassins.

At the time of this writing the fate of Osama bin Laden remains unknown. Likewise the structure of Al-Qaeda has been under severe attack by the political, military, and economic forces of the civilized world.

NOTES

1. In an odd twist of history, in the 1970s the Israelis would bomb Krak des Chevaliers because it was a stronghold of Palestinian terrorists.

2. The constant reference to "crusaders" is not unusual. The radical Muslims continue to see any activity of the West in the Middle East as an extension of the eleventh- to twelfth-century crusades. It must be remembered that their entire focus is on religion and everything is seen in the context of religion.

3. In fact, the United States has not occupied the al-Aqsa mosque, nor has Israel, which, recognizing the religious significance of the mosque has carefully preserved its sanctity. Unfortunately, because of its proximity to the "wailing wall" incidents are frequent. It is particularly venerated by the Muslims because it was built in A.D. 709 to commemorate the site where Muhammad left his horse before ascending to the top of Mt. Zion and being caught up to the seventh heaven. It is the third most significant site in Islam, after the mosques in Mecca and Medina.

Chapter 14

CONCLUSION

One might usefully divide the military history of the Islamic peoples into three broad periods, the Great Conquest, the Ottoman era, and the post-colonial or modern period. These broad divisions capture the most significant events by the most militarily significant of the Islamic peoples and nations. Each of these general eras bears an overriding question for the reader of history. The questions come easily, but the answers will not—still, we have attempted to address them.

The great Arab conquests of the seventh and eighth centuries were simply astonishing and without precedent—or antecedent. Never before or since in history has such an unlikely people as the nomadic tribes of Arabia produced such an astonishing wave of conquests. In a few years the proud old Sassanid Empire was destroyed, and the mighty Byzantine Empire humiliated and reduced to a shadow of its recent past. The lands that now form Afghanistan, the state of Kashmir, Iran, Iraq, Syria, Jordan, Israel, Egypt, Libya, Algeria, Tunisia, Morocco, and Spain all fell to Muslim armies.

The Arab armies were not numerous, not terribly well armed, and of no better "warrior stock" than their adversaries. Nor did they enjoy a particularly superior military tradition—they fought well against cavalry armies, infantry armies, archers, well-drilled troops, rough hordes, and every conceivable combination. It is difficult to suggest that they consistently fielded better tactical leaders, and the Emperor Heraclius, an early opponent, was an able strategist, and one with the resources to make them tell.

In spite of these odds, the conquests seem to have been limited only by the speed of the advancing armies. Setbacks were few, and those minor. The obvious question for the modern reader is how did such an extraordinary chain of events come to pass? At least two plausible answers emerge.

The first explanation for the Arab conquest is simply that time and chance favored them. It is quite true that Persia was exhausted by a long foreign war followed by a useless struggle for the succession. This circumstance allowed Muslim armies to defeat the old empire with a minimum of difficulty. Likewise, the Byzantines were equally exhausted and torn by internal strife—particularly religious strife—that diluted what should have been an invincible defense to the attacking armies of the Prophet. With Byzantium reeling, the African coast had no other real defense. The Visigoths in Spain were merely occupiers, not a developed civilization, and so they crumbled as well. This "time and circumstance" explanation to the Arab victories can at least rationalize the Muslim successes. It does not, however, explain how quickly and thoroughly the conquered areas accepted or adapted to Islam. One can challenge the degree of Islamization in any way desired, but the new rulers achieved a sufficient grasp of each of their conquests to use it as a recruiting base for the next.

One can make a point that the real victor in the conquests was not the Arab warlords, but Islam itself. Over the centuries warlords and nations would arrive and depart with dizzying speed. Many were capable, but none enjoyed a success as incredible as the religious success of Islam. Simply put, Islam may have sped the conquests, but it also showed much greater staying power. It is useful to realize that the power of Islam was separate from much and more permanent than that of the armies with which it rode.

This brings us to the second possible explanation for the success of the Arab Conquests, and that is that God, or Allah, arranged it. This explanation can explain the miraculous successes and combination of circumstances at least as well as the idea of mere fortunate happenstance. It does not, however, explain why the conquests stopped when they did. Why did God stop the Arabs in France? Why did Byzantium hold for 700 years?

The divine explanation of the conquests is probably even less satisfactory to Western readers than the time-and-circumstance rationale. Modern Westerners don't like to think that any God ordains wholesale murder, slavery, and pillaging, which has been the case within parts of the Islamic world. Many of the same Westerners have been trained to believe that all cultures are equal if not identical, and the idea that an orthodox strain of a dominant world religion offers conversion or death and has done so in the past, is beyond their comprehension.

The Turkish centuries are remarkable in their own way, but not miraculous. The Turks had been steppe nomads who operated purely as tribal warlords. When they occupied the principal lands of the thirteenth-century Arab Conquests they were merely the most recent set of raiders to erect their series of feuding petty city-states and sultanates. By the time the Crusaders and the Mongols had blown through the Middle East, the Turks emerged as the one great Mediterranean power. Indeed, the empire of the Ottomans closely resembles that of the Romans, with the center "flipped" one sea to the east. The Turks, being steppe peoples by heritage, were more concerned with the lands bordering the Black Sea than the Mediterranean, although once their eastern frontiers seemed secure, their attentions shifted rapidly and ominously west.

The Ottoman success, however, is remarkable. An early run of capable sultans solidified the idea of a strong imperial government and pushed the frontiers of Turkish authority toward the territorial limits of its Byzantine predecessors. With able leadership, great resources, an imperial tradition, and a lack of any particularly formidable opponents the Turks became the greatest single military and economic power in the world. Between 1500 and 1600 Ottoman strength had grown to the point that it could be checked only at the fringes. Turkey employed the largest and most modern military in the world—her siege trains and Janissary regiments were the very last word in military professionalism.

The great question about the Ottomans is of course—"What happened between 1600 and 1700?" In that time period the Turks lost neither key territories nor any great economic prizes, but their might and influence so declined that they were no longer counted as being a great power, and still less "the" great power. How did this happen?

The story of Turkish decline is really one of European ascension rather than any great downfall of the Ottomans. It is true that the crack Janissary corps had become palace soldiers by then, and it is true that viziers were the true authority rather than the Sultans themselves. These may be symptoms of the greater fault, which was a pronounced Turkish inertia, for power was growing elsewhere. By 1700 Austria and Russia, the European monarchies that directly confronted Islam, had developed much more rapidly than the Sublime Porte. Modern sailing ships were beginning to make galleys obsolete, and the Europeans' disciplined musketry made the great bulk of the Sultan's feudal levies useless. The West developed a new corps of officers through the idea of the educated military professional who owed his allegiance to his regiment through his monarch. Most of the Sultan's soldiers were temporary levies with tribal rather than national identities. As such, they were not the best material to form into disciplined regulars who could best exploit the new musket's massed firepower. Nor did they ever develop much emotional identity with the distant, and usually alien Porte. It was one thing to be a Russian, in a Russian regiment, defending Russia in the army of the Russian czar, and another thing to be an Egyptian, brigaded with Persian levies, fighting in Bosnia for a Turkish Sultan.

The balance of military power and domination shifted from the Islamic world to the West when the Turks failed in their last great effort to take Vienna. This shift had two causes. The first was the formation of national states and national governments in the West, which provided a sense of national identity to their people and their armies. The second reason was the explosion of scientific learning in the West unparalleled in the Islamic World.

While Europe aggressively modernized and developed its military techniques and technologies, the Islamic world was less aggressive in these pursuits. The innovation that produced the first organized artillery corps and the Janissaries had slumped into a lethargy generated by an inclination to traditionalism, the lack of an educated population, and a high incidence of governmental corruption.

Since 1945 the technological advancements of the West have produced weapons systems highly attractive to Eastern potentates. Islamic states have, in order to defend themselves from one another, obtained modern weapons systems from the West. As they've fought with one another since 1945 they have demonstrated an equal incompetence in their use of these weapons that permits something approaching an equilibrium. On the other hand, when on the battlefield, they face a Western state, which here includes Israel, they are totally outclassed.

In addition, the Islamic world has not been stable. Political instability, civil wars, political assassinations, and military coups have marked the history of almost every Islamic state since 1945. One legacy of the Ottoman Empire and colonial occupations is that national boundaries differ from ethnic boundaries. This has produced ongoing problems as various groups struggle for their national identities against oppressive governments intent on preserving those boundaries. Further instabilities arise because of conflicting territorial claims that literally stretch back thousands of years.

The national governments that have formed since 1945 are, for the most part, either monarchies or the dictatorships of warlords. To support these governments, whose legitimacy faces constant challenge, their rulers have brought in a flood of modern military equipment, technology, and advisers to train their soldiers to operate them. These rulers have recognized that in order to compete in the modern world, as well as to prevent total domination by the West, they must abandon much of their cultural predisposition toward traditional Islamic methods and solutions. The ancient Islamic cultural imperatives no longer provide an adequate basis upon which to establish a stable government in a world flooded with Western ideas and ideals. This influx of Western ideas and material has, by its very nature, produced internal stresses in the Islamic world.

Though little state-based nationalism exists, this intrusion of the West into the Middle East, invited and uninvited, has produced what one might call Islamic nationalism. The rise of this xenophobic, Islamic nationalism, which is widely called fundamentalism, presents the Islamic world with a military paradox.

The fundamentalists wish to establish and maintain a purely Islamic culture. To do this they feel they must purge the "Frank" from their society. They have taken up arms against the West, making their conflict with the West essentially a religious conflict, as they show no visible intention to conquer and occupy the West. The first paradox is that because of the overwhelming military power of the West, if they are to engage in a conventional war they must adopt Western military systems and equipment. The problem arises in that this equipment requires an educated populace to operate and maintain it. The education necessary is in itself Western, and by spreading it through their population those wishing to purge Western influences from their society bring in still further Western influences. Inevitably this training opens up the eyes of their otherwise illiterate populations to the world of ideas outside Islam.

This literacy process destabilizes both the Islamic state the fundamentalists want and the regimes of various dictatorial Islamic potentates. In that sense, a natural alliance arises between dictators and fundamentalists to purge Western influences. The concept of democracy threatens the dictator's absolute authority to rule and, arguably, is an anathema to Islam, which in its ideal form has the state ruled by a religious leader, not by the will of the populace.

Stepping beyond that, if one then assumes that these militant fundamentalists have mastered the operation and use of Western equipment the third problem that arises is that they are incapable of operating successfully against a Western army. The Arab-Israeli wars and the Gulf War clearly demonstrate the overwhelming superiority of Western forces and the utter inability of Muslim troops to face the West in a conventional war.

Here lies yet another paradox. Because they cannot compete with the West in a conventional war, many in the Islamic world have moved toward the unconventional alternative, including two diametrically opposed approaches. The first is the weapon of mass destruction and the second is a variety of forms of unconventional warfare.

Among those choosing weapons of mass destruction, one currently finds only the nuclear-armed Pakistan as the possessor of the "Muslim Bomb." Saddam Hussein's Iraq is known to be working on nuclear, biological, and chemical weapons. Libya is also thought to be working on them. In addition to huge amounts of money, the development, deployment, and maintenance of these weapons also requires further Western influences penetrating into these countries that lack the national human and educational resources necessary to produce them.

In addition, the Islamic world generally recognizes overt national use of weapons of mass destruction as an invitation for an overwhelming counterstrike by the West. Most likely this is why Saddam Hussein did not use his chemical weapons arsenal against the Allied army that liberated Kuwait. There is, however, no guarantee now that the President Bush has called for a change of regime that Saddam Hussein will exercise the same restraint. Having nothing to lose, he may well use whatever weapons of mass destruction he has in his arsenal. The same standoff exists between India and Pakistan and must influence the development of military thought in the Islamic world.

For this reason, and their inability to face a Western army on the battlefield, fundamentalists who feel compelled to strike militarily at the West, have turned to the unconventional form of warfare known as terrorism. By operating outside the parameters of the classic nation-state and the system of warfare between nations, these fundamentalists believe they can hide from Western retaliation. They believe that they can disarm the West's military might by hiding behind the burkas of Muslim women and the West's unwillingness to kill innocents to defend its own interests. They believe that, without a nation-state as a declared enemy, the West no longer has the will to declare civilian populations legitimate targets and to strike them with the ferocity displayed during World War II. The evidence, to date, indicates that they may be right.

As a result, the fundamentalist terrorists are not only willing to launch what might be considered "conventional" attacks with guns, suicide bombers, and airplanes filled with fuel and helpless passengers, they also have shown their interest in developing and acquiring weapons of mass destruction. This has been amply supported by recent discoveries in Afghanistan that clearly indicate that Al-Qaeda had an aggressive program to acquire all sorts of those devices.

One must add to this mix the concept of the jihad. The jihad has evolved from its historical context of a religious war of massed armies and become the cry of the fundamentalist terrorist. It adds a terrible dimension to unconventional warfare. It gives the murderer a reputation that goes beyond anything experienced in any of the world's armies.

All this indicates that the Western and Islamic worlds are moving into a new relationship that will be marked by military action. This is a third phase in the relationship between the Islamic and Western worlds. The first came as the Islamic world expanded at the expense of the Christian world, conquering by the sword those lands it now occupies. It was a relationship of a military dominant Islamic world to a military inferior West. The second phase appeared in the nineteenth century when the militarily dominant West oppressed and divided up Islamic world. The third phase is developing today and it is, again, a military relationship. Indications are that this relationship will be marked by suicidal attacks by dedicated Muslim fanatics and a multitude of responses by an enraged West.

The result of this will surely be that Muhammad's division of the world into *Dar ul Islam* (the Land of Peace) and *Dar ul Harb* (the Land of War) will cease to be as he had originally conceived it. The global reach of the covert terrorist, striking at will, assures that all of the non-Islamic world can be subjected to murderous attack. Similarly, the global reach of the United States and other Western powers guarantees that no corner of *Dar ul Islam* will be safe from a furious response. Pinprick strikes by fanatics with exploding tennis shoes, individually, will probably not provoke massive strikes. However, the cumulative impact of repeated strikes, great and small, may eventually force the democracies to abandon their moral imperatives and respond with anger and the justification of self-preservation.

The oil-based Western economy will force the industrial nations to continue to push themselves on *Dar ul Islam*. This guarantees a constant level of angst among the Islamic fundamentalists about the purity of *Dar ul Islam* and guarantees that they will seek to strike back.

In this light, the biblical prophetic voices that reach us from Revelations about a great battle at Armageddon begin to move from the mystic to the believable. An inescapable tension between the Islamic and Western worlds arises from the essence of what is Islam and the overwhelming allure of what is the West. The fundamentalists of the Islamic world believe that they are in danger of being overwhelmed by the modern world and are turning to the military to lash out against their perceived enemies. They are utterly incapable of facing the West on the open battlefield, for to do so would only hasten the obliteration of what they are attempting to preserve. They have only one military option open to them, and that is the hope that terrorism will force the West to withdraw from *Dar ul Islam.* But that hope is futile so long as the Western economies depend on oil from the Middle East.

Although political and religious murder are the current tools of fundamental Islam, reason for some optimism does exist. The "Jihad"-shouting fundamentalists are simply religious or political extremists who deny the realities of the world around them. Islam will never be a dominant cultural force in the world until it accepts the reality that it cannot conquer by force of arms, still less so by murder. The fundamentalists offer only death, poverty, and misery. In time it is almost certain that modernized Muslim governments will provide their people with better ideas. History has always been kind to good ideas and harsh to bad ones. Most recently freedom has defeated the empty ideas of the Soviet Communist empire with nothing much more than blue jeans and rock-n-roll. It is probably not an accident that the young people of fundamentalist Iran are desperate for Western music and clothes and pressing against their fundamentalist, theocratic government for a voice in their own future.

BIBLIOGRAPHY

Arnold, A. *The Fateful Pebble, Afghanistan's Role in the Fall of the Soviet Empire.* Novato, CA: Presidio, 1993.

Atkinson, R. *Crusade: The Untold Story of the Persian Gulf War.* Boston: Houghton Mifflin, 1993.

Beehler, Commodore W. H. *The History of the Italian-Turkish War.* Annapolis, MD: Naval Institute Press, 1913.

Bergquist, R. E., Major. *The Role of Airpower in the Iran-Iraq War.* Maxwell AFB, AL: Air University Press, 1988.

Borovik, A. *The Hidden War.* New York: Grove Press, 1990.

Bradford, A. *The Great Siege Malta 1565.* Harmondsworth, Middlesex: Penguin Books, 1971.

Bridge, A. *Suleiman The Magnificent, Scourge of Heaven.* New York: Granada, 1983.

Delbrück, H. *Medieval Warfare.* Lincoln, NE: University of Nebraska Press, 1990.

El-Edroos, Brigadier S. A., *The Hashemite Arab Army 1908–1979.* Amman, Jordan: Publishing Committee, 1980.

Fidi, R. A. *Concise History of the Muslim World,* New Delhi: Kitabbhavan, 1997.

Field, M. *Inside the Arab World.* London: Murray, 1994.

Forbes, A. *The Afghan Wars, 1839–1842 & 1878–80.* London: Seeley, 1906.

Fregosi, P. *Jihad in the West, Muslim Conquests from the 7th to the 21st Centuries.* New York: Prometheus, 1998.

Friedman, N. *Desert Victory: The War for Kuwait.* Annapolis, MD: Naval Institute Press, 1991.

Fromkin, D. *A Peace to End All Peace: The Fall of the Ottoman Empire and the Creation of the Modern Middle East.* New York: Avon Books, 1989.

Furneaux, R. *The Breakfast War.* New York: Crowell, 1958.

Galeotti, M. *Afghanistan: The Soviet Union's Last War.* London: Frank Cass, 2001.

German General Staff. *Der Balkankrieg 1912/13.* Berlin: Mittler & Sohn, 1914.

Glubb, Sir J. *Soldiers of Fortune, The Story of the Mamlukes.* New York: Dorset, 1973.

Glubb, Sir J. *The Great Arab Conquests.* London: Quartet Books, 1980.

Gorfdienko, A. N. Война в Афганистане. Из книги: Войны второй половины XX века. Minsk: Literature, 1998.

Gromov B. V., General-Colonel. Ограниченный контингент. Moscow: Progress, 1994.

Groueff, S. *Crown of Thorns, The Reign of King Boris III of Bulgaria 1918–1943.* Landham, MD: Madison, 1987.

Hallion, R. B. *Storm over Iraq: Air Power and the Gulf War.* Washington, D.C.: Smithsonian Institution Press, 1992.

Harl-El, Shai. *Struggle for Domination in the Middle East, the Ottoman-Mamluk War 1485–91.* New York: Brill, 1995.

Heathcote, T. A. *The Afghan Wars, 1839–1919.* London: Osprey, 1980.

Herzog, C. *The Arab-Israeli War: War and Peace in the Middle East from the War of Independence through Lebanon.* New York: Vintage Books, 1982.

Hiro, D. *The Longest War: The Iran-Iraq Military Conflict.* New York: Routledge, 1991.

Hitti, P. K. *History of the Arabs From the Earliest Times to the Present.* London: Macmillan, 1956.

Hourani, A. *A History of the Arab Peoples.* Cambridge, MA: Belknap Press of Harvard University Press, 1991.

Immanuel, Lt. Col. *Der Balkankrieg 1912/13.* Volumes 1, 2, & 3. Berlin: Mittler & Sohn, 1913.

James, C. *An Universal Military Dictionary in English and French in Which are Explained the Terms of the Principal Sciences that are Necessary for the Information of an Officer.* London: T. Egerton, 1816.

Karsh, E. *The Iran-Iraq War: A Military Analysis.* London: Adelphi Paper, 1987.

Karsh, E. *The Iran-Iraq War: Impact and Implications.* New York: St. Martin's Press, 1989.

Keddie, N. R. *Roots of Revolution, An Interpretive History of Modern Iran.* New Haven: Yale University Press, 1981.

Knight, I. *Marching to the Drums, From the Kabul Massacre to the Siege of Mafkeng.* London: Greenhill, 1999.

Laffin, J. *Holy War: Islam Fights.* London: Grafton, 1988.

Lewis, B. *The Muslim Discovery of Europe.* New York: Norton, 1982.

Macdermott, M. *A History of Bulgaria 1393–1885.* London: Allen & Unwin, 1962.

Pascu, S. *A History of Transylvania.* New York: Dorset Press, 1982.

Payne, R. *The Dream and the Tomb: A History of the Crusades.* New York: Dorset Press, 1984.

Pickthall, M. *The Meaning of the Glorious Koran.* New York: Dorset Press, date unknown.

Porch, D. *The Conquest of Morocco.* New York: Knopf, 1983.

Preston, R. M. P. *The Desert Mounted Corps, An Account of the Cavalry Operations in Palestine and Syria, 1917–1918.* Boston: Houghton Mifflin, 1921.

Rajee, F. *Iranian Perspectives on the Iran-Iraq War.* Tallahassee: University Press of Florida, 1997.

Robinson, J. J. *Dungeon, Fire and Sword: The Knights Templar in the Crusades.* New York: Evans, 1991.

Runciman, S. *A History of the Crusades.* Cambridge: Cambridge University Press, 1954.

Runciman, S. *The First Crusade.* New York: Cambridge University Press, 1980.

Sabini, J. *Armies in the Sand: The Struggle for Mecca and Medina.* New York: Thames and Hudson, 1981.

Schurman, J. G. *The Balkans Wars, 1912–1913.* Princeton, N.J.: Princeton University Press, 1914.

Shaw, S. J. *History of the Ottoman Empire and Modern Turkey.* Cambridge: Cambridge University Press, 1976.

Slatin, R. C. *Fire and Sword in the Sudan.* New York: Negro Universities Press, 1969.

Stoye, J. *The Siege of Vienna.* New York: Holt, Rinehart & Winston, 1964.

Watson, B. W., George, B., Tsouras, P., and Cyr, B. L. *Military Lessons of the Gulf War.* London: Greenhill, 1991.

Wheatcroft, A. *The Ottomans.* New York: Viking, 1993.

Wise, T. *The Wars of the Crusades, 1096–1291.* London: Osprey, 1978.

Wolpert, St. *A New History of India,* New York: Oxford University Press, 1977.

Zulfo, 'Ismat Hasan. *Karari, The Sudanese Account of the Battle of Omdurman.* London: Frederick Warne, 1980.

INDEX

About the Authors

GEORGE F. NAFZIGER, Ph.D., Captain USNR-Ret., has authored numerous books and articles on the subject of military history. Nafziger is a former Director of the Napoleonic Society of America and the Napoleonic Alliance. He is also owner of The Nafziger Collection, a publishing house specializing in the Napoleonic Wars and World War II history.

MARK W. WALTON is an independent researcher. With degrees from Miami University of Ohio and Temple University, he has had a life-long interest in history. He currently lives near Indianapolis. This is his first book.